Family Enterprise in the Asia Pacific

IN ASSOCIATION WITH THE GLOBAL STEP PROJECT

The success of passing a family business from one generation to another depends not only on instilling business ideas and leadership in future generations, but, and perhaps more importantly, it depends on engendering the entrepreneurial spirit in those business leaders to come; this is the practice of transgenerational leadership. Successful Transgenerational Entrepreneurship Practices, more commonly known as the STEP Project, was put in place to help facilitate family enterprising. An innovative research initiative that spans the globe, it offers insight, partnership and solutions for current and future family leaders. In the STEP Project, academics of entrepreneurship and business collaborate with prosperous multigenerational family businesses to explore and identify those practices that will help family business grow and prosper through three key tenets: venturing – launching new businesses; renewal – revitalizing existing businesses; and innovation – introducing new products and processes. By creating a stream of powerful practices and cases that empower families to build their entrepreneurial legacies, the members of the STEP Project are rapidly moving their discoveries from research into practice.

Current STEP Partners

Europe
- Alba Graduate School of Business, Greece
- ESADE, Barcelona, Spain
- HEC, Paris, France
- Jönköping International Business School, Sweden
- Lancaster University, Lancaster, England
- UCD, Dublin, Ireland
- Universita Bocconi, Milan, Italy
- University of Edinburgh, Edinburgh, Scotland
- University of Jyväskylä, Jyväskylä, Finland
- Universitaet St. Gallen, St. Gallen, Switzerland
- Universitaet Witten/Herdecke, Germany
- Universiteit Antwerpen, Antwerp, Belgium
- University of the Western Cape, South Africa (Joint Venture with Jönköping)

Latin America
- Fundação Dom Cabral, Brazil
- Universidad Adolfo Ibáñez, Chile
- Universidad de Los Andes, Colombia

- PUCMM, Dominican Republic
- Universidad San Francisco de Quito, Ecuador
- Tecnológico de Monterrey, Mexico
- INCAE Business School, Costa Rica/Nicaragua
- IESA, Venezuela
- Inter American University of Puerto Rico
- CENTRUM, Pontificia Universidad Católica del Perú

Asia Pacific
- Chinese University of Hong Kong, Hong Kong
- Nankai University, Tianjin, P.R. China
- Sun Yat-Sen University, Taiwan
- Sun Yat-Sen University, Guangzhou, P.R. China
- Kyungpook, National University, Korea
- Waseda University, Japan
- Queensland University of Technology, Australia
- Bond University, Australia
- Indian School of Business, Hyderabad, India
- UNIRAZAK, Malaysia
- Bangkok University, Thailand

Family Enterprise in the Asia Pacific

Exploring Transgenerational Entrepreneurship in Family Firms

Edited by

Kevin Au

The Chinese University of Hong Kong

Justin B. Craig

Bond University, Australia

Kavil Ramachandran

Indian School of Business, India

IN ASSOCIATION WITH THE GLOBAL STEP PROJECT

Edward Elgar

Cheltenham, UK • Northampton, MA, USA

Published by
Edward Elgar Publishing Limited
The Lypiatts
15 Lansdown Road
Cheltenham
Glos GL50 2JA
UK

Edward Elgar Publishing, Inc.
William Pratt House
9 Dewey Court
Northampton
Massachusetts 01060
USA

A catalogue record for this book
is available from the British Library

Library of Congress Control Number: 2009941242

ISBN 978 1 84844 792 9

Typeset by Servis Filmsetting Ltd, Stockport, Cheshire
Printed and bound by MPG Books Group, UK

Contents

v

Preface

Family businesses and business families have been studied by anthropologists, sociologists, and historians for a long time. But, as a field of research among business scholars, the study of family enterprises is young. It has, however, expanded very quickly over the last decade along all dimensions.

The field started among entrepreneurship researchers because family members become involved as the entrepreneurial firm grows, and ownership, governance, and management of the business become a shared endeavor of the family over time. So, when entrepreneurship researchers started asking what happens in the long run to the successful entrepreneurial venture, they naturally began examining family firms. But family business studies are now being published by researchers in strategy, organization, finance, accounting, and economics aside from those in entrepreneurship and small business.

Geographically, research in the field began mainly in North America. But studies are now being conducted and cover family businesses in all continents. In terms of education, young and future researchers are now graduating with PhDs focused on family business studies. And prominence is being given to the field through the establishment of research centers and research chairs.

So far, most of the studies have been conceptual or empirical. Conceptual research has relied mainly on using mainstream theories of organization or management to explain how family involvement changes the policies, structure, behavior, and performance of the firm. This is the normal route for a new field to gain legitimacy. But, as a result, the assumptions about what goals family firms pursue and how they pursue them are constrained by the assumptions and logic underlying the mainstream theories of organization or management. Empirical research, on the other hand, must be guided and is, thus, restricted by conceptual development in terms of the hypotheses tested and the differences between family and non-family firms targeted. For example, the most popular mainstream theories applied to family business are agency theory, resource-based view, stewardship theory, transaction cost economics, stakeholder theory, and behavioral theory. Each of these theories has its own assumptions, framework of analysis, logic, measures, and hypothesis testing methodology. While they provide well defined paths for family business researchers, they also constrain our thinking and investigations. Therefore, I believe that, until our thinking about family business or the business family transcends the mainstream theories, the field will continue to be seen as primarily a niche area where mainstream theories are being applied to a different context.

For the field to break out and establish itself as its own discipline, we must first expand the horizons of our discourse and question the applicability to the family enterprise of the assumptions, frameworks, and logics of the mainstream theories. But the questioning and expanded discourse must be based on rigorous evidence. I believe that this can come only from qualitative research of which the case study is one approach.

Thus, I am very glad to see the global cooperation through the STEP Project to gather research-oriented case studies of family firms. This will eventually form a very large, international, cross-cultural qualitative database. I strongly believe that only through the extension of academic discourse as a result of examining qualitative data will family business researchers discover all the intricacies and subtleties in family business logic and behavior unexplainable by mainstream theories. And it will be through these observations that different assumptions, frameworks, and logic evolve and give family business studies its own discipline.

I am also quite excited about the project's focus on entrepreneurship because I believe that, in our dynamic globalized economies, almost all markets, except maybe regulated monopolies, are contestable. Therefore, businesses can disappear overnight. That, in fact, happened to my own family; a joint venture of ours disappeared when our joint venture partner was acquired by the firm against which the joint venture was competing. As a result, I believe very strongly that instilling entrepreneurial drive and developing entrepreneurial capabilities in succeeding generations are the requisites for family enterprises to prosper from generation to generation.

Having said this, however, I have a few suggestions that I hope the participants in the STEP Project will consider if they have not already thought about them. They are not about the individual case studies included in this volume but about the grand design. The first is with respect to sampling. The family firms examined in this volume appear to be all successful ones. Logic says that if B then A does not imply if A then B – because successful family firms do them does not imply that doing them ensures success. The evidence would be more conclusive if, to the collection of best practices, is added verification that family firms fail when they do not follow the best practices. Therefore, I encourage STEP researchers to include some family firms that failed to maintain their entrepreneurial capabilities across generations and examine how the practices of these firms are different from those of the successful ones. The second is also with respect to sampling.

Eventually, for quantitative analyses of the data, variance conditions must be met. Therefore, I hope that STEP has a grand design to make sure that the database developed will provide sufficient variances for quantitative analysis in the future. Not doing so would be regrettable because it would deprive the field of a very valuable research resource, especially since it would not take that much more effort to do it. Third, empirical studies, especially quantitative ones, have consisted mainly of cross-sectional studies. By their nature, cross-sectional studies have problems establishing causality. Thus, it would benefit the field tremendously if the project researchers were to collect longitudinal data by returning to a selected set of family firms repeatedly.

It seems clear that the STEP Project is and will continue to be the focal point for research about maintaining entrepreneurial capabilities across generations. To the project researchers, for the continuing intellectual stimulation and what they have already accomplished, the family business research community owes a heavy debt.

JESS H. CHUA
AUGUST, 2010
CALGARY, ALBERTA

Acknowledgments

This book is a collective effort by scholars, entrepreneurs, and administrators who are interested in family entrepreneurship in Asia. The editors and the contributors would like to thank Babson College and its staff for supporting the Asia Pacific Consortium of the Global STEP Project. Like many research collaborations, this consortium emerged out of serendipity when Professor Robert Eng, who headed up Asia research and development for Babson, discussed collaboration with the Center for Entrepreneurship of the Chinese University of Hong Kong. With common interest discovered, Professor Tim Habbershon and Robert Nason of the STEP Project then took over and worked with the Center to put together a research workshop. This workshop was fortunate in attracting more than a dozen scholars to come and discuss the theory and method behind the STEP Project. It also stimulated the interest of the attendants to organize a family summit in Asia, building on Babson's experience in similar summits in Europe and South America. After the workshop the scholars conducted research on business families and a year later shared their findings in the first family summit held in Hong Kong. Their studies result in the present volume.

We would like to thank all the families and scholars who came to the workshop and summit. Their support and comments encouraged us in this cross-national endeavor. In particular, Mervyn Morris originated the idea of an edited book and actually drafted the book proposal to the publisher. He worked jointly on a chapter but did not serve as an editor due to time constraints. Roger King, Kuang S. Yeh, T.J. Wong, Joseph Fan, and Beeleng Chua served as speakers, moderators, and organizers in the Hong Kong workshop and summit. In addition, Hyunsuk Lee and Jangwoo Lee were supportive of the consortium and hosted the second family summit in Seoul. We are also grateful to sponsors and the schools behind the project. Particularly, Prudential Insurance, *Wall Street Journal Asia*, and the *Hong Kong Economic Journal* supported the workshop and summit in Hong Kong. The Indian School of Business organized the first Asian Conference on Family Business to support the STEP scholars in their work. Bond University invited STEP scholars to visit their campus to nurture a collaborative spirit. When we worked on this edited volume, the support and direction given by Mattias Nordqvist and Thomas M. Zellweger as well as the editorial team of Edward Elgar was invaluable.

This volume is an attempt to stimulate more interest on family business in Asia and hopefully more research will appear in the near future.

KEVIN AU
JUSTIN B. CRAIG
KAVIL RAMACHANDRAN

Contributors

Kevin Au is Associate Professor of Management at the Chinese University of Hong Kong. He also serves as the associate director of the Center for Entrepreneurship. His research interests are international management, entrepreneurship, family business, social network, and cross-cultural research methodology.

Shyh-Jer Chen is Professor of the Institute of Human Resource Management of National Sun Yat-sen University, Taiwan.

Wenting Chen was Teaching Assistant of School of Business of Sun Yat-sen University, China, and is now with School of Business Administration, Dongbei University of Finance and Economics, China.

Hsi-Mei Chung is Associate Professor of Department of Business Administration of I-Shou University. His research interests are organizational theory, strategic management and international business management.

Justin B. Craig is a co-director of the Australian Centre for Family Business and Associate Professor (global strategy, entrepreneurship and family business) in the Business Faculty of Bond University. His research interests are family enterprising and entrepreneurial behavior.

Mimi Fu was a student at the Sun Yat-sen University, China. She is now a Lecturer at Guangdong University of Foreign Studies, China.

Wayne Irava is a Research Associate at Australian Centre for Family Business at Bond University.

Rachna Jha is a Research Assistant at the Indian School of Business, Hyderabad.

Weiwen Li is Assistant Professor of the Department of Business Administration, Sun Yat-Sen University, China. His research interests are international entrepreneurship, corporate government, family business and CEO succession.

Ya Li is Associate Professor at the Institute of Modern Management (IMM) at Business School of Nankai University.

Xinchun Li is Professor at Department of Business Administration at Sun Yat-sen University, China, and was formerly the Dean of the Business School. His research interests include theory of the firm, family business, entrepreneurship and strategic alliances.

Danming Lin is Vice President of Shantou University. He is also professor at the Shantou University Business School, China. His current research focuses on strategic issues on the applications of information technology in China.

Yuan Lu is Professor of Management at the Chinese University of Hong Kong. His research interests include international strategic alliance and decision-making in Chinese enterprises.

Ken Moores is Professor in Management (Family Business) and Director of the Australian Centre for Family Business in the Faculty of Business of Bond University. His research interests include management accounting, finance, strategic planning, corporate governance, and leadership development in family businesses.

Mervyn Morris is a Lecturer in Management at the Queensland University of Technology Business School. He has worked in administrative and managerial roles in the public and private sectors across a variety of industries. His research interests include entrepreneurship, gender, and structure and agency in management.

Kavil Ramachandran is Thomas Schmidheiny Chair Professor of Family Business and Clinical Professor of Wealth Management at the Indian School of Business. His research interests include family business governance, challenges of professionalization of family business, growth strategies and new enterprise management.

Bing Ren is Associate Professor of Department of Business Administration of Nankai University.

Sachin Waiker is a writer at the Kellogg School of Management, Northwestern University.

John Ward is Clinical Professor at the Kellogg School of Management, Northwestern University. He is an active researcher, speaker and consultant on family succession, ownership, governance and philanthropy. He is the author or co-author of several leading texts on family business, including *Keeping the Family Business Healthy*, *Strategic Planning for the Family Business*, and *Perpetuating the Family Business*.

Bin Yang is Professor in the Human Resource Department of Nankai University. His research interests include strategic human resource management, labor relations, enterprise evolution, corporate governance, business history and comparative business.

Kuang S. Yeh is Professor of Organization Management in the Department of Business Management at National Sun Yat-sen University, Taiwan. He also serves as a deputy minister of the Research, Development and Evaluation Commission of the Executive Yuan. His research interests include organization theory, business ethics, corporate governance and economic sociology.

Hang Zhu is Associate Professor in the Department of Tourism and Hotel Management at Sun Yat-Sen University, China.

1. Introduction

Kevin Au, Justin B. Craig and
Kavil Ramachandran

Driven by Babson College, a world renowned entrepreneurship school located in Boston in the United States of America, the Successful Transgenerational Entrepreneurship Practices (STEP) Project is an international research study that focuses on corporate entrepreneurship in family businesses. Transgenerational entrepreneurship is the nomenclature used by a coterie of scholars whose interest is to work with families in business to understand, improve, and consequently, it is hoped, help them maintain their entrepreneurial capabilities across generations. This effectively means that the STEP research lens is focused on the processes and outcomes of corporate entrepreneurship in the family context, rather than on the succession of management and ownership, which has predominated family business research to date.

The research project began in 2005 with a group of academics from six leading European business schools collaborating to develop and implement a case-based research framework and methodology. The model put forward was replicated in 2006 by a group of like-minded South American scholars from premier institutions and was launched in the Asia-Pacific region in 2007.

This book is a compilation of chapters authored by STEP Asia-Pacific founding partners.[1] These partner-institution scholars and the families with whom they have worked have interpreted their observations around a particular dimension, or in some cases multiple dimensions, of the overall research framework that is common to all involved in the global STEP Project. The following chapters, therefore, can be useful in a variety of contexts. Consistent with the STEP philosophy of upholding the highest scholastic integrity, each case is action research based rather than being positioned as what would typically be referred to as a teaching case. However, having introduced this caveat, there is ample opportunity and sufficient scope, as will become evident, to use each case to facilitate classroom discussion at undergraduate, graduate and executive education levels. The purpose of each of the following chapters, therefore, is to broadly interpret a common research question in order to introduce key findings to extend or challenge existing theoretical frames and further the understanding of the uniqueness of the family business context. Following a brief overview of family business in the countries of the three Asia-Pacific regions in which the featured case families reside, this introductory chapter outlines the theoretical and methodological basis of the STEP project and highlights several emerging themes.

FAMILY BUSINESS IN THE ASIA-PACIFIC REGION

Asia-Pacific countries have a comparatively short history of economic development, which means that, though there are exceptions, family businesses in this region have shorter histories than their longer established Western regions counterparts. This is particularly true of India, Hong Kong, Taiwan and mainland China (the latter three countries being commonly referred to as Greater China). In formal academic settings, Australian business schools have a longer history of studying family businesses than their Asian counterparts; in fact, the use of modern paradigms to study family business is still relatively new to Asia, and this is especially so for schools in Greater China. Consequently, there are many challenges ahead for family business stakeholders, not only those internal to the firm. The encouraging news is that interest in this area is growing rapidly. In this section, we briefly canvass the context, status and challenges of family businesses in three Asia-Pacific regions, specifically, Australia, India and Greater China.

Australia[2]

In Australia, many of the businesses that have morphed into considerable family firms were established immediately post World War II (Moores and Mula 1993) and the majority of these remain family owned and operated. These family firms not only operate in a wide diversity of industries, but importantly, have a presence in small, medium and large sectors.

More specifically, using a narrow definition of family business, the Business Longitudinal Survey (BLS) carried out by the Australian Bureau of Statistics finds that at least half of all businesses in Australia are family businesses (ABS 1997, quoted in Moores and Mula 2000). These firms were then estimated to have a combined wealth of AU$3.6 trillion, and to employ 50 percent of the private sector workforce (Smyrnios and Walker 2003). In a more recent study, the overall wealth of Australian family businesses was estimated to be approximately AU$4.3 trillion (Smyrnios and

Dana 2006). Significantly, while not all family firms are small, they constitute approximately 67 percent of the small and medium-sized enterprise (SME) sector in the Australian economy (Kotey 2005), and it is important to acknowledge that over half of Australia's top 500 private companies are family owned (Matterson 2002).

The significance of family firms in the Australian market is therefore evident and these statistics are not appreciably different from those reported in other countries (Astrachan and Shanker 1996; Morck and Yeung 2003). However, Australian family firms are relatively young in comparison to family firms from old world economies such as Europe and Japan. The majority of Australian family firms currently still have the founding generation in some position of authority, monitoring or control. The founders are those family members who are often accredited as being the entrepreneurs, and while the founders are entrepreneurial at first, their entrepreneurial capacity typically declines over time.

Apart from the reported poor survival records of family businesses, there are a number of unique challenges that beset even those that do manage to survive. Failure to understand and manage these challenges, particularly during transition periods, often results in conflicts that are destructive to both the firm and the family. These may contribute to the high mortality rate of family-owned firms. Some of the most difficult issues for family businesses occur at transition points, particularly generational changes. Failure to understand the difference between the family system and the business system, failure to run the family business on a proper business basis and failure to handle the transition to the next generation are seen as three critical challenges for family businesses.

To address these challenges, Moores and Mula (1993) sought to explain the management and control of second (and later) generation Australian family firms in terms of three stages: collectivity, formalization and control, and elaboration of structure. They found that the pattern of strategy, structure and control of family-owned businesses across the three stages generally reflected an increasing level of sophistication in management and systems as firms developed from collectivities to more elaborate structures.

Despite their significant contribution to the Australian economy, Australian family-owned firms have not been subject to the extensive research necessary to increase the understanding of them (Moores and Mula 2000). They warrant greater research and analysis, of a sort that is separate from research into the small business sector because family firms vary in size from small owner-manager firms to large multinational corporations (Moores and Barrett 2002). This is particularly evident in the Australian economy where family names like Murdoch, Packer, Smorgon and Fox all lead large corporations that are renowned in Australia and the throughout the global business community.

Like family businesses across the world, Australian family businesses, in order to survive across generations, need to maintain an entrepreneurial mindset within every generation (Sirmon and Hitt 2003). Generational leaders need to be entrepreneurs for business growth (Schwass 2005). With the majority of Australian family firms on the verge of generational transition (Smyrnios and Dana 2006), the question currently being asked is whether the founder's entrepreneurial drive can be retained and perpetuated over incoming generations. Recognizing the family resources and practices that perpetuate an entrepreneurial mindset across generations is paramount (Irava 2009). This is because the inability to remain entrepreneurial not only contributes to the demise of family firms, but may also have catastrophic effects on national economies, including that of Australia.

Survival of the family firm across generations is difficult to maintain. While some have mastered the art of transition (Miller and Le Breton-Miller 2005), the majority of family firms in Australia share the same fate as others around the globe that do not make it to or past the third generation hurdle (Hoy and Vesper 1994; Miller et al. 2004). Notwithstanding its relatively recent beginnings, in commercial terms, Australia too has only a small percentage of family firms that reach the third generation, with nearly 50 percent being identified as unlikely to become later generation firms (Smyrnios and Dana 2006).

India

Family businesses have played a key role throughout the evolution and development of the Indian economy. During the early years of India's independence, when start-up capital was scarce, many traders set up manufacturing companies to take advantage of emerging entrepreneurial opportunities. Largely deriving from the trading communities, these were essentially family businesses and included names such as Birla and Murugappa. Under the control of a licensing regime that restricted the free flow of resources into many potential entrepreneurial opportunities, most of these family businesses diversified into unrelated areas. However, competition was limited and competitiveness was less of an issue than it is today.

The tipping point for the Indian economy came in 1991 when the government was forced to remove restrictions on the entry of new firms and effectively opened up the economy. This unleashed a new level of entrepreneurial energy across the country, resulting in the emergence of a new pool of first generation entrepreneurs.

During this time, two major changes took place simultaneously. First, Indian family businesses, along with others, were forced to restructure themselves, which increased competitiveness. Initially, the choice was simple: to perform or to perish. Several business families chose the former and undertook innovative ways to restructure not only their portfolios but also their individual business operations. This required some of the fundamental qualities of entrepreneurship propounded by Schumpeter (1934), one of which was innovations in processes.

Second, a new generation of entrepreneurs emerged from established family businesses. These alert individuals identified market opportunities and had big dreams. Since they belonged to business families, they had initial advantages such as superior access to resources, a higher level of confidence to manage risk and, importantly, relevant exposure to and understanding of the process of doing business. While members of entrepreneurial families were the first to take the initiative, many others who took a 'wait and watch' attitude soon followed, with plans not only to expand or modernize their existing businesses but also to venture out with new business ideas.

In spite of the dominant role played by family business in the Indian economy, academic interest in this area has been insignificant, primarily because of the broad brush categorization of family enterprises as small, orthodox and unprofessional. Ramachandran and Kirtania (2009) found that half of the top 50 firms listed in the National Stock Exchange are family businesses. Their share in the economy steadily goes up as relatively smaller sized firms are considered for analysis. The top 500 family firms in India grew at an astonishing rate (435 percent in sales, 677 percent in profit and 462 percent in net worth) during the period from 1990–2009 while their non-family counterparts grew at about 60 percent during the same period (Ramachandran and Kirtania 2009). The same research found that the relative growth in contribution to GDP was similarly significant. In essence, the critical role played by family businesses in the entrepreneurial transformation of India has remained substantial over the years.

There are several challenges faced by Indian family businesses. Some of these are not unique to the Indian context, because, like all families in business, they too need to manage three key stakeholders (family, management and owners) whose goals do not necessarily align. However, some challenges are particular to India and can be linked to the rapid growth of the economy and the challenges of transformation that must be managed by family businesses while playing a key role in this globally significant emerging economy.

Like many maturing family businesses around the world, professionalization is a major challenge faced by most Indian family businesses. This is particularly so because of the speed at which changes are required in both the mindset of the family executives who run the business and in the choice of relevant systems and processes and their acceptance in the organization. In most cases, family entrepreneurs with limited experience or exposure to the functioning of well managed large organizations tend to be concerned and hesitant about making the required transition. The challenges are greater if the executive is not from the family. Since most Indian family businesses are not only controlled, but also operated by family members, the challenge of professionalization can be influenced by the quality of family governance that they have in place. Agreement on the nature and extent of decentralization of decision-making on a variety of topics is not always certain.

Family governance is still an important challenge, covering a range of issues such as business ownership structure, leadership succession, retirement and family wealth management. While most families in India tend to adopt an amoebic model of division of ownership in every generation, this is either not handled smoothly or cannot be achieved because of structural problems. Many Indian families tend to set up as many separate business units as there are male members (and females too in many cases today). The concept of family entrepreneurship, which was previously restricted to establishing separate business units, is rapidly changing, with the focus shifting towards exploiting attractive investment opportunities. The assumption is shifting from 'self-employment' to entrepreneurial opportunities.

In essence, India's rapid transformation in recent years has been powered to a great extent by family entrepreneurship. While some families encourage, if not actually compel, the younger generation to enter and build existing businesses, an emerging option is for the new generation to separate ownership and management and venture out on their own without interfering in the operations of the existing businesses. There is growing interest and preparedness among business families to understand the unique challenges of managing a family business and to bring about necessary changes. The high level of interest and excitement devoid of huge inhibitions is a reflection of the arrival of a welcome era for family business in India. Still, as highlighted in the Australian context, very few firms continue to survive beyond three or four generations, reflecting the enormity of the challenge of transforming and institutionalizing them.

Greater China

Social and historical factors have contributed to the low status of family business in Greater China. In their country's struggle towards modernity, the Chinese have suffered as a result of feudalism, in which family cronyism played an important part. Since World War II, the adoption of

Western practices and technology has enabled Chinese societies to develop and modernize rapidly. Hong Kong and Taiwan were industrialized in 30–40 years whereas it took China less than 30 years to achieve this. A result of this perceived haste to imitate the more advanced nations is that a large number of traditional values and systems, unless transformed (Lau 1978), are being looked down upon, shuffled aside or actively ignored (Au 2007). Despite the role that the family plays in the success of a significant proportion of businesses, many family businesses, particularly those that are listed and prominent, tend to conceal or evade questions about their family background out of fear that people will stigmatize them as traditional and undermine their achievements.

Perhaps because of the negative connotations associated with the family business label, Chinese businessmen do not organize themselves around their identity as a family business even though the Chinese have established scores of associations along lineages and hometowns. Without advocates such as an association to plead their case, the weaknesses of family businesses, such as nepotism and family infighting, are played up and even ridiculed in the media, in business analysis and even in popular soap operas. The impression that family businesses in Greater China are mostly small, unprofessional, backward, nepotistic and fraught with questionable business practices is prevalent and accepted as a common fact. Academics should be responsible for correcting such misunderstandings, but institutional ranking pressure has distracted them from this objective and directed their attention to researching and publishing works related to more mainstream subjects (Meyer 2006). Family business has been virtually ignored, perceived only as a niche, unfashionable subject in local academia. Similarly, business school pedagogy concentrates on teaching students to develop a career in incorporated companies, further demeaning the existence and achievements of family businesses.

Fortunately, there are signs that the tide has turned. After three decades of development, founders of private companies on the mainland have reached retirement age. They are joined by the first generation of many Hong Kong and Taiwanese family firms. Succession has now become a pressing issue that is commanding the attention of family firms. Private bankers and family business advisers are also recognizing the change and are expanding into the market. Meanwhile, a few prominent research papers, such as that by Anderson and Reeb (2003), have spurred local academics to turn their attention to the growing field of family business and explore the needs of the community. In addition, several forward-looking organizations have begun to educate and transform family businesses in the region.[3]

Scholars who studied why Chinese entrepreneurs were competitive and able to achieve an economic miracle among 'the four Asian tigers' and the ASEAN countries found that Chinese family businesses were able to exploit familial ties to start companies, make swift deals and react quickly to market needs (Lau 1978; Redding 1990; Wong 1988; Weidenbaum and Hughes 1996). Family businesses continue to be as prevalent today and many of them have since grown to be substantial and even prominent companies. Anecdotal evidence suggests that two-thirds of the listed firms in Hong Kong are family businesses. Yet, formal and rigorous statistics do not exist. Research still cites historical data in relation to family businesses (for example, Carney and Gedajlovic 2002; Claessens et al. 2000).

Despite the strengths observed among Chinese family businesses by the above scholars, the weaknesses of family businesses have drawn criticism, particularly since the Asian financial crisis in the late 1990s. Nepotism has been widely associated with Chinese family businesses. For instance, Claessens et al. (2000) found that East Asian economies are dominated by large, oligarchic family firms. Families hold a tight grip on a network of businesses through a pyramidal structure. They concentrate wealth around themselves, which can promote crony capitalism, the exploitation of smaller shareholders and political rent-seeking. The rigidity of family businesses and their unwillingness to evolve was highlighted in studies on failure in leadership and ownership succession. Moreover, Fan et al. (2007) found that Hong Kong public firms on average suffered from a 56 percent loss in their market return in a five-year period prior to a succession. Taiwanese firms suffered similarly, although to a lesser extent. They attributed this huge value destruction to the difficulties of transferring specialized assets such as founders' personal networks across generations, and thus, to problems and conflicts heirs would likely confront with other stakeholders after succession. These phenomena show that the general public's negative perceptions of Chinese family firms may have a kernel of truth.

Because Greater China, like India and Australia, has a short history of development, some of the challenges of family businesses are common to all. First of all, Chinese family businesses are grappling with the issue of professionalization. Hong Kong and Taiwan family firms have introduced a significant number of professional managers and financiers, but many family businesses are still inward-looking and have not considered outside talent. In numerous cases, qualified outsiders simply prefer to work for multinational corporations or the government. The situation is more acute in mainland China as private companies only began to emerge after the Open Door Policy in the late 1970s (Lee and Li 2009). There is a lack of capable managers, and the one-child policy left many families with only one chance to produce a competent heir. Related to professionalism are a string of business issues regarding the growth of firms, including corporate governance, innovation and international expansion. Without enough professionals and adequate management, family firms are haunted by the problem of growth (Carney and Gedajlovic 2002; Yeung and Olds 2000).

Growth is by no means related just to business. Many of the first generation entrepreneurs have reached retirement age and still continue to work. They desperately need a proper family governance structure in order to bring in and groom new leadership, to separate family issues from the company board, to prepare for succession and perpetuate the family's entrepreneurship spirit. The problem is that communication within the Chinese family is usually top-down, with power concentrated in the hands of the traditional older generation. Meanwhile, members of the younger generation are often educated overseas and tend to prefer a different style of communication and to have a different vision for themselves and the family. Therefore, initiating discussions on family governance topics, such as a family council or a family office, is particularly difficult. This leads many among the younger generation to opt to work outside the family and leaves the founders to seek other routes to preserve the business and family wealth such as, for instance, seeking the help of private equity firms (Lansberg and Gersick 2009). In the worst case scenario, however, disputes can erupt between parents and children or brothers and sisters. Such family sagas are not uncommon in the popular press. In sum, Chinese family businesses face many challenges related to expansion, building brands, innovation and going global (Ahlstrom et al. 2004; Yeung 2006).

STEP RESEARCH THEORETICAL FRAMES

Apart from some sporadic contributions in special issues of *Entrepreneurship Theory and Practice* and the *Journal of Business Venturing* (Poza 1988; Gartner 1990; Hall et al. 2001; Habbershon and Pistrui 2002; Zahra et al. 2004; Kellermans and Eddleston 2006; Naldi et al. 2007), an area that receives particularly little attention is entrepreneurship in family firms (Wortman 1994; Chrisman et al. 2005). In many family firms, ownership and management are maintained across several generations and a key challenge for long-term survival is to sustain the entrepreneurial spirit. All firms regularly need to renew their way of doing business in order to stay competitive as they risk losing their entrepreneurial capacity when they mature (Eisenhardt and Martin 2000). However, family firms face additional challenges with regard to entrepreneurship. For instance, little is known about how family business governance structures with highly concentrated power and a long-term intergenerational perspective affect entrepreneurship (Hall et al. 2001). Some scholars see family firms as a setting where entrepreneurship flourishes, while others argue the opposite, that is, that family firms are conservative, introverted, inflexible and lack entrepreneurial spirit (Zahra 2005). Most agree, however, that there is a need for research on entrepreneurial processes in family firms, and especially on how entrepreneurship can be maintained and practiced across generations (Habbershon and Pistrui 2002; Zahra et al. 2004).

The STEP research project aims to investigate transgenerational entrepreneurship in family firms. Importantly, this means a dual unit of analysis, where we introduce the business family unit along with the more traditional firm unit of analysis. Combining literature on corporate entrepreneurship, especially entrepreneurial orientation, with the research-based view, and literature on family firms with a particular focus on values, continuity, culture and governance, we investigate two broad research questions:

- How do business families and family businesses generate and sustain entrepreneurial performance across generations?
- How does entrepreneurial performance relate to the continuity, growth and transgenerational entrepreneurship of business families and family businesses?

The STEP initiative, therefore, emerged from an observation that the family business field has not explicitly identified the entrepreneurial potential of the family ownership group nor adequately delineated the strategic requirements for families in wealth creation (Habbershon and Pistrui 2002). While empirical evidence suggests that families play an important role in the venture creation process (Timmons 2004), little attention is given to the family perspective in the entrepreneurship literature (Aldrich and Cliff 2003). The family's entrepreneurial contribution and its justification to the family firm remain largely absent although the family is a distinct unit of analysis capable of sustainable entrepreneurial behavior over time (Cruz et al. 2006). Entrepreneurship in general has been under-researched in the family business context (Eddleston et al. 2008).

STEP METHODOLOGY

The STEP research strategy is to start with in-depth case research and then move into quantitative data collection and analysis. Nordqvist and Zellweger (2010) lay out the details and the rationales of such a strategy. Essentially, a qualitative approach helps better to grasp and expand the meaning of key concepts (such as entrepreneurial orientation (EO), resource-based view (RBV) and familiness), facilitates multi-level analysis of family businesses and underscores the heterogeneity of various family businesses. The research team in each country studied at least one family business, using, as a point of departure, a common conceptual framework. The approach is 'abductive', which is essentially a mix of inductive and conductive approaches (Alvesson and Sköldberg 2000). STEP research teams were encouraged to capture and interpret additional emerging aspects and dimensions for transgenerational entrepreneurship. In so doing, our study serves the dual purpose of comparing our initial theoretical understanding with real-life cases and using the emerging observations to refine, develop and improve the theoretical framework.

The STEP teams followed a set of stringent procedures to ensure data quality and comparison across the cases.[4] Specifically, there are procedural requirements with regard to the sampling of firms, selection of interviewees, research process and reporting of findings. In essence, STEP creates a purposeful sample in which businesses varying in size and industry are studied so long as they fulfill specific criteria that qualify them as significant, multi-generational family businesses. Each business has multiple actors to be interviewed. The actors, in any combination, would include the controlling owner or owners, the CEO, different generations, non-family top management, and, if deemed necessary, a significant non-family owner. The teams conducted interviews following an interview guide that covered the background of the family and the business, entrepreneurship and resource profiles, family influence on these profiles and performance. The teams received training before they started the study. To provide the context for interpreting the interviews, the teams also studied secondary materials relating to the companies, such as websites and documents, as well as the historical, political, economic and industrial development background of the countries in which the companies operate.

After the interviews, the teams transcribed the verbatim records and followed a specific structure in writing a master case document (30 to 50 pages). This document served as the 'data' storehouse for subsequent analysis, leading to the proposal of emergent ideas and interpretations, other reflections, and possible explanations on views different from the initial conceptual model. The chapters in this book are a combination of records from a selection of Asia-Pacific case studies, analysis with regard to the initial conceptual model and alternative views concerning family entrepreneurship.

The Asia-Pacific teams followed the method as outlined by the STEP consortium. Each of the teams conducted semi-structured interviews in 2007–08. This book features five families from Greater China, four families from Australia and two families from India. Table 1.1 summarizes the main features of the families and the main business of each family. The families and their businesses vary in terms of their history and

Table 1.1 *Families studied and the main features of their business*

Family	Greater China					Australia				India	
	Mok	Lee	Sun	Chen	Han	Deague	Belcher	Dennis	Battaglia	Rao	Shah
Company name	Automatic Manufacturing Limited	Lee Kum Kee Corporation Limited	Dawu Business Group	Menshy Group	Jong-Shyn Ship-building Company	Asia-Pacific Building Corporation	Sands Management Group	Dennis Property Limited	Base Group Development	GMR Group	Shakti Group
Major locations of operation	Hong Kong; Dongguan, PRC	Hong Kong; Guangzhou, PRC	Xushui County, Hebei Province, PRC	Liuzhou and Chenghai, PRC	Kaohsiung, Taiwan	Melbourne and other major cities, Australia	Gold Coast, Australia	Victoria and other states, Australia	mainly Australia, also Argentina	All over India; also overseas	India
Founding year/ number of generations	1976/2	1888/5	1989/2	?1979/2	1985/2	early 1900s/6	1981/2	1965/3	1967/2	?1978/2	1947/2
Generations in business	First & second	Third & fourth	First & second	First & second	First & second	Fourth & fifth	First & second	First, second & third	First & second	First & second	First & second
Industry	Advanced manufacturing	Sauces and condiments; health-care products	Mainly livestock and agriculture	Mainly automobile battery	Ship-building	Mainly construction	Management rights; tourism	Land development; construction	Diversified; property development	Diversified; mainly infrastructure & manufacturing	Diversified; Mainly cooking spices and health-care

the industries in which they are involved. They are all privately held and are medium to large in size. All of them exhibit prominent features that deserve research attention. For instance, the Lee family of Lee Kum Kee has the distinction of having the top ranking brand in the Chinese sauce and condiment market while the Rao family of the GMR Group is a leader in India's infrastructure development sector.

As stipulated in the interview guide, several decision-makers, including family and non-family members, were interviewed; in some cases they were interviewed several times. In the case of the Mok family of Hong Kong, for example, John Mok, one of the founders of Automatic Manufacturing Limited (AML), and William Mok, a second-generation family member, were interviewed together with three top managers (see Table 2.1 in Chapter 2). Like the other cases from China and India, the interview was conducted primarily in the local dialect (Cantonese in this case) together with English in some instances, as many interviewees received some of their education overseas and used English to express themselves at times. The quotes are translated from Cantonese into English, with the best attempt being made to retain the underlying meaning of the original.

STEP ASIA-PACIFIC CASES: EMERGING THEMES

The cases assembled in this book provide a rich analysis of 11 family businesses. The robust theoretical foundation and sound methodology utilized here enable us to make informed observations, which in this section we will do by first introducing each case study and then making a concluding statement.

The Deague family case featured by Justin Craig, Wayne Irava and Ken Moores in Chapter 7 introduces the idea of learning entrepreneurship by osmosis. The process of 'knowledge accrual through osmosis' has ensured that the next generation of Deagues has been socialized into all aspects of their portfolio of businesses. As such, the case shows how the Deague family has been able to attain and maintain a competitive advantage by being innovative and leveraging their distinct familiness. The case outlines the way in which the unyielding pursuit of innovation and creative solutions, which is endemic throughout the business and across generations, is at the heart of the Deagues' business success.

The family business learning and life cycle framework is the focus of Chapter 10 on the Battaglia family, also by Justin Craig, Wayne Irava and Ken Moores. This case shows how the sibling partnership of the second generation learned business and learned to lead the family business while the incumbent generation learned to let go. Interestingly, the case canvasses some of the conflicts between the twin brothers and between them and the patriarch. Insights gleaned are related to how siblings approach and handle differences of opinion between themselves and between their generation and the incumbent generation. What is noteworthy – as reported by both generations – is that the long intentional apprenticeship or incubation period required of the next generation has both advantages and disadvantages. The matriarch openly expressed concern that one or both sons would not return to the family fold in a contributing way once they had pursued their own entrepreneurial ventures. Both sons report how they eventually understood their parents' wisdom in giving them considerable scope to pursue various ventures using family funds without being overly concerned with producing stellar financial results. The family is now positioned to benefit from the strong foundation it has built and the considerable trust and mutual respect that exist amongst all the family members. They remain prudent investors who rely heavily on their understanding of the industry life cycle in their core business.

Craig et al.'s Belcher family case (Chapter 8) highlights how the first (and second) generation Belchers have overcome (and continue to overcome) issues related to the liability of newness in their family business. The Belcher family pioneered and helped legitimize a new industry while simultaneously maintaining a competitive advantage. The discussion provides insights into how they have been able to accomplish this 'against the odds' achievement.

In Chapter 9 on the Dennis Family Corporation, the final case from Australia, Mervyn Morris focuses his lens on 'incremental entrepreneurship' in the transition from the first to the second generation. The role of professional governance is highlighted as being instrumental in ensuring that members of the second generation successfully continue the entrepreneurial spirit of the family business (albeit in a different style), adding value to the firm in an 'incremental' manner.

Chapter 4, featuring the Sun family, by Bing Ren, Bin Yang and Ya Li of Nankai University, highlights how families in business in China are developing the enterprise economy by linking their success with the happiness and wealth of the larger community. The authors help us understand the enterprise challenges relating to formal and informal institutions that have both helped and hindered the Sun family's growth and opportunities over a period of 30 years. As such they complement the RBV and EO dimensions with what they refer to as 'the institutional factor'.

The second Greater China case by Weiwen Li, Yuan Lu, Danming Lin and Kevin Au (Chapter 5) concerns a family business located in mainland China. Menshy Battery Ltd, based in Shantou, is the largest exporter of motorcycle batteries in China. It uses nanotechnology to outcompete

Japanese and Korean companies. This case shows how fast-changing environments may quickly render an entrepreneur's capabilities obsolete and how a family business can overcome this difficulty through the renewed entrepreneurial dynamism of the overseas-educated incoming generation. In particular, it highlights the importance of building a top management team with diverse knowledge and skills to introduce new technologies.

The third case from Greater China transports readers to Hong Kong where the largest Chinese sauce and condiment producer, Lee Kum Kee, has its headquarters. Xinchun Li, Hang Zhu, Wenting Chen and Mimi Fu discuss how the third and fourth generations have overcome the challenges arising from family disruptions and expanded their business to China and many other countries. Learning from past family conflicts, the Lee family focused on building family governance structures to promote family cohesion and sustain its entrepreneurial spirit. Combining a formal structure and constitution with informal cultural values, their sophisticated family governance structure provides the necessary resources to enable transgenerational entrepreneurship in the future.

Kevin Au also studied Automatic Manufacturing Ltd in Hong Kong (Chapter 2). The first generation of the Mok family founded a business around the manufacture of advanced equipment. The company grew with the development of Hong Kong industries in the Pearl River Delta. In the process, it groomed a cadre of professional managers and established a corporate governance system that is the envy of their peers. To continue the family's entrepreneurial spirit, AML is at present using the resources it has built to encourage the second generation family members to spin off from the family business and test their wings as entrepreneurs, and to eventually lure them back to take over AML from the first generation. Such a systematic approach, though still under experiment, has the potential of becoming best practice for other family businesses.

The last case from Greater China features Taiwan's Han family and the Jong-Shyn Shipbuilding Company. Chapter 6, contributed by Hsi-Mei Chung, Kuang S. Yeh and Shyh-Jer Chen of the National Sun Yat-sen University, illustrates how the Han family successfully transformed itself and boldly entered the highly value-added yacht market in 2003. The chapter highlights how the next generation continued the founder's entrepreneurial legacy. The family's ability to adapt to change and its ability to recognize technology innovation have had a significant influence on the transfer of entrepreneurship in this family business.

The GMR Group from India, which is discussed in Chapter 11 by Kavil Ramachandran, John Ward, Sachin Waiker and Rachna Jha, is representative of the new generation family business in India. De facto a first generation entrepreneur, the group's founder G.M. Rao explored multiple business opportunities while expanding the existing business. He ultimately saw his dream of building an empire realized in the rapidly expanding area of infrastructure, particularly in the construction of airports and roads. He recognized early on the need to ensure governance both in the business and the family and has introduced accepted governance principles such as a detailed family constitution. The family continues to identify new entrepreneurial opportunities while leaving operational responsibilities to non-family professionals. These systematic approaches have helped the family to grow entrepreneurially while keeping familial relationships intact.

The second case from India, written by Kavil Ramachandran, features the midsized Shakti Group (Chapter 12). This is the amazing story of a refugee entrepreneur from Pakistan who migrated to India with a large family at the time of the country's independence, and of his struggle to survive. He kept his family together while exploring different small business ideas and finally succeeded in developing a unique spice mix product for those consuming tobacco. Lacking clear governance guidelines, the family experienced a bitter split as the second generation entered the business, at a time when it was doing very well financially. The case captures the approach taken by the entrepreneur and his two sons to rebuild the business and bring accepted family and business governance structures to the business. They have diversified into the health-care, food and entertainment businesses and now achieve the same turnover and profits that they had enjoyed as a group before the split, all within the span of a few years. The two brothers continue to scan for entrepreneurial opportunities while simultaneously professionalizing their growing portfolio of businesses.

EMERGING THEMES

The families featured in this collection provide rich insights into what is considered the most complex form of business in the world. Though the three regions, Australia, India and Greater China, all have relatively short histories in commercial development terms, it can be concluded that family businesses that involve multiple generations are the minority, and the reasons for this are many. Challenges related to dealing with an expanding family concurrently with a growing business; the related issue of professionalism, which neccessitates the introduction of new ways of conducting business that in many cases are in direct contrast to the incumbents' methods; the introduction of outside experts, including non-family directors; and the introduction of new generations with new ideas into the business were all unveiled as common concerns of the featured family businesses in the three regions.

In terms of family governance, a small number of the case families adopt practices that are proven in the West and establish governance structures such as family councils and other family forums to separate family issues from business issues. However, others are either too small or are still in the process of evaluating the appropriateness of these practices to their own contexts. Chinese business families, in particular, face the added issue of communication within the family, as the founding generation tends to be more traditional and to have a starkly different background to that of the incoming generation, which is increasingly being exposed to Western ways of doing business as a result of a Western university education. Additionally, next generation family members are ever more aware that they can pursue professional careers outside their own family business, requiring the incumbent leadership to find ways to attract them back to the family business and continue the family legacy. How to nurture the incoming generation to be future leaders stewarding the family and the increasingly complex business is evidently a challenging issue for all the families operating in the Asia-Pacific region featured here.

There are also indications of a synthesized model emerging that is based on a combination of traditional values and modern organizational structures and systems. Given the pace of transformation of the Asia-Pacific region and the emergence of a new class of family entrepreneurs, it is natural to expect the new generation of family businesses of this region to have some unique experiences to offer to the rest of the world.

NOTES

1. Most of the families participated in a regional summit in 2008. For details see entre preneurship.baf.cuhk.edu.hk.
2. Information for this section was sourced from previous works, significantly those of Professor Ken Moores and Dr Wayne Irava from the Australian Centre for Family Business at Bond University.
3. For example, the Family Business Network Pacific Asia, India and Australia chapters were established in 2009, 2005 and 2007 respectively (www.fbnpa.org; www.cii.in; www.fambiz.org.au).
4. Details are available on www.stepproject.org ; also Nordqvist and Zellweger (2010).

REFERENCES

Ahlstrom, D., M.N. Young, E.S. Chan and G.D. Bruton. 'Facing constraints to growth? Overseas Chinese entrepreneurs and traditional business practices in East Asia'. *Asia-Pacific Journal of Management*, 21:3 (2004), 263–85.

Aldrich, Howard E. and Jennifer E. Cliff. 'The pervasive effects of family on entrepreneurship: toward a family embeddedness perspective'. *Journal of Business Venturing*, 18:5 (2003), 573–96.

Alvesson, M. and K. Sköldberg (eds). *Reflexive Methodology: New Vistas for Qualitative Research*. New York: Sage, 2000.

Anderson, Alistair R. and David M. Reeb. 'Founding family ownership and firm performance: evidence from the S&P 500'. *Journal of Finance*, 58:3 (2003), 1301–27.

Astrachan, Joseph H. and Melissa Carey Shanker. 'Myths and realities: family businesses' contribution to the US economy – a framework for assessing family business statistics'. *Family Business Review*, 9:2 (1996), 107–23.

Au, K. 'Self-confidence does not come isolated from the environment'. *Asia Pacific Journal of Management*, 24 (2007), 491–6.

Carney, M. and E. Gedajlovic. 'The co-evolution of institutional environments and organizational strategies: the rise of family business groups in the ASEAN region'. *Organization Studies*, 23:1 (2002), 1–29.

Chrisman, James J., Jess H. Chua and Pramodita Sharma. 'Trends and directions in the development of a strategic management theory of the family firm'. *Entrepreneurship Theory and Practice*, 29:5 (2005), 555–75.

Claessens, S., S. Djankov and L.H.P Lang. 'The separation of ownership and control in East Asian corporations'. *Journal of Financial Economics*, 58:1–2 (2000), 81–112.

Cruz, C., Timothy G. Habbershon, M. Nordqvist, C. Salvato and Thomas Zellweger. 'A conceptual model of transgenerational entrepreneurship in family-influenced firms'. International Family Enterprise Research Academy, Jönköping, 2006.

Eddleston, Kimberly A., Franz W. Kellermanns and Thomas Zellweger. 'Corporate entrepreneurship in family firms: a stewardship perspective'. United States Association for Small Business and Entrepreneurship, San Antonio, Texas, 2008.

Eisenhardt, K.M. and Jeffrey A. Martin. 'Dynamic capabilities: what are they?' *Strategic Management Journal*, 21:10–11 (2000), 1105–21.

Fan, J.P.H., M. Jian and Y.H. Yeh. 'Succession: the role of specialized assets and transfer costs'. Working paper. Chinese University of Hong Kong, 2007 (http://ihome.cuhk.edu.hk/~b109671/index.html; last accessed November 2009).

Gartner, William B. 'What are we talking about when we talk about entrepreneurship?' *Journal of Business Venturing*, 5:1 (1990), 15–28.

Habbershon, Timothy G. and Joseph Pistrui. 'Enterprising families domain: family-influenced ownership groups in pursuit of transgenerational wealth'. *Family Business Review*, 15:3 (2002), 223–37.

Hall, Annika, Leif Melin and Mattias Nordqvist. 'Entrepreneurship as a radical change in the family business: exploring the role of cultural patterns'. *Family Business Review*, 14:3 (2001), 193–208.

Hoy, Frank and Trudy G. Vesper. 'Emerging business, emerging field: entrepreneurship and the family firm'. *Entrepreneurship Theory and Practice*, 19:1 (1994), 9–23.

Irava, Wayne J. 'Familiness qualities, entrepreneurial orientation and long-term performance advantage'. Doctoral dissertation, Bond University, 2009.

Kellermanns, F.W. and K.A. Eddleston. 'Corporate entrepreneurship in family firms: a family perspective'. *Entrepreneurship Theory and Practice*, 30:6 (2006), 809–30.

Kotey, Bernice. 'Goals, management practices, and performance of family SMEs'. *International Journal of Entrepreneurial Behavior & Research,* 11:1 (2005), 3–24.

Lansberg, I. and K. Gersick. 'Tradition and adaptation in Chinese family enterprises: facing the challenge of continuity'. Lansberg Gersick and Associates, 2009.

Lau, S.K. 'From traditional familism to utilitarianistic familism: the metamorphosis of familial ethos among the Hong Kong Chinese'. Chinese University of Hong Kong, Social Research Centre, Hong Kong, 1978.

Lee, J. and H. Li. *Wealth Doesn't Last 3 Generations: How Family Businesses can Maintain Prosperity.* Hackensack, NJ: World Scientific, 2009.

Matterson, H. 'How to cash in and still keep a finger in the pie'. *Weekend Australian,* 26–27 October 2002.

Meyer, K.E. 'Asian management research needs more self-confidence'. *Asia Pacific Journal of Management,* 23 (2006), 119–37.

Miller, Danny and Isabelle Le Breton-Miller. *Managing for the long Run: Lessons in Competitive Advantage from Great Family Businesses.* Boston, MA: Harvard Business School Press, 2005.

Miller, Danny, Isabelle Le Breton-Miller and Lloyd P. Steier. 'Toward an integrative model of effective FOB succession'. *Entrepreneurship Theory and Practice,* 28:4 (2004), 305–28.

Moores, Ken and Mary Barrett. *Learning Family Business – Paradoxes and Pathways.* Aldershot: Ashgate Publishing Company, 2002.

Moores, Ken and Joseph Mula. *Managing and Controlling Family Owned Businesses: A Life Cycle Perspective of Australian Firms.* Gold Coast: Australian Center for Family Business, 1993.

Moores, Ken and Joseph Mula. 'The salience of market, bureaucratic, and clan controls in the management of family firm transitions: some tentative Australian evidence'. *Family Business Review,* 13:2 (2000), 91–106.

Morck, Randall and Bernard Yeung. 'Agency problems in large family business groups'. *Entrepreneurship Theory and Practice,* 27:4 (2003), 367–82.

Naldi, Lucia, M. Nordqvist, K. Sjoberg and Johan Wiklund. 'Entrepreneurial orientation, risk taking, and performance in family firms'. *Family Business Review,* 20:1 (2007), 33–47.

Nordqvist, M. and T. Zellweger. 'A qualitative research approach to the study of transgenerational entrepreneurship' in M. Nordqvist and T. Zellweger (eds), *Transgenerational Entrepreneurship: Exploring Growth and Performance in Family Firms across Generations.* Cheltenham, UK and Northampton, MA, USA: Edward Elgar, 2010, 39–57.

Poza, Erneston J. 'Managerial practices that support interpreneurship and continued growth'. *Family Business Review,* 1:4 (1988), 339–59.

Ramachandran, Kavil and Ansuhree Kirtania. 'Family Businesses – Their Performance and Contribution to Indian Economy Post Liberalization'. Family business working paper, Indian School of Business, Hyderabad, 2009.

Redding, S.G. *The Spirit of Chinese Capitalism.* Berlin: Walter de Gruyter, 1990.

Schumpeter, Joseph A. *Theory of Economic Development.* Cambridge, MA: Harvard University Press, 1934

Schwass, Joachim. *Wise Growth Strategies in Leading Family Businesses.* Basingstoke and New York: Palgrave Macmillan, 2005.

Sirmon, David G. and Michael A. Hitt. 'Managing resources: linking unique resources, management, and wealth creation in family firms'. *Entrepreneurship Theory and Practice,* 27:4 (2003), 339–58.

Smyrnios, Kosmas X. and Lucio Dana. 'The MGI family and private business survey 2006'. RMIT University, Melbourne, Australia, 2006.

Smyrnios, Kosmas X. and R.H. Walker. 'Australian family and private business survey'. The Boyd Partners and RMIT, Australia, 2003.

Timmons, J.A. *New Venture Creation: Entrepreneurship for the 21st Century.* Boston, MA: McGraw Hill, 2004.

Weidenbaum, M.L. and S. Hughes. *The Bamboo Network: How Expatriate Chinese Entrepreneurs are Creating a New Economic Superpower in Asia.* New York: Martin Kessler, 1996.

Wong, S.L. *Emigrant Entrepreneurs: Shanghai Industrialists in Hong Kong.* Hong Kong: Oxford University Press, 1988.

Wortman, M.S. 'Theoretical foundations for family-owned business: a conceptual and research-based paradigm'. *Family Business Review*, 7:1 (1994), 3–27.

Yeung, H.W.C. 'Change and continuity in Southeast Asian ethnic Chinese business'. *Asia-Pacific Journal of Management*, 23:3 (2006), 229–54.

Yeung, H.W.C. and K. Olds. *Globalization of Chinese Business Firms.* Basingstoke: Macmillan, 2000.

Zahra, Shaker A. 'Entrepreneurial risk taking in family firms'. *Family Business Review,* 18:1 (2005), 23–40.

Zahra, Shaker A., James C. Hayton and Carlo Salvato. 'Entrepreneurship in family vs. non-family firms: a resource-based analysis of the effect of organizational culture'. *Entrepreneurship Theory and Practice*, 28:4 (2004), 363–81.

2. The Mok family of Hong Kong: incubating the next generation of entrepreneurs

Kevin Au

INTRODUCTION

Automatic Manufacturing Limited (AML) is a pioneer among manufacturers in Hong Kong. It has become known for high-quality manufacturing and refrains from price competition. Its success, to a great extent, can be attributed to the effective governance and management systems it has built to promote excellence in learning and innovation. This chapter first describes the structures and processes that contribute to AML's outstanding performance and then examines the system that the founding family has created to foster the entrepreneurial spirit in the next generation. This system has three distinguishing features: (1) it provides the incentive as well as a launching pad for the incoming generation to take risks and grow as independent entrepreneurs; (2) it gives willing AML employees the opportunity to join the spin-off ventures of the incoming generation; and (3) it forms part of an integrated plan to enable the incoming generation eventually to take the helm at AML.

Accordingly, this chapter answers the question of 'families as engines for entrepreneurship' raised in the STEP research project (Nordqvist et al. 2010) by illustrating how AML addresses 'change, growth, and the creation of the new'. In addition to addressing this central question, this study strives to enrich our understanding of family business in East Asia by giving a first glimpse into family portfolio entrepreneurship (Sieger et al. 2009), the idea of 'open innovation' and family firm innovation (Chesbrough et al. 2006), and spin-offs into new ventures with family support (Erikson et al. 2003).

In the following pages, we will first briefly review the relevant literature. Next, AML and the Mok family will be introduced and analyzed based on the STEP research framework. Finally, we will discuss the implications of the analysis for family businesses and non-family businesses in Asia and beyond.

THEORETICAL BACKGROUND

According to Claessens et al. (2000), East Asian economies are controlled by large, oligarchic family firms. They warn that wealth concentration of this kind breeds crony capitalism and stimulates political rent-seeking. Corporate governance reform might prevent collusion and is important for economic development. While most people endorse better governance, Steier (2009) cautions against confusing entrepreneurial establishments with oligarchies. Over-exuberance in corporate governance can kill activities related to innovation and entrepreneurship in family businesses. In other words, one must be careful not to throw the baby out with the bathwater. Instead, the key is to encourage the dynamism of family businesses while ensuring that their operations become more equitable and more transparent to non-family investors. This is important because although owner-founder entrepreneurs typically rely on the family for important resources during the start-up phase, this activity, as Steier observed, is largely underreported.

In East Asia, family and familial ties are the means for starting and growing companies (Redding 1996; Whyte 1996). A family member may choose not to take up the baton in the main company but may instead start a new business by borrowing human, financial and social capital from the family, inside or outside the umbrella of a family (holding) company (Arregle et al. 2007). As STEP researchers would put it, familiness acts as the reservoir of resources that family members can take advantage of to add new firms to existing activities (Nordqvist et al. 2010). The case of AML epitomises the ways in which a Hong Kong family business and its familiness contribute to innovation and entrepreneurship. Research on several relevant areas is discussed below within the context of family business to highlight the possible significance of studying AML.

Family Portfolio Entrepreneurship

Multiple business ownership or a development of a portfolio of entrepreneurial interests is a way of achieving growth (Wilkund and Shepherd 2008). Carter and Ram (2003) argue that portfolio entrepreneurship is meaningful in the family context, as family dynamics influence the engagement of portfolio strategies and the implementation process. They call for more studies into the actual process of portfolio entrepreneurship. Recently, Sieger et al. (2009) conducted in-depth case studies on several families within the STEP framework, and proposed that family resources, including business and political networks, tacit knowledge and the entrepreneurial skills and competencies of the business families, are conducive to portfolio entrepreneurship activities. Moreover, they also argued that reputation is an independent resource of a family insofar as it can enhance the effects of the above resources. Another recent study by Plate et al. (2010) interprets portfolio entrepreneurship as 'corporate diversification'. They investigated a German business family that grew from a small business into a multi-billion dollar conglomerate. Their analysis reveals that building an entrepreneurial organization based on the 'dominant logic' (Prahalad and Bettis 1986) of the family is crucial for portfolio entrepreneurship. Familiness is thus affirmed as a factor behind portfolio entrepreneurship.

However, spin-offs as a form of portfolio entrepreneurship have not yet been investigated. Given that 'portfolio entrepreneurship takes different forms and performs different functions for entrepreneurs' (Carter and Ram 2003, 373), studying AML's spin-offs into new ventures controlled by family members will reveal details of the ways in which family angels manage their investments and attempt to raise the chances of success for a new venture.

Innovation in Family Business

Innovation is emphasized in family businesses in order to achieve change and growth and to bring in new leadership from the succeeding generations (Poza 2007). Miller and Le Breton-Miller (2005, Table 1-4) have documented findings that suggest that family firms in the US invested more in machinery and R&D and spent more on employee training and compensation than non-family firms. Craig and Moores (2006) found that established family firms place considerable importance on innovation when reacting to uncertain environments. Though they are just emerging as a new force of capitalism, family businesses in China are also recommended to innovate in order to sustain their businesses (Lee and Li 2009). Carlock and Ward (2001) suggest that they identify a totally new market or form new business alliances. On the other hand, Miller and Le Breton-Miller (2005, 131) argue that family businesses should pursue a strategy that includes 'path-breaking innovation, leveraging of discovery, commercialization of innovations tailored to key markets, and creative destruction' in order to be long-lasting innovators.

However, creating value from innovations and new technologies requires complementary assets to take the innovation through the stages of development, commercialization, marketing and distribution. The firm that generates the innovation might not always have all the pieces of the value chain in-house; therefore, some inter-firm and outside transactions are necessary and desirable. Family businesses should thus utilize new ideas and innovation both internally and externally. That is to say, innovation and renewal in family businesses can be much more open. This brings us to the concept of open innovation, which refers to the use of purposive inflows and outflows of knowledge to accelerate internal innovation and expand the markets for the external use of innovation (Chesbrough et al. 2006). Open innovation presents a new avenue for understanding innovation in corporations. Yet, the angle of open innovation in family businesses has not been much discussed, and more research attention is required on spin-offs from family businesses.

Family Angels

Angel investors provide funding to support early stage ventures, thereby influencing their development trajectory. Family angels are found to behave differently from non-family angels. Erikson et al. (2003) studied Finnish family angels and found that they were more conservative than non-family angels and did not expect to exit from their investments. Another stream of related research concerns the ways in which venture capital firms, as professional investors, evaluate family and non-family businesses. Upton and Petty (2000) found that venture capitalists who invested in transition funding ranked the existence of a successor as a top criterion, followed by a firm's growth potential and strategic plan. Silva (2006) found that venture capitalists viewed family businesses as a source of deal flow and were willing to structure deals differently (such as accepting more debts instead of equity) to accommodate a family's need to maintain ownership.

It is widely believed that, among the ethnic Chinese, the family is central to the funding of new ventures and their growth (for example, Redding 1996). Ahlstrom et al. (2004, 273) observed that 'overseas Chinese owners of large firms historically have funded their firms internally'. However, there is some recent evidence to indicate that this may not always be the case. Au and Kwan (2009) show that Chinese entrepreneurs seek initial funding from their families rather than outsiders only if they expect to have lower transaction costs and a lower level of family interference in their businesses. Therefore, the literature suggests that family angels are common, but we are still not sure how the investments are initiated. Investigating the AML case gives insights into how family angels make their investments and raise the chances of success for a new venture.

CASE OVERVIEW

Automatic Manufacturing Limited

AML was founded in 1976. It provides integrated manufacturing services for medical and health-care devices, automotive electronics, telecom products, industrial controls and home automation products. Innovation and quality are the two pillars of AML. Despite being a medium-sized company, it has won numerous innovation and quality awards and is widely regarded in the industry as an advanced manufacturer. What is more, as a result of its outstanding corporate governance, the Hong Kong Institute of Directors gave the 'Director of the Year' award to AML's co-founder and chairman, John Mok in 2005. John is also the founding chairman of the Hong Kong Medical and Healthcare Devices Industry Association.

AML currently employs more than 3000 people, of which 260 are engineers. Its major manufacturing plants are located in Dongguan, China and it has set up an office in Shanghai. In addition to its main business, AML has a technology joint venture called SGAI [1] and two spin-offs into new ventures by the second generation.

The three co-founders, John Mok, Peter Mok and Meg Mok, collectively own AML. John Mok and Peter Mok are brothers, and Meg is John's wife. Together with the co-founders, the top management team also includes K.M. Chow, James Li, Erik Lee and Asso Lee (see Table 2.1). AML's board of directors consists of three categories of directors: non-executive directors (NED), independent non-executive directors (INED) and executive directors (ED). The chairman and vice chairman of AML are NEDs. The corporate management coaches and internal auditors are INEDs. EDs are members of the top management team, which includes general managers and assistant general managers.

The Mok Family

The father of Peter and John was in the shipping business. Peter (the eldest son) and John (the youngest) have two brothers, Andrew and James, and two older sisters. Andrew and James established a garment business, and Andrew retired in 2007. John and Meg do not have any children. Peter has three sons, Carmel, Anthony and Simon, and Andrew has two children, Mirin and William.

All the male members of the current generation of the family worked for several years in AML after graduating from college. They were coached by the top management team. All three of Peter's sons started and ran

Table 2.1   Overview of AML's top management team

Management team member	Post	Date joining AML	Date of joining TMT or becoming director	Responsibility
John Mok (JM)	Chairman of BoD	1976	1976	General management and strategic decision-making. Has solid experience in engineering and manufacturing of electronics and biomedical products
Peter Mok (PM)	Vice Chairman of BoD	1976	1976	Mechanical technology, global marketing, strategic alliance and joint ventures
Meg Mok (MM)	Director of BoD	1976	1976	Finance, purchasing, personnel management and administration
William Mok (WM)	Associate Director of BoD	2000	2007 (Assistant Director); 2008 (Executive Director)	Finance and business networking
K.M. Chow (KM)	Corporate General Manager	2003	2003 (Corporate General Manager)	Developing growth strategies, heading the corporate university and coaching new division start-ups; importing technology for product development
James Li	Divisional General Manager	1983	1992 (Divisional General Manager)	Office and telecom equipment
Erik Lee	Divisional General Manager	1999	2000 (Divisional General Manager)	Medical devices
Asso Lee	Divisional General Manager	N.A.	2001 (Divisional General Manager)	Home automation and industrial controls

their own spin-off companies as owners/managers in joint ventures with American and European partners. William, on the other hand, works for AML as an executive director, taking care of legal and intellectual property matters, corporate finance and angel investment. John, as one of the co-founders, made it clear that it was the wish of the founders eventually to step down and become non-executive directors and owners. He expected the members of the top management team to be able to run and grow the company divisions without constant attention from the founders. He also expected succession to occur when the second-generation members succeeded in their spin-offs and merged their companies with AML.

CASE ANALYSIS

As mentioned earlier, the two focal issues of this analysis are to examine the structures and processes leading to AML's innovation and to introduce the experimental spin-off system that is being tested by the founding family. To put things in context, we begin by reviewing Hong Kong's industrial development and the history of AML.

Original Equipment Manufacturing and Lack of High Technology in Hong Kong

From the mid-nineteenth century through the 2000s, Hong Kong went through several different stages of development, evolving from a fishing village into an entrepôt, then into an export manufacturing center, and, after China's Open Door Policy, into a business service and financial center. Many people attribute its success to a laissez-faire approach to governance dating back to the days of the British colonial government. This essentially means that the government relies on market forces to lead economic development and that governmental interventions are kept to a minimum (Goodstadt 2005).

Hong Kong manufacturing firms made use of Hong Kong's comparative advantage to produce labor-intensive goods for export after World War II. The influx of industrialists from Shanghai during the Chinese civil war, the rebuilding of war-torn Western countries and the drop in trade barriers in the 1950s accelerated Hong Kong's development. As in the case of other countries, small firms in Hong Kong were born in the manufacturing sector. What is exceptional is that these manufacturing firms remained as small and medium-sized enterprises (SMEs) while continuing to grow in the competitive export market (Au et al. 2006)[2] by turning their small size into an advantage. Most of the firms were original equipment manufacturers (OEMs) who took orders for labor-intensive goods from overseas buyers, using the latters' designs and incremental technology. Relying on their social networks, small firms were able to obtain information, technology and capital in an efficient way. As a result, they were competitive because they were flexible, capable of reacting quickly to market changes, and, at the same time, low cost. This network-based economy has been attributed to Chinese cultural values (Redding 1996).

China's Open Door Policy in the late 1970s transformed Hong Kong's economy – and the SMEs – in the 1980s and 1990s. Many manufacturers, AML included, enjoyed huge growth and expanded rapidly, using the cheap labor and abundant land available in China. In the process, SMEs split value-added activities according to a 'front shop, back factory' model, with their sophisticated services in Hong Kong and production facilities in the Pearl River Delta of southern China. The wealth created in the delta was plowed back into Hong Kong, with the result that domestic services, real estate and the stock market all enjoyed a boom. Although the Open Door Policy allowed industries to expand and prosper, it unfortunately did not motivate SMEs to upgrade their technology or improve their value-added activities in, say, technology, design and branding. Past success became a barrier to change. As labor and rent became increasingly expensive, with little value added in their business, SMEs engaged in OEM were no longer competitive. The Asian Crisis in 1997 put a halt to the boom. Many SMEs, and Hong Kong as a whole, were hard-hit.

Observing the lack of technology development in the past, the Hong Kong government established programs to promote technology. However, without a clear policy or resolve, the fiscal deficit following the Asian Crisis and the handover of Hong Kong in 1997 combined with several political events to intensify the conflict between the government and vested interests in society with regard to the direction and necessity of governmental intervention in innovation and technology development.[3] Despite this, years of investment in technology are starting to bear fruit in the form of some embryonic industrial clusters. There are also voices in support of technology as essential for Hong Kong's future. Moreover, ever since China promulgated a national policy of using technology to advance the country in 2008, many Hong Kong manufacturers have begun to accept and realize that there is an immediate need for change. AML, which had technology and quality as its foundation, was a rare breed among its peers.

Development of AML

John Mok studied physics at university and worked for a semi-conductor company for two years after graduation. He then joined a computer manufacturer and was promoted to the position of manufacturing manager. During the same period, Peter worked in sales and business development at a large multinational company. Exposure and travel led him to predict that there would be a large demand for advanced machine tools and engineering plastic. He suggested the idea of starting a company to address this demand to John and Meg, who worked in administration for the same company as her husband.

In the beginning, AML focused on mold making and engineering plastic. The Moks soon found that the market for these advanced products was small. However, they discovered that there was a large market for low-tech, non-engineering plastic, which was widely used in producing plastic flowers. They gained a foothold in this market and expanded into manufacturing and product assembly, making remote-controlled toys and electrical appliances. The market was simple in terms of technology and low in terms of its profit margin, but large in terms of volume.

In 1979, AML was incorporated as a limited company. However, the Moks reckoned that even though the business was profitable, there were hundreds of OEMs in Hong Kong. They felt they would be better off if they leveraged their knowledge and decided to steer AML towards producing more sophisticated products, such as electronic controls. This way, they could stay ahead in technology, enjoy a higher margin and avoid fierce price competition. To do so, AML would have to focus on reducing defects and raising production quality. However, they found it difficult to run two very different kinds of manufacturing operations and decided to sell their low-tech divisions. As John put it, 'one factory cannot have two different systems of quality'.

They sold their mechanical manufacturing and toy production divisions one after the other in the early 1980s. In 1985, in addition to selling more advanced office electronic equipment and industrial controls, they obtained GMP certification (a compliance standard for producing medical equipment) after several years of effort and were able to bring medical and surgical products to the market. They never looked back, and since that time, they have constantly made technology and quality improvements in their manufactured products. With regard to strategy, they focused increasingly on R&D and product design.

In the 1980s, AML expanded into mainland China, taking advantage of lower costs and the abundance of engineers.[4] With the rapid expansion of the company, the Moks decided in 1996 to adopt a multi-divisional structure for the business. A top management team (TMT) system, made up of a general manager and several assistant general managers, was set up. Formulated upon the proven experience of AML in the early years, or a 'dominant logic' (Prahalad and Bettis 1986), the TMT system had evolved by 2000 into one in which a manager was assigned to guard each of the three 'fences': market development and sales (the top fence), R&D and product design (the middle fence) and production and quality control (the bottom fence). The corporate structure now reflects this setup (see Figure 2.1). Each manager needs different qualities and skill-sets. The Moks have given autonomy to the team and stepped back from daily operations. The TMT is responsible for planning and controlling the divisions under a structure and system that is governed by the board of directors at the headquarters of the group.

The Moks designed the governance structure, began several of the second-generation activities in the company and run the board. AML also took up new initiatives such as the joint venture SGAI and installed new structures to strengthen their know-how and create a learning culture. A case in point is the Automatic Manufacturing Limited University, established in 2002, for which they brought in Dr K.M. Chow. The university covers eight different specialties, including corporate strategy and planning, marketing and sales, research and development and project management. Each specialty has a 'professor', a researcher and a research assistant. Their primary responsibility is to introduce 'modernization' and new advancements to AML. Since it opened its doors in 2003, the university has also pursued new knowledge, customized it and provided training and coaching to employees. The employees take exams and undergo monthly auditing exercises and quarterly benchmarking. Awards are given to those who perform well.

Structures and Processes Leading to Innovation in AML

The success of AML can be seen as having three major themes: its philosophy towards competition, its learning culture and a structure that facilitates autonomy.

(a)   Competitive philosophy
From the outset, AML strived to manufacture products using technology and technological innovations. The founders were highly educated. Also, through their experience of working for major corporations, they developed the ability to understand the market and recognize new opportunities. They were not interested in engaging in price competition for OEM contracts as most local firms did. Even though it could earn larger profits using less capital in a shorter period of time as an OEM, AML realized that this business model might not be sustainable over time as the market or customers shifted their interest. They decided instead to proactively stay ahead of the pack by taking over additional production processes

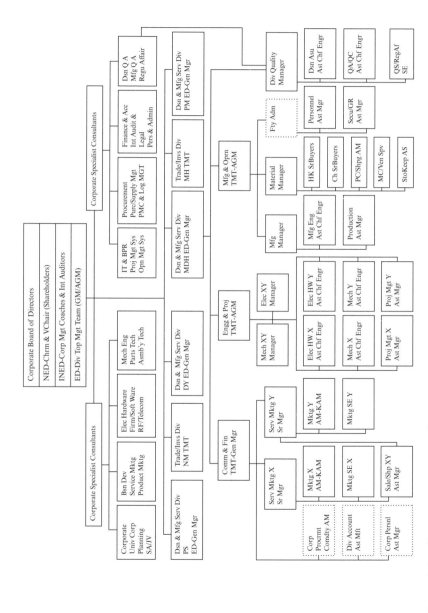

Figure 2.1   Corporate structure of AML

from clients. John said, 'As our customers planned to shift more and more of their production processes overseas, we understood that we could develop ourselves to take over more value-added production for them.'

Thus, AML acquired new production technology and gained access to the new market for medical devices through investments in R&D. In this way, they exercised more control to reduce risk in their business.

(b)   Learning culture

Knowledge is at the core of AML's competitiveness. The founders have created a learning culture and established an internal university to facilitate and develop new knowledge. AML's workforce is knowledge-intensive and its managers are encouraged to study and improve their knowledge. This emphasis is best reflected in a story related by Michelle Lum. She recalled that she was on an important and difficult business trip in the US while she was in the process of doing her EMBA at the university. Michelle said, 'When John found that an exam was coming up in my EMBA, he urged me to take the first flight back while he stayed behind to solve the problem.'

In order to tap into advanced technology and gain the capability to manufacture the latest products, AML has actively sought opportunities to form joint ventures, invest in new technology as a corporate angel (supporting new teams in exchange for the right to do manufacturing), encourage spin-offs from AML and liaise with universities. A prime example of the effectiveness of this approach is the development of the award-winning 3-Dimensional Stem Cell Bioreactor.[5] The medical division, along with the marketing and sales team headed by Michelle, designed the product using technology from Imperial College in the UK. The bioreactor is now housed under a new company called MediHealth Ltd, with Michelle leading the marketing and sales function.

(c)   Autonomy

AML has a group of loyal senior managers who have grown along with the founders. James and Michelle have each taken up leadership roles in their divisions and have the autonomy to make strategic decisions within their own areas. James, for instance, focuses on quality leadership in his division. His motto is 'no quality, no business', but this same focus is not required of other divisions. These divisions are wholly-owned subsidiaries of AML. James is attached to two companies, AML Comtech and Excel Tech. A profit center structure appears to have been put into operation successfully with professional managers in charge.

One worry, of course, is whether autonomous units that are innovative themselves can share their development and cross-fertilize with other units to make new and unique products for AML. The alarming examples of Philips and 3M speak to such a danger. Without adequate integration devices, AML may turn out many new products but lose the opportunity to churn out cutting-edge products. Although neither Michelle nor James talked about cross-fertilization directly, the top managers of the divisions are frequently consulted by and responsible for specific management functions for the corporate division. Michelle, for instance, is responsible for corporate marketing apart from her divisional duties. Divisional knowledge is thus shared with the corporate and other divisions. In addition, the internal university and the corporate board may enhance such functions. According to K.M. Chow, a knowledge management system is set up to record lessons learned from any division for cross-division learning. The corporate division also sends consulting teams to the different divisions to help solve their problems. Several integration devices are thus present in AML.

Spin-Offs by the Incoming Generation

AML has been experimenting with a scheme that encourages their second-generation family members to spin off new businesses from the parent company. It is a unique way to develop transgenerational entrepreneurship. This scheme can be divided into several distinct stages.

Stage 1   Members of the incoming generation finish college, gain outside working experience and then pursue a relevant postgraduate degree, such as a Master of Science or MBA degree.

Stage 2   They join AML as trainees for three to four years and are coached by department managers in the three major business processes (or fences) of the organization, namely, operations, engineering and marketing.

Stage 3   They advance to supervisory or managerial positions in their divisions and serve on the TMT. Meanwhile, the division head, the founders and experts from the internal university create an environment that can be described as an 'incubation nursery', where the company philosophy, social capital, knowledge and business skills are transferred to the incoming generation. Accordingly, apart from learning the entrepreneurial values of the family, the business and governance experience they gain at AML also helps the new generation to develop sophisticated management skills and business vision and prepares them to form start-up teams with like-minded AML employees.

Stage 4 When they have gained sufficient experience, generally in their early thirties, they formulate a business idea (in a related but non-competitive area) and present a business start-up plan to their parents, uncles or aunts in the Mok family business. Approved plans first receive seed money from the parents of the proposer. The start-up teams are composed of members of the incoming generation and often, but not necessarily, former employees of AML.

Stage 5 If the potential of the concept is proven using the seed money, AML provides a substantial 'loan' (USD1 million or more) to fund the spin-off of a 'joint venture' with AML. The new ventures must be large enough to challenge the skills of the incoming generation and make it worth the time and the risk involved. A large enough venture also forces the next generation to be concerned about ensuring the spin-off's survival and to look for clients themselves. The prudent yet risk-taking nature of the founders is reflected in their thoughtful decision-making with regard to the size of the loans.

Stage 6 In this stage, AML continues to provide support to the new ventures. When the ventures have grown and attained a certain size, the incoming generation will merge their own companies with AML via share exchange agreements. After the mergers, they will continue to operate their own divisions (or spin-offs) as executive directors. At the same time, they will also serve on the board of the AML Group as non-executive directors, governing the top management teams that are already in place in the existing divisions.

Currently, two male members of the incoming generation have gone through the early stages of this process and spun off a power tool company and an electronics product company under their own brands. They are focused on growing their companies. Two younger members of this generation are at the 'incubation' stage at AML. William has said that he admires his cousins' success and dreams of spinning off his own company one day. The Moks have now formalized the scheme and opened it to the offspring of senior managers.[6] Despite its ambition and sound logic, Stage 6 of this scheme has not yet been tested. The final judgment has yet to be cast.

Transgenerational Entrepreneurship Potential and Future Challenges

The founders have a long-term vision for the company. They are open to new ideas and have designed a succession plan largely on their own without the close involvement of outside professionals. As they build AML into a sophisticated company, the succession plan will be gradually implemented. The members of the second generation have all been well-educated overseas, and while they are currently learning the ropes and testing their wings as entrepreneurs or professional managers, they have expressed their interest in continuing the family business. Key managers who understand the spirit of AML are in place to take up individual divisions. They are given the autonomy to run the divisions on their own and to demonstrate strong corporate entrepreneurship. Despite the above strengths, the Mok family and AML have to deal with several challenges in the implementation of the last stage of their spin-off scheme:

- It remains to be seen whether key managers will stay and work for the second generation, particularly given the fact that loyal managers and close aides have yet to be offered stock options. A scheme to address this issue is still in the planning stages and will be implemented when the company makes its IPO in the next few years. Will giving these senior executives the autonomy to run their own show, combined with the loyalty and respect they have for the first generation be enough to retain them? Distributing stocks of a private company may not be a major motivator, as the stocks may not have a real exit point. Further, going public takes some years of preparation and is a complicated process for any family business.

- Some close connections have been forged between members of the TMT and the second generation, as the former have served as mentors to the latter. Another tie between the second generation and the management was formed when former employees from AML were asked to join the two spin-off companies. These TMT members have considerable experience of working in AML and may identify closely with AML. Nevertheless, we might anticipate a 'struggle' between new team members when they start working with incumbent managers and their successors.

- A fundamental question remains as to whether the second generation shares the same vision for the future as the outgoing generation of the Mok family. In the instance of future sibling competition or discord, trustworthy outside directors or experts (such as long-term family friends with succession experience and respected, retired managers) may be able to step in as 'umpires' to set up evaluation criteria and 'officiate' the race (Carlock and Ward 2001). This can help to avoid accusations of bias or unfairness. In AML's case, the dearth of outsiders, especially at the board level, may put the implementation of the final stage of the scheme at risk.

AML's founders have made great strides in developing the TMT (whose members are about 15 years younger than themselves) and subsequently the members of the incoming generation (who are about 30 years younger). Now it is time for them to contemplate the process of letting go. AML's founders have gradually removed themselves from daily duties and spend more than half of their time in voluntary social and charitable work, education and mentoring other entrepreneurs, thereby giving more room to the TMT and the incoming generation. It seems that they are moving in the right direction.

Given the sibling partnership structure, it might also be necessary for the three founders to arrive at a consensus to act together. The founders might take on new duties to facilitate the transition of the business and sustain transgenerational entrepreneurship. One possibility is to set up a family council whereby members of the Mok family can participate in family affairs and articulate the family's values. John jokingly suggested that they 'develop a "shrine" for the family'. Obviously, this shrine would be dedicated to the living, not to their ancestors.

DISCUSSION

The spin-off scheme of AML could not have succeeded if the incoming generation had not inherited the resources and the beliefs of the founders, particularly their belief in quality, technology and entrepreneurship. Moreover, the scheme's success is also due to the company's learning culture, strong R&D infrastructure, good governance and a cast of loyal managers who were willing to mentor the young inside AML. For example, James mentored Carmel for about two of his six years in AML. James believes that the relatively secure and nurturing internal environment at AML allowed Carmel to pick things up gradually and learn better than he would have done outside the company. In his own words, 'A person may be asked to sign a cheque without knowing what accounting is.' The environment at AML helps them to learn why. Michelle also mentored Carmel shortly before he spun off his own venture. Believing that Peter could teach him about business better than she could, she instead taught him about managing people, focusing on areas like fairness and how to develop competent employees. Clearly, the Mok family and the family business are resource pools which contribute to the success of the scheme.

The scheme has the potential to be a best practice for solving problems in creating new streams of value across generations (Nordqvist et al. 2010). It also has profound implications for research on family portfolio entrepreneurship, open innovation and family angels. First, it provides enough room and incentive for members of the incoming generation to return to and develop their careers in the parent company. Second, it fosters in the incoming generation the values of innovation and entrepreneurship. The second generation of the Mok family received sophisticated management training, inherited social capital from the founders and recruited AML employees to their start-up teams. Such an incubation process increases the chances of success of new ventures. Third, it is an unobtrusive way to renew AML as new business ideas are brought in to enhance the existing knowledge without a direct challenge to the status quo. When the ventures are spun off, like-minded employees can also join the startups. Thus, personnel renewal also takes place. Fourth, the spin-off process challenges the second generation to establish themselves and achieve success, thereby gaining legitimacy within the family and among the top managers of AML for the day that they take over the helm of the business from the founders. It also promotes healthy competition among the members of the incoming generation over the question of succession. Last but not least, the support of AML and the family in helping them to build their careers and their own leadership abilities increases the likelihood that the members of the second generation will identify with the family and decide to carry on its entrepreneurial spirit.

NOTES

1. SGAI was formed with Sagentia to tap into advanced engineering consulting. Sagentia hires more than 150 PhDs in Cambridge and is one of the world's pre-eminent technology management and product development companies. In 2002, lacking an understanding of Chinese culture, Sagentia decided to form a joint venture with AML to reduce costs associated with cultural differences. SGAI has been successful and AML benefits from Sagentia's technological know-how.
2. In the 1970s, an average manufacturer had 25 employees. Yet, the average number of employees decreased to less than 16 by 1989 (Au et al. 2006).
3. Research and development is a public good that the private sector cannot provide sufficiently. In Hong Kong, however, suggestions or even a mere discussion of any 'violation' of the laissez-faire doctrine are seen as favoring a particular sector or vested interests.
4. Since 1990, the Dongguan plant has become AML's manufacturing base. In the early stages of their China expansion, production was based in China and design in Hong Kong. In 1991, however, AML moved product design to Dongguan. Product design requires a lot of engineering time in testing, optimization and tinkering. As more university graduates from northern China moved to the south in search of job opportunities, AML was able to take advantage of the newly available talent. Meanwhile, the primary design team and product planning remained at the company's headquarters in Hong Kong, where there was a free flow of information and versatile engineers.
5. More about the 3-Dimensional Stem Cell Bioreactor. Traditionally, replacement skin has been cultured using a two-dimensional machine; that is, using a small healthy piece of 2D skin. The cultured skin looks similar to skin in vivo. However, the cells of the new

skin do not appear natural. The 3-dimensional incubation machine better represents the microenvironment of living tissues. Therefore, the skin cultured using the 3D machine is very similar to the skin in vivo in the sense that the cultured cells of the skin can grow like the skin in a human body.
6.   John Mok explained this point in a talk he gave to the author's class in August 2009.

REFERENCES

Ahlstrom, D., M.N. Young, E. S. Chan and G.D. Bruton. 'Facing constraints to growth? Overseas Chinese entrepreneurs and traditional business practices in East Asia', *Asia Pacific Journal of Management*, 21:3 (2004), 263–85.

Arregle, J.L., M.A. Hitt, D.G. Sirmon and P. Very. 'The development of organizational social capital: attributes of family firms', *Journal of Management Studies*, 44:1 (2007), 73–94.

Au, K. and H.K. Kwan. 'Start-up capital and Chinese entrepreneurs: the role of family', *Entrepreneurship Theory and Practice*, 33(2009), 889–908.

Au, K. et al. 'Innovation policy and high growth startups'. Research report. Chinese University of Hong Kong Centre for Entrepreneurship, 2006 (www.cuhk.edu.hk/centre/entrepreneurship).

Carlock, R. and J.L. Ward. *Strategic Planning for the Family Business*. Basingstoke: Palgrave, 2001.

Carter, S. and M. Ram. 'Reassessing portfolio entrepreneurship', *Small Business Economics*, 21(2003), 365–71.

Chesbrough, H., W. Vanhaverbeke and J. West. *Open Innovation: Researching a New Paradigm*. Oxford: Oxford University Press, 2006.

Claessens, S., S. Djankov and L.H.P. Lang. 'The separation of ownership and control in East Asian corporations', *Journal of Financial Economics*, 58:1–2 (2000), 81–112.

Craig, J. and K. Moores. 'A 10-year longitudinal investigation of strategy, systems, and environment on innovation in family firms', *Family Business Review*, 19 (2006), 1–10.

Erikson, T., R. Sørheim, and B. Reitan. 'Family angels vs. other informal investors', *Family Business Review*, 16:3 (2003), 163–71.

Goodstadt, Leo F. *Uneasy Partners: The Conflict between Public Interest and Private Profit in Hong Kong*. Hong Kong: Hong Kong University Press, 2005.

Lee, J. and H. Li. *Wealth Doesn't Last 3 Generations: How Family Businesses can Maintain Prosperity*. Hackensack, NJ: World Scientific, 2009.

Miller, D. and I. Le Breton-Miller. *Managing for the Long Run: Lessons in Competitive Advantage from Great Family Businesses*. Boston, MA: Harvard Business School Press, 2005.

Nordqvist, M., T. Zellweger and T. Habbershon. 'Transgenerational entrepreneurship', in M. Nordqvist and T. Zellweger (eds), *Transgenerational Entrepreneurship: Exploring Growth and Performance in Family Firms across Generations*. Cheltenham, UK and Northampton, MA, USA: Edward Elgar, 2010, 39–57.

Plate, M., C. Schiede and A. von Schlippe. 'Portfolio entrepreneurship in the context of family owned business', in M. Nordqvist and T. Zellweger (eds), *Transgenerational Entrepreneurship: Exploring Growth and Performance in*

Family Firms across Generations. Cheltenham, UK and Northampton, MA, USA: Edward Elgar, 2010, 96–122.

Poza, Ernesto J. *Family Business*, second edition. New York: Thomson, 2007.

Prahalad, C.K. and R. Bettis. 'The dominant logic: a new linkage between diversity and performance'. *Strategic Management Journal*, 7 (1986), 485–501.

Redding, S.G. 'Weak organizations and strong linkages: managerial ideology and Chinese family business networks', in G.G. Hamilton (ed.), *Asian Business Networks*. Berlin: de Gruyter, 1996, 27–42.

Sieger, P., R. Nason, T. Zellweger and M. Nordqvist. 'Family portfolio entrepreneurship'. Paper presented at Babson College Entrepreneurship Research Conference. Boston, MA, 2009.

Silva, J. 'Venture capital investments in family businesses: the financier perspective', in J.E. Butler (ed.), *Venture Capital and the Changing World of Entrepreneurship*. Greenwich, CT: Information Age, 2006, 239–48.

Steier, L.P. 'Familial capitalism in global institutional contexts: implications for corporate governance and entrepreneurship in East Asia', *Asia Pacific Journal of Management*, 26 (2009), 513–35.

Upton, N. and W. Petty. 'Venture capital investment and US family business', *Venture Capital*, 2:1 (2000), 27–39.

Wilkund, J. and D.A. Shepherd. 'Portfolio entrepreneurship: habitual and novice founders, new entry, and mode of organizing', *Entrepreneurship: Theory & Practice*, 32 (2008), 701–25.

Whyte, M.K. 'The Chinese family and economic development: obstacle or engine?', *Economic Development and Cultural Change*, 45:1 (1996), 1–30.

3. Lee Kum Kee Corp. Ltd (HK): 120 years and going strong

Xinchun Li, Hang Zhu, Wenting Chen and Mimi Fu

INTRODUCTION

A long-established family business in China, Lee Kum Kee (LKK) Group (Hong Kong) has evolved from its modest beginnings as a small oyster oil producer 120 years ago into a large group company with subsidiaries in Hong Kong, the United States, Malaysia and China. The group is today in the hands of the fourth generation of the Lee family. Over the years, it has faced challenges posed by common family succession issues. The company also experienced difficulties at different periods due to a decline in entrepreneurship, but it ultimately got back on track as a result of successful transgenerational entrepreneurship.

It is often the case that family businesses suffer from a loss of entrepreneurial spirit and disruption post-succession; thus, it is remarkable that the LKK family continues to produce entrepreneurs generation after generation to lead the family business. Now, after 120 years in business, the entrepreneurial Lee family is drawing on its experience and focusing on building a solid foundation for transgenerational entrepreneurship in the future.

The LKK family's efforts are oriented towards improving family governance as a means to sustaining the family's entrepreneurial spirit and promoting close cooperation within the family and towards providing resources to ensure the firm's continued entrepreneurship. These are the two main challenges facing Chinese transgenerational family businesses, and the Lee family has tried to address them head on.

BACKGROUND AND CASE OVERVIEW

Cultural Background

The strong cultural background and traditions that influence Chinese society present two constraints for transgenerational entrepreneurship in Chinese family businesses.

(a) Wealth dissipation resulting from the equal distribution of wealth and assets among the sons of the family

One of the direct causes for the dissolution or demise of many Chinese family businesses after succession is the dissipation of financial and human capital post-succession. Redding (1993) observed that the equal allocation of a family's wealth among the offspring brought about a diffusion of leadership. Even in a highly united family, when leadership is divided between four or five people, there is a tendency to diverge from the shared goal of the family and take new directions instead, which may ultimately cause the breakdown of the firm. Fukuyama (1995) also criticizes the deep-rooted Chinese tradition of distributing the family inheritance equally between the offspring, which poses enormous difficulties in developing a large firm.

(b) Difficulty of preserving the entrepreneurial spirit across generations

There is a Chinese saying: 'One generation sets up the business, the second preserves it, while the third causes its extinction.' This vividly describes the prevailing realities that explain the loss of entrepreneurial spirit in transgenerational transmission. There are deep cultural roots behind this reality. On the one hand, accumulating wealth for future generations motivates the efforts of many entrepreneurs, and this one-way altruistic tendency manifested by family business leaders results in a moral hazard for future generations (Schulze et al. 2003). On the other hand, the entrepreneurial spirit is inherently difficult to acquire through formal education, and many entrepreneurs neglect to cultivate this spirit in their children because they are fully occupied with their businesses.

The Family and the LKK Group

The Lee business family, with a history of more than 100 years, is now in its fifth generation (see Figure 3.1). The family traces its origins to Qibao Chung Lek village in Xinhui, Guangdong province. The firm's founder, Lee Kum Sang, left the village in his youth and drifted to Nanshui, Zhuhai where he settled down and began cooking and selling oysters for a living. He inadvertently invented a delicious oyster oil, and in 1888, he established

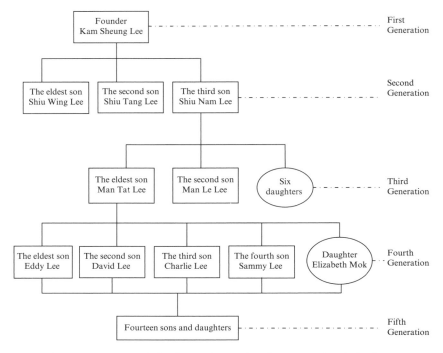

Note: Squares represent male family members and ovals represent female family members. The figure lists only blood descendants of Lee.

Figure 3.1   The structure of the LKK family

the LKK Oyster Oil Workshop, thus launching a family business that has carried on for over 120 years.

After Lee Kum Sang's death, his three sons inherited the family business. His eldest son, Shiu Wing, was not keen on running the business, so it was co-managed by his two younger sons, Shiu Tang and Shiu Nam. While the descendants of Shiu Wing and Shiu Tang joined the business at an early age, Man Tat, the eldest son of Shiu Nam, followed his father's instructions and started an independent external business. After his father's retirement, however, Man Tat Lee was invited to join the family business. In 1972, Man Tat's cousins attempted to buy out Shiu Nam Lee's shares. Man Tat convinced his father to prevent the takeover and subsequently helped his father secure his cousins' shares. This resulted in a family rupture, with the members of the two other branches of the family quitting the firm.

Shortly after completing the acquisition, Shiu Nam Lee handed over the management of the business to Man Tat. Man Tat then invited his younger brother, Man Le, who was working elsewhere at the time, to join the management of the family business and presented him with a considerable portion of the company's shares as a gift. However, in 1980, there was a dispute between the two brothers, and Man Le demanded a stock settlement that eventually led the two to court. Man Tat won the case and bought his brother's shares.

Man Tat's first four children graduated from colleges in the United States in the 1980s. Responding to their father's call, they joined the company upon graduating. After gaining business experience in both the family firm and other firms, Man Tat's fourth son, Sammy Lee, started a new business for the family in 1992 – Southern LKK (now renamed Infinitus China Ltd). The family business has developed significantly through the joint efforts of the two generations and become a major player in the condiments and health products industries, employing nearly 5000 people. Southern LKK, the subsidiary company, was even named among the 'Best Employers in Asia' and 'Best Employers in China' in 2005 and 2007.

At present, Man Tat Lee and his wife hold a majority of the shares of the LKK Group, while the remaining shares are divided equally between their four sons (there is no publicly available detailed break down of shares held by family members). The group's seven-member board of directors is composed of Man Tat Lee, his four sons and two outside directors. In 2006, all the family members (with the exception of Elizabeth Mok) quit the management of the sauces business and hired a team of professional managers to run it. Management of the health products business, however, remained in the hands of Sammy Lee. As they gradually removed themselves from the daily management of the business, the family members became increasingly committed to building a family governance system. In 2003, the LKK family established a family council and set up several standing bodies of family affairs under it (see Figure 3.2). Currently the family council is composed of Man Tat Lee, his wife and their five children.

Industry and Business

The LKK Group has a presence in two industries – the condiments industry and the health-care products industry. The LKK Sauces Group is engaged in the production and sale of condiments, including oyster oil and sauces, worldwide, while the LKK Health Products Group primarily produces and sells herbal health-care products, skin-care products and other health products in mainland China.

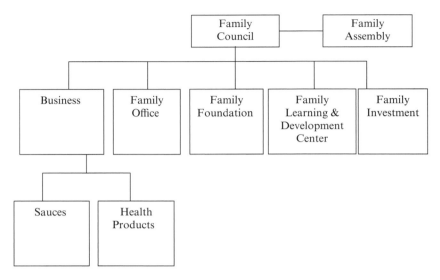

Figure 3.2   The Lee family governance structure

(a)   The seasoning industry and LKK's sauce business
The market for condiments varies according to the cultural background and eating habits of a particular place. LKK's sauces are generally targeted at the Chinese market and other markets where similar dietary habits prevail. As the Macao and Hong Kong markets were limited in scope, the group had already expanded its business overseas by the 1980s, targeting Chinese communities in Southeast Asia and the United States. At the same time, the group made its foray into other markets in the region that had a similar food culture, such as Japan. LKK's seasoning is currently the leading brand of Chinese seasoning in Hong Kong and in key international markets. In recent years, LKK seasoning's market share in Hong Kong has risen as high as 37 percent, while its oyster oil has an 80 percent market share in North America. LKK also has the distinction of creating the first Asian seasoning brand and the world's first brand of oyster oil.

In the 1980s, LKK Group began to invest in mainland China, building factories and distribution networks. It built raw material facilities in Dalian and Fuzhou and production facilities in Guangzhou and in the Xinhui district of Jiangmen City. Its sales and market position in mainland China gradually improved. As a result of its intensified focus on business development in mainland China, LKK has become one of the three major nationwide brands.

(b)   The health products industry and LKK's health products business

Health-care products cover a wide range, from food to medicine. In China, the health-care products market grew rapidly from the 1990s onwards due to the rise in income of Chinese residents, motivating many companies to enter the industry. For example, during the three-year period from 1993 to 1995, the number of companies manufacturing health-care products in China increased 30-fold, to about 3000.[1] However, firms in the industry varied greatly with regard to quality and integrity and the prevalence of false propaganda and advertising led to difficult times for the industry from 1994 to 1998. Many businesses failed; only those with a reputation for honesty survived.

Initially, the health products business was jointly established by LKK and the First Military Medical University. In 1998, the army withdrew from the business, and the company became wholly owned by LKK. In the early days of the business, it employed the direct sales model to expand its markets. In 1998, when the state enacted a ban on direct sales, LKK was prepared for the transformation. It opened stores in large and medium-sized cities across the country and grew steadily. After it obtained a direct sales license in February 2007, it began to operate a direct marketing business in 14 cities in Guangdong Province, offering three types of products (a total portfolio of 39 products). The business was once again on a fast development track.

The health products business has maintained a low profile since its establishment and has developed steadily though its annual sales figures have never been published. Southern LKK's 'Infinitus' brand ranked 62nd in the World Brand Laboratory's (WBL) 'China's 500 Most Valuable Brands' list in 2005 at the World Brand Conference, the highest ranking in China's health-care industry.

FAMILY BUSINESSES

Transgenerational Entrepreneurship in LKK

The development of the LKK Group can also be seen as a process of transgenerational entrepreneurship. Entrepreneurs emerged in each successive generation, which not only helped tide the firm over a series of crises, but also contributed to sustainable growth. The entrepreneurial spirit embodied in the joint leadership of the company by the third and fourth generations is a typical manifestation of transgenerational entrepreneurship.

(a)   The entrepreneurial activities of the first generation
The founder, Kam Sheung Lee, set up the LKK Oyster Oil Workshop in Nanshui, Zhuhai after he discovered a unique method of making oyster oil. This established the reputation of LKK oyster oil. However, disaster hit in 1902, when the LKK oyster oil workshop was reduced to ashes in a fire in Nanshui. After this tragedy, Kam Sheung Lee and his family moved to Macau and rebuilt LKK there.

(b)   The entrepreneurial activities of the second generation
Kam Sheung Lee's sons, Shiu Nam and Shiu Tang were the second generation leaders of the business. They took over the management of the company and not only promoted new products successfully, but also expanded the market for their products. In 1920, LKK developed shrimp paste, which was widely welcomed in the market. The company also began gradually to explore potential markets elsewhere. In 1932, LKK expanded its oyster oil production and sales business to Hong Kong and set up offices there, and its scale of production increased. In 1946, the company shifted its headquarters to Hong Kong.

(c)   The entrepreneurial activities of the third generation
After the third generation took over the management of the firm, LKK initially entered a period of stagnation. Man Tat Lee, who had returned to the family business, had different ideas and a different vision for the business than those of several of his cousins, which made it difficult for him to achieve his entrepreneurial ambitions. Although LKK had gradually expanded its business to some markets in Southeast Asia in the 1950s, its high-end product line meant that only the wealthy could afford and enjoy its products. As a result, until the 1970s, there was no major increase in sales volume, and the firm continued to have manually operated workshops staffed by no more than 20 people.

When Man Tat Lee bought his cousins' stock in the company, his lack of capital required him to pay for the purchase in installments and operate with negative equity. However, after he took over the reins of the company, he re-launched a number of entrepreneurial activities. He began to extend the product lines and made innovations in production processes. In 1972, LKK took advantage of the establishment of Sino-American diplomatic relations and introduced the low-price 'Panda' oyster oil, which received a warm welcome in the mass market. LKK subsequently went on to promote more than 10 kinds of sauce products. Around the same time, Man Tat Lee began to focus on modernizing production by introducing advanced machinery, thereby expanding the scale of operations.

However, a second rupture within the family occurred in 1980, leaving him both physically and mentally exhausted. When his plan to build a plant in Taipo, Hong Kong, ran into trouble due to lack of funding, he himself put up HK$80 million towards the purchase, landing LKK in financial difficulty.

(d)   The joint entrepreneurial activities of the third and fourth generations
After the fourth generation entered the family business, the two generations worked closely together, enabling LKK to step successfully into the fast growth lane.

i. Entrepreneurial activity in the condiment businesses   At this stage, a lot of innovative products were introduced into the expanding product line, including the high-end XO sauce. XO sauce was originally inspired by a recipe that included scallops, ham and dried shrimp, which was served in upscale Hong Kong restaurants and later imitated by many other eateries. LKK observed this consumption trend and developed the LKK XO sauce, focusing on quality and flavor and promoting it as a high-end product. The unprecedented success of XO sauce improved the market for Chinese sauces. Today, the LKK Sauces Group produces more than 10 varieties of sauce and more than 200 different kinds of seasonings.

Innovation is also reflected in the packaging of its products. The company broke with tradition and introduced a tube with an inverted vertical design for its high quality oyster oil. The tube's flow control valves made dispensing the oil very convenient, and it was well received by consumers. Further, targeting the middle-class youth market, LKK introduced a variety of convenience food sauce packets, such as spicy bean curd sauce, fish-flavored eggplant sauce, and so on.

The company also rapidly expanded its sales reach. From the 1980s onwards, the LKK sauces business steadily built its international market, first entering the US market and setting up factories there, and then foraying into Japan, Europe and other markets. Currently, LKK's sauces are sold in more than 80 countries and regions worldwide, such that it has become synonymous with the phrase, 'Where there are Chinese, there is LKK'. After China opened its doors, LKK quickly seized the opportunity to develop its business in the mainland. From 1980 onwards, LKK built factories in mainland China, laid distribution networks, invested several billion RMB and rapidly became the third largest seasoning brand in that market.

ii. A new venture: the health products business   Since its establishment, Southern LKK has constantly introduced innovations in marketing, product development and management and overcome various challenges; in the process it has grown by leaps and bounds.

When Southern LKK introduced its first batch of products, sales were sluggish. Sammy Lee reconsidered his sales strategy and introduced the direct marketing model, which was used by very few companies in China at that time, to expand the market. In 1998, the country's ban on direct marketing put an end to LKK's dependence on this sales model. Confronted with the ban, Southern LKK made a critical transformation and decided to establish stores throughout the country, thus surviving a second crisis. Prior to 1998, there were 41 direct sales companies across the country; however, after the government ban on direct marketing, 37 of them disappeared.

In 1998, confronted with the ban on Southern LKK's direct marketing model and the exit of its partners, Sammy Lee adopted the innovative 'auto-pilot' leadership model.[2] Through a continuous focus on team-building and trust-building, Sammy Lee established a highly engaged workforce and achieved a degree of empowerment rarely seen in family businesses. This inspired an unprecedented degree of enthusiastic employee participation, innovation and initiative throughout the organization. As one employee put it, 'it seems as though we have started a business with the boss'.

Southern LKK has always maintained a strong commitment to R&D and attached great importance to the joint research and development of traditional Chinese herbal medicine products in conjunction with innovative institutions. In July 1996, Southern LKK, in partnership with the Hong Kong University of Science and Technology, established the Hong Kong Traditional Chinese Medicine Research Center; in 2000, the Natural Medicines Research Center was launched in collaboration with the First Military Medical University; and in 2003, a letter of intent was signed with Tsinghua University with the aim of accelerating research on herbal health products. Since its foundation, the company has developed three categories of products, comprising more than 20 varieties of innovative products altogether, such as Infinitus herbal health products, Zhi Ya herbs and daily necessities, Wei-ya Chinese herbal skin-care products, and so on.

In 2003, Southern LKK successfully obtained three international certifications – GMP, ISO9001: 2000 and HACCP (international certification of food safety systems) – a rare achievement in the Chinese herbal health products industry. By the end of 2005, Southern LKK increased its capital to more than 100 million yuan to expand its production facilities. The oral liquid production line designed and constructed by Southern LKK was China's first fully automated oral bottle production line and also complied with GMP standards. In 2009, the second phase of the plant was completed, yielding an annual output of 10 billion yuan. The success of Southern LKK has helped LKK evolve into a large, diversified business group and furthered its mission of 'carrying forward China's excellent health culture'.

LKK's Entrepreneurial Orientation

During the period of close cooperation between the third and fourth generations, LKK Group demonstrated a considerable degree of entrepreneurial orientation in terms of initiative, risk-taking tendencies, innovation and autonomy (Lumpkin and Dess 1996). With the entry of the fourth generation into the company, LKK became more proactive than ever in searching for new market opportunities. At this time, the group entered major markets such as the US, Japan and Europe and also began actively to seek new business opportunities. Supported by the family, Sammy Lee explored several industries such as food and beverages, property management and so on, eventually finding success in developing the health products market.

During this period, the group was also more active in taking risks. It made large investments in new markets. LKK built factories in Guangzhou, the Xinhui district of Guangdong, Fuzhou, Dalian and the US. In 1996, LKK Sauces Group built a massive production facility in Xinhui covering over 280 acres, with a first-phase investment of 500 million yuan, and then followed this with an additional investment of 200 million yuan. In 2005, LKK Xinhui Health Products Group's plant was completed with an investment of over 100 million yuan and began production.

In the case of projects whose prospects were unclear, the family's strategy was to redouble its initiatives and efforts. Sammy Lee explained the thinking behind the '6677 principle' that the family adopts towards their new ventures thus: 'When we are making investments or starting businesses, it is not with 100 percent certainty that we act, but with the feeling of 6677 – that it is about 60 or 70 percent certain – and we act decisively, even if we fail.'

The establishment of Southern LKK jointly by LKK and the First Military Medical University is a typical example of the '6677' principle. LKK's optimism about the market for traditional Chinese herbal health products was infectious, with the result that a letter of intent was signed within an hour of a meeting between the two parties, and an official contract was signed one month later, without any counsels present.

Innovative activities were also occurring at a fast pace throughout the whole group. Not only were R&D investments in new ventures being made, but many new products were also introduced in the existing businesses. Innovation could be seen in the development of new products, design of new packaging and adoption of new sales and leadership models, all of which boosted growth across the group. During this period, the members of the fourth generation, who had entered the company one after the other, became the backbone of the group's development and expansion. The important mission of developing the US market was entrusted to David Lee; Charlie Lee was in charge of the development of the Chinese market; Eddy Lee and Elizabeth Mok vigorously led R&D and the promotion of seasoning products, while Sammy Lee was in charge of exploring new business opportunities (see Table 3.1). The family members of the fourth generation have enjoyed a high level of personal discretion in their respective areas. For example, in developing the US market, David Lee made the independent decision to open up the market via promotions rather than try his best to collect accounts receivables, while Sammy Lee constantly received the backing of his family as he explored new business opportunities.

When analyzing transgenerational entrepreneurship in LKK, we can see that entrepreneurial orientation is affected by two factors: first, whether the firm is controlled by an individual who has an entrepreneurial spirit; and second, whether the family members work closely together. The former is the powerhouse of entrepreneurial activities in a family business, while the latter provides a favorable resource base for those entrepreneurial activities.

Taking a historical perspective, we can see that from the first to the third generations, control of and involvement in the business became dispersed and some family members lost their entrepreneurial spirit. Among the three brothers of the second generation, one was not interested in joining the family business, though it is fortunate for the family that two of the brothers carried on the entrepreneurial spirit.

However, even after the advent of the third generation when the family business was jointly managed by the cousins, Man Tat Lee's efforts to promote entrepreneurship were constrained, as most of the members were satisfied with the status quo. As a result, the business entered a period of stagnation marked by a lack of entrepreneurial orientation. This situation continued until Man Tat Lee and his children took control of the firm. The concept of 'constant entrepreneurship' proposed by Man Tat Lee boosted entrepreneurial activities at this stage in the company's history when the third and fourth generations worked together to develop the business. Summing up his thoughts on both

Table 3.1   Overview of the fourth generation of the LKK family

Fourth generation	Position in family	Major and educational institution	Year of joining the business	Role in the business	Experience and former duties
Eddy Lee	The eldest son of Man Tat Lee	Food Science and Technology, University of California	1980	Former Chairman, LKK Sauces Group	Helped his father develop Asian sauces; mainly responsible for the promotion of Chinese food seasonings
David Lee	The second son of Man Tat Lee	Business Administration and Marketing, University of Southern California	1982	Chairman, LKK Sauces Group	In 1982 helped LKK enter the US market; in 1991 established the LKK factory in Los Angeles, California; in charge of the LKK real estate business
Charlie Lee	The third son of Man Tat Lee	Chemical Engineering, University of Southern California	1985	Former Chairman, LKK Sauces Group (China)	Formerly in charge of production, logistics and the Chinese market
Sammy Lee	Fourth and youngest son of Man Tat Lee.	Financial Management, University of Southern California	1986	Chairman and CEO, LKK Health Products Group	Was responsible for human resources and financial management of LKK Group; founded the LKK Health Products Group in 1992
Elizabeth Mok	Daughter of Man Tat Lee	Food Science, University of California	1982	Technology Director of Food Safety, LKK Sauces Group	Responsible for quality and food research.

Source: The Lee family.

business development and family continuity, Man Tat Lee said, 'It is impossible to hold the business still, and yet keep entrepreneurship and innovation alive.' The family also regards 'constant entrepreneurship' as its core belief and an integral part of the business education of its offspring.

The family's entrepreneurial activities are closely tied to cooperation between family members. The two periods of disruption in the family business exerted heavy penalties – the family paid a high price for the acquisition of stocks in the company and was left with negative equity, with the result that investments in entrepreneurial activities were constrained. During the second family disruption, the huge expenditure on the acquisition of the business was nothing less than snow combined with frost for a firm that was short of money. What was worse, business operations were frozen for a time during the takeover proceedings. For six consecutive years, litigation consumed the time and energy of the entrepreneur and LKK's pace of expansion and innovation slowed down, while the heavy debt burden was borne by both the family and the business for more than a decade.

In contrast, the ensuing era of cooperation between family members provided strong support in terms of both human and financial capital for entrepreneurial activities. The fourth generation of LKK demonstrated their leadership of the company by driving both innovation and expansion and gave it a strong entrepreneurial orientation. Because of the deep trust among the family members, they were able to create a culture of empowerment and discretion, which allowed the business quickly to capture valuable market opportunities and explore opportunities for innovation. The accumulation of financial capital also provided strong support for managing risk. For example, during the growth of the health products business, the family's capital position gave the new venture a better chance of survival. Close cooperation within the family contributed to the family's concentrated and efficient use of resources and bolstered its entrepreneurial activities. Man Tat Lee, the third-generation entrepreneur of the family, continually points out that 'harmonious families breed prosperity'.

Family Governance in LKK

In its bid to improve the family's management of the company, LKK has sought to learn from past experience in solving the problems that commonly confront family businesses in China: first, prevent disruption and promote cooperation among family members; and second, sustain the family's entrepreneurial spirit and business orientation.

(a)   Promote cooperation and prevent disruption

Adhering closely to the belief that 'harmonious families breed prosperity', the LKK family has deliberately designed its family governance structure to promote cooperation and prevent disruption.

First, with regard to preventing disruption and interference in the family business, the family has a policy in the form of a constitution and unwritten rules. The constitution of the LKK family states that only those with a consanguineous relationship to the LKK family have the right to inherit the shares of the business and that family shareholders can only make an internal transfer of shares within the family in case of a withdrawal. On the one hand, these provisions ensure that the control of the business remains with the family. On the other hand, they also prevent passive shareholders from holding up the business as a way to force the successor and the family to allow them to sell their shares. There are also unwritten rules regarding marriage that are aimed at preventing potential crises and ruptures. According to Man Tat Lee, 'divorce is not allowed, a second wife is not allowed and getting married late is not allowed, and those in violation of the regulations must quit the board'.

Second, the family has established a family council for better communication between its members. In 2003, the LKK family set up the family council to deal specifically with its internal affairs. The committee was composed of core family members. According to Sammy Lee, 'The reason that a lot of problems emerge inside many families is that family members are unable to communicate. We put in tremendous effort to foster family unity and communication to create a platform on which anything about the family can be brought up for open discussion.'

The council helps family members make a distinction between their roles within the family and their roles as shareholders, directors of the board or managers, so that 'even if some family members do not want to be shareholders or want to exit management in the future, they could still take part in family activities as family members'. Thus, the council ensures that communication and solidarity between family members is maintained.

The family council meets four times each quarter to discuss important family issues. Their efforts to create an atmosphere of free and open communication have resulted in family members becoming increasingly engaged and involved in the council. The family has also built multi-level communication platforms, such as a family assembly comprising the whole family; 'super mother groups', in which exchanges on parenting take place; a family education committee, where educational arrangements for the future generation are discussed and so on.

Third, the family places great importance on strengthening shared values. Man Tat Lee has emphasized the value of 'considering the interests

of others' both in the education of children and the treatment of employees and business partners. 'Considering the interests of others' essentially
means to 'stand in another's shoes'. It is the core value of the family and its
businesses. An individual's ability to put this value into practice and represent the interests of the whole family is an important selection criterion
for each member of the family council.

Strengthening values has become a critical issue for the family council.
In its bid to transmit these core values from generation to generation,
the family has put its beliefs down in writing. In his book, *The Power of
Considering on Behalf of Others*, Sammy Lee describes three key elements
of this core value: empathy, being concerned about the feelings of others
and helicopter thinking (which refers to considering the overall interests of
the whole family).

(b)   Sustain the family's entrepreneurial spirit and business orientation

The LKK family has adopted the lofty goal of 'promoting China's excellent food culture and carrying forward China's excellent health culture' as
its mission. In this way, it hopes to unite members of future generations
and fire their entrepreneurial enthusiasm. The family has also established
ceremonies to inspire entrepreneurship. For example, Man Tat Lee
combined the traditional Tomb Sweeping Day festival and an event to
recognize employee excellence in a single annual ceremony that celebrates
entrepreneurship, in which all family members take part.

In cultivating future generations and ensuring the continuation of
the entrepreneurial spirit, the LKK family is seeking to learn from the
experiences of previous generations. The third and fourth generations
of the family were confronted with a challenging and difficult business
environment, which in turn, shaped and tempered their entrepreneurial
spirit. Man Tat Lee was originally excluded from the family business by
his father and worked elsewhere on his own for a long period; the fourth
generation joined the firm at a time when the family business was in difficulty; and the support given to Sammy Lee when he launched his new
venture was very limited at first – he had to start from a position of debt.
In contrast, some members of the second and third generations lost their
entrepreneurial spirit because they enjoyed a position of comfort right
from the beginning. For this reason, the family's constitution states:

> In case the fifth generation joins the family business, a minimum of three to five
> years of work experience outside of LKK is required, and the procedures of
> recruitment are the same as those that are followed for non-family employees.
> Upon joining LKK, the fifth generation of Lees are treated just like any other
> employee; moreover they are not immune to punitive actions if they underper-
> form or commit an offence.[3]

In this way, the family can avoid cases of one-way altruism (from one generation to the next), while strengthening the next generation's entrepreneurial spirit.

Recognizing that future generations are growing up in a different environment, the family has also tried to replace old ideas and traditions with new ones. Sammy pointed out that the traditional emphasis on working from a 'sense of responsibility' does not resonate with the new generation; rather, the focus should be on capturing their interest: 'Change the word from push to pull – interest coupled with ability, that is how a good entrepreneur will be nurtured.'

The family also pays attention to educating the younger generations about the traditional family business. Under the auspices of the family learning and development center, Elizabeth Mok, who has mastered the oyster oil recipe, is carrying out the 'Oyster Oil 101' project, which introduces the next generation to the business and its products, teaches them about the traditional business and motivates them to participate in the family business.

By improving family governance, the family tries to distinguish between the roles of family members, shareholders, the board of directors and top managers. For example, not only must family members who wish to enter the business undergo a 'survival test', there are also strict requirements for family members who are on the board of directors. Family directors must be members of the family council, they must be interested in the business and must have appropriate abilities. The family's willingness to set these strict conditions at the two levels of governance and management reflects its intention of ensuring that only those family members with an entrepreneurial spirit take over the leadership of the family business.

Descendants who have no intention of engaging in the family business are supported in establishing their own businesses according to their interests. The family council is currently planning to add a new feature to support new ventures of family members under the category of 'family investment'. It is considering the establishment of full program standards for such ventures, from business plan to investment, and making the support for start-ups stricter and more institutionalized.

DISCUSSION

The LKK Group's 120-year history shows a positive correlation between entrepreneurial activities and business growth. With an effective family governance structure in place, the family can use its familiness (Habbershon and Williams 1999) to promote transgenerational entrepreneurship. As the practices of the LKK family demonstrate, family governance can play two key roles in supporting transgenerational entrepreneurship, maintaining close cooperation within the family and sustaining the entrepreneurial spirit.

Maintaining Close Cooperation within the Family

The belief that 'harmonious families breed prosperity' is the outcome of profound retrospection on the part of the LKK family and their understanding of the relationship between family continuity and entrepreneurial activities. Disruption within the family dissipates resources and constrains the firm's entrepreneurial activities. By contrast, close cooperation within the family is more likely to promote entrepreneurship in the firm. This is not only because the accumulated wealth of the family can provide badly needed capital for investment, but also because it can provide urgently needed management resources and entrepreneurial skill (Penrose 1959), so that the family can act quickly, with complete trust and empowerment, to seize market opportunities.

As is the case with many business families, close cooperation between the third and fourth generations of LKK has been based largely on the close *guanxi* (relationships) between core family members and their pursuit of a common goal during difficult times. However, the foundation for such cooperation could be eroded through the proliferation of family, scattered equity and control and increasingly distant *guanxi* between family members. The two family disruptions in LKK are examples of this: the first occurred between cousins, and the second, between the elder brother and sister-in-law. Maintaining close cooperation between family members through effective family governance seems even more challenging and necessary in the future. Thus, the family emphasizes that its current focus on family governance is 'for the fifth and sixth generations and the continuation of the family'.

The governance structure established by the LKK family is different from a traditional family governance structure, which is dependent on *guanxi* and paternal authority. It places greater emphasis on the construction of communication platforms and contracts within the family as well as on reciprocal altruism and the enforcement of values as ways to promote trust between members.

These methods to strengthen family social capital (Nahapiet and Ghoshal 1998) can help to achieve greater scalability, avoid the limitations of traditional family governance structures and support future cooperation between family members even if *guanxi* and family authority weaken. Thus, the advantage of having the whole family jointly supporting the business is maintained. The combined application of formal and informal governance methods has also prepared the family for ambiguity and variability in the future (Carson et al. 2006).

Sustaining the Entrepreneurial Spirit

The LKK family is 'lucky' because outstanding entrepreneurs emerged in every generation. This helped to maintain the continuity of the business and promote transgenerational entrepreneurship. The family is aware of the laws behind this 'luck' and tries to apply them to family governance.

Family governance impacts a family's ability to sustain entrepreneurship in two respects. On the one hand, it can provide an institutional basis for the continuation of entrepreneurship by preventing one-way altruism from parent to offspring through a formal family constitution, preventing moral hazards from occurring among future generations (Schulze et al. 2003) and enhancing formal and informal entrepreneurship education through the family council. On the other hand, it can integrate the resources and wisdom of the whole family, thereby promoting entrepreneurship education and support for entrepreneurial activities among future generations. This kind of collective nurture can provide a reliable and lasting basis for sustaining the entrepreneurial spirit.

THE FUTURE

As the firm grows, the continuation of entrepreneurial activities will become increasingly dependent on the promotion of capable non-family members to leadership positions. One clear sign of this was the appointment of the first non-family CEO of the Sauces Group in 2006. This CEO built a professional management team to run the business, while the family retained control only at the board level. This trend raises problems in two areas for the LKK Group: the maintenance of entrepreneurial orientation and the maintenance of entrepreneurial spirit following the disengagement of the family from management of the company.

How is Entrepreneurial Orientation to be Maintained after the Family Disengages itself from the Management of the Company?

The family is tackling this problem on two fronts. First, family members can serve as strategic decision-makers who will continue to promote the firm's entrepreneurial orientation and can also act as entrepreneurial culture communicators.

Second, the family can motivate and empower non-family managers and leaders. LKK's core values may be embraced by non-family members, creating a closer emotional bond between family and non-family members and increasing their dedication to the company. The 'auto-pilot' leadership model emphasizes trust and empowerment, giving non-family managers room to apply their talent. Southern LKK has demonstrated the validity of this model.

How is the Entrepreneurial Spirit to be Maintained after the Family Disengages itself from Management?

The recent exit of family members from the management of the family business is part of the process of establishing its family governance structure and does not mean that the family will be forever or entirely separated from the management of the business. In fact, the ongoing 'Oyster Oil 101' project launched by the family demonstrates that it is keen to foster future business leaders among the fifth generation. It also hopes that even if the members of future generations of the family decide not participate in the management of the existing business, they may wish to start new businesses. In addition, the family is also facilitating entrepreneurial activities at the level of corporate governance, such as the cultivation of an entrepreneurial culture.

CONCLUSION

The LKK family, with its 120-year history of entrepreneurship, is a powerful example of an entrepreneurial family that is building the foundation for transgenerational entrepreneurship. Their quest to achieve this goal highlights the significant role of family governance in preventing disruptions within the family and sustaining its entrepreneurial spirit.

NOTES

1. *International Business Daily*, 2007.
2. 'Auto-pilot' is a leadership model that was applied and tested by Sammy Lee. In Chinese, it translates to 'automatic gear', and Sammy used it to draw an analogy to his leadership model which encouraged staff to take the initiative. The spirit of the model is 'invisible leadership', a concept that derives from the book *Tao De Jing* by Lao Tze. In his book, Lao Tze described four kinds of rulers: 'the best rulers are scarcely known by their subjects; the next best are loved and praised; the next are feared; the next despised. When the best rulers achieve their purpose, their subjects claim the achievement as their own.' Sammy sought to adopt the way of the best ruler and applied this to his leadership

model, which comprises of six key factors: the mentor's mind and skills; an atmosphere of deep trust; selecting the proper talent; a high degree of empowerment; an efficient team; and a shared goal. The model has helped the firm develop highly engaged employees and build a strong foundation to overcome challenges

3. 'Passing on the legacy: family business succession', *Hong Kong Industrialist* (2008), 5:18.

REFERENCES

Carson, S.J., A. Madhok and T. Wu. 'Uncertainty, opportunism, and governance: the effects of volatility and ambiguity on formal and relational contracting', *Academy of Management Journal*, 49:5 (2006), 1058–77.

Fukuyama, F. *Trust: The Social Values and the Creation of Prosperity*. New York: Free Press, 1995.

Habbershon, T.G. and M.L. Williams. 'A resource-based framework for assessing the strategic advantages of family firms', *Family Business Review*, 12:1 (1999), 1–25.

Lumpkin, G.T. and G.G. Dess. 'Clarifying the entrepreneurial orientation construct and linking it to performance', *Academy of Management Review*, 21 (1996), 135–72.

Nahapiet, J. and S. Ghoshal. 'Social capital, intellectual capital, and the organizational advantage', *Academy of Management Review*, 23:2 (1998), 242–66.

Redding, S. Gordon. *The Spirit of Chinese Capitalism*. Berlin: de Gruyter, 1993.

Penrose, E.T. *The Theory of the Growth of the Firm*. New York: John Wiley, 1959.

Schulze, W.S., M.H. Lubatkin and R.N. Dino. 'Toward a theory of agency and altruism in family firms', *Journal of Business Venturing*, 18:4 (2003), 473–90.

4. The Sun family (Dawu Group): passing the helm to the wise

Bing Ren, Bin Yang and Ya Li

INTRODUCTION

Family business is an important organizational form that has greatly helped to advance China's economic development in the past 30 years (Boisot and Child 1996). However, in the case of many Chinese family firms, ownership and management are difficult to maintain across generations, and a key challenge for their long-term survival is to sustain their entrepreneurial spirit and transgenerational potential. Relative to the West, the interrelationship between entrepreneurship and transgenerational potential in Chinese family enterprises has not been sufficiently examined, and the way in which Chinese family enterprises expand entrepreneurially and are sustained is still poorly understood.

Under the Asia STEP research project, we conducted an in-depth analysis of one Chinese family business enterprise, the Sun family enterprise (also called Dawu Business Group) in northern China. The case study examined the Sun family's unique approach to entrepreneurship, their familiness resource pools and the important role of institutional contexts in shaping the enterprise's growth. This chapter will discuss the significant findings from this research and their theoretical and managerial implications.

Our research shows that the entrepreneurial orientation and familiness resource pools of the Sun family enterprise have significantly driven its entrepreneurial performance. In addition, the findings reveal a third factor that also exerted a significant influence, namely, the institutional factor. As a consequence of institutional influence, the Sun family business went through a series of unique entrepreneurial processes, with unusual consequences.

This chapter will tell a story on 'passing the helm to the wise'. To use an analogy, the Sun family was like a small boat sailing down a stream and encountering many dangers, but ultimately getting itself on the right track. There are many small boats in China, but not all of them are able to introduce entrepreneurial concepts and appropriate controls after a crisis. The Sun family is an example of a family that has been able to endure and survive a crisis, and, as such, is a rich and interesting example of an entrepreneurial family.

CASE OVERVIEW

In the early 1980s, Liu Huiru, the wife of Sun Dawu, the eventual founder of the Sun family business, contracted six acres of wasteland to plant fruit and sunflowers and raise 1000 chickens and 50 pigs with an investment of 20,000 RMB. At that time, Sun Dawu was a clerk in the Agricultural Bank of Xushui County, a small town in Hebei Province in northern China. In 1989, Sun Dawu resigned from his job at the bank, joined his wife and established Hebei Dawu Farming and Stock Breeding Ltd. When the Chinese government began to deregulate markets and allow alternative forms of economy, such as private businesses, to develop, the Sun business family seized the chance to grow its business, and ultimately expanded the small firm into a constellation of businesses under the umbrella of the Dawu Business Group. Most of the businesses in this group were related to agriculture, with 100 percent ownership control in the hands of the Sun family.

In May 2003, however, Sun was charged with 'illegally soliciting deposits from the public' and imprisoned, together with his two younger brothers Erwu and Sanwu. In a dramatic change of fortune, in November of the same year, Sun was released on probation and recovered control of the business, local governments and individuals having vouched for his innocence and petitioned for his release. From then on, he began to study the family business transmission mechanism and proposed a system he called the 'private enterprise constitutional monarchy' in the family enterprise. In February 2005, the first company election was held in the Dawu Group. Sun Dawu was elected Chairman of the supervisory board, Sun Erwu, Chairman of the board of directors, and Liu Ping, the general manager.

As of 2008, after over 20 years of development, the Dawu Group had an annual turnover of 300 million RMB. It had seven subsidiary companies focusing on breeding, planting, fertilizer processing, water and beverages, education and tourism. Except for the Dawu Middle School (an educational institution), all the other subsidiaries were profit-making businesses. The pillar of the group was its feed manufacturing business, which comprised nearly half of the assets and total annual revenues of the Dawu Group. The group had a total of 1600 employees in 2007.

FAMILINESS RESOURCE POOLS

Entrepreneur's Personal Values

The first generation leader, Sun Dawu, had distinctive personal values that became unique resources in the Sun family enterprise. His value system helped shape the ways of doing business in the family and was the first driver of the family enterprise's growth. Sun believed that Confucianism resonated with his ideas of managing the Dawu Group. The group built a memorial temple in honor of Confucius and also made it a point to teach employees about Confucianism.

The family enterprise adopted a unique corporate citizenship culture. In the Dawu enterprise, people were encouraged to have a kind and gentle disposition and refined manners, to believe in justice and truth and to act with humanity and reason. Sun insists that power and money only embody wealth, not the value of life; instead, the value of life exists in effort, knowledge and devotion. Sun believes that the people who dare to take responsibility are the real bosses.

Sun's dream is to establish a Dawu town. The family enterprise links business development with benefit to employees, customers and, most importantly, farmers and communities in the surrounding villages. The company's goal is not merely the pursuit of profit, but rather, the pursuit of mutual wealth and sustainable development. The enterprise has demonstrated its commitment to this mission by consistently adopting socially responsible behavior in the community throughout the years.

The Familiness Factor in Leadership

The impact of familiness on leadership in the Sun family enterprise has been positive and has enhanced the integrity and growth of the enterprise. Familiness in leadership has been achieved through the combination of the core leadership of Sun Dawu and the loyal and harmonious leadership of family and non-family members. Leadership of this enterprise was also characterized by a combination of first-generation and second-generation leadership. Sun, the first-generation leader, was akin to the 'godfather' within the family enterprise and exerted a significant influence on the whole family. He successfully transformed the family business from a small firm into a large business conglomerate. His leadership and charisma were highly respected by his son Sun Meng and other family and non-family leaders.

Sun Erwu and Liu Ping are the enterprise's leaders, elected after Sun Dawu resigned from the top position. Compared to Sun, they are less influential in terms of their charisma and thinking. However, they are young, energetic and motivated to further develop the enterprise. Importantly, they believe that Sun's Confucian beliefs are a good foundation for running the family enterprise, and thus also adhere to Sun's value system and strive to maintain a consistent corporate citizenship culture. The second-generation leaders are more closely attuned to the general public and are more adaptable to learning from different management teachings and new business environments.

Sun Meng, the only son of Sun Dawu, is another important figure in the leadership structure of the enterprise. He was elected as president of Dawu Middle School and was elected as one of 13 board directors in 2004. Among the next generation leaders, Sun Meng is the most closely aligned with Sun Dawu's personal value system and is also the most loyal to Sun's Confucian beliefs. He staunchly follows his father's principles, and expects teachers at Dawu Middle School to be guided by similar principles in their work. Even though he is perhaps less influential than his father and the other second-generation leaders in the group, he is ambitious about taking on more responsibilities and has striven to become ever more capable and competent. Driven by his father's influence, he has sought to pursue higher goals.

The harmonious familiness that characterized the group's leadership is especially significant in the case of two non-family leaders, Liu Jinhai and Li Wensheng, who are the general managers of two important subsidiary firms. These two non-family members are in line with Sun Dawu's value system. They have manifested their respective personal competencies in managing the subsidiary businesses and introduced new capabilities, such as a strong executive capability. Liu Jinhai and Li Wensheng are also ambitious. They appreciate the company's governance mechanism, which gives non-family members an equal opportunity to pursue higher positions in the group. Table 4.1 profiles the leadership structure of the family business group.

Knowledge and Skills

Since the Dawu Group was founded, it has steadily increased the level of scientific and technological input into the business. The group has recruited talent from colleges and universities since 1992 and trained them to become the company's technical backbone. Selected trainees were sent to Shijiazhuang Feed Research Institute to study feed production technology and to Hebei Institute of Animal Veterinary Sciences to study dissection and testing technology related to fowls and livestock. Trainees were also sent to Hebei Agricultural University and China Agricultural University to learn fowl-breeding technology.

The company also trains enterprise leaders. It organized a training program in public relations in the Department of Philosophy at Hebei

Table 4.1   Leadership profiles of the Sun family enterprise

Name	Title	Notes
Sun Dawu	Owner of the group; Chairman of the supervisory board	First-generation leader
Sun Meng	President of Dawu Middle School, member of the supervisory board	Family member, son of Sun Dawu
Sun Erwu	Chairman of the board of directors	Second-generation leader, younger brother of Sun Dawu
Liu Ping	CEO of the group and member of the executive board	Second-generation leader, relative of the Sun family
Liu Jinhai	General manager of the feed production subsidiary firm, member of the executive board	Non-family leader
Li Wensheng	General manager of the fertilizer subsidiary company and member of the executive board	Non-family leader

University for the top cadre of the company. The family enterprise also recruits talented people from outside the family as top leaders. This outsourcing strategy has created two non-family general managers in two important subsidiary companies which have become the backbone of the Dawu Business Group.

Innovative Governance

In 1992, Sun Dawu pointed out that a private company need not be called 'private', and that private only refers to a form of production and management, whereas the aim of Dawu Group is to create social wealth. During Sun's time in prison, his son Sun Meng and the family's relative, Liu Ping, led the group, but it was under great pressure and showed a deficit for the first time. In 2004, after serving a four-month prison term, Sun Dawu began to think about a system that could effectively sustain the family business across generations. He studied the system of constitutional monarchy in other countries and believed that it could help family businesses achieve long-term sustainability.

The private enterprise constitutional monarchy that Sun established in the Dawu Business Group has a three-pronged governance structure comprising a supervisory board, a board of directors and an executive board. It separates monitoring rights, decision-making rights and management rights, giving monitoring rights to the supervisory board, decision-making rights to the board of directors and management and operating rights to the executive board.

The supervisory board is composed of key family members whose seats are hereditary. It also includes lawyers and key consultants of the group. The directorate and executive board are both composed of top executives elected by the group. The three boards in the constitutional monarchy form the decision-making structure of the Dawu Business Group, with the respective boards responsible for specific aspects of the business. The board of directors makes strategic decisions relating to business development. The executive board is responsible for strategy execution and for daily operations. The supervisory board is a monitoring unit, and the chairman of the supervisory board can impeach members of the board of directors and the executive board in the event that these boards' managements are in violation of company regulations.

The system of constitutional monarchy also holds that family members on the supervisory board have no right to peculate enterprise assets and that the board of directors can only propose investment projects that require less than one-third of the total annual income of the previous year. In cases where the proposed investment exceeds this limit, the board of directors must call for a three-party meeting to jointly decide whether the investment can be made. Figure 4.1 illustrates the decision-making structure and the respective rights and responsibilities of each of the boards in the group's private enterprise constitutional monarchy.

The constitutional monarchy forges a strong and stable relationship between the business family and the family business. It has clear rules governing what each board can do. With these rules in place, the enterprise has created a good organizational environment for growth and development. The business can run smoothly under both family and non-family leadership. The business family need not worry about whether there are capable family members to lead the enterprise as the constitutional monarchy system allows for capable non-family members to pursue leadership positions. Non-family leaders and employees are pleased with the system as well because they have the opportunity to be promoted to high levels of leadership and even become top leaders in the group. Liu Ping, CEO of the group, shared her views on this system.

> The chairman of Dawu Group is elected by the staff, not appointed. Even though the chairman (or other leaders) may keep achieving the company's goals, he still needs to continuously strive to do better since the chairman is elected every four years, and more capable leaders may emerge to challenge his position. This system encourages, or forces, the enterprise leaders to work harder. (Liu Ping, CEO, Dawu Group)

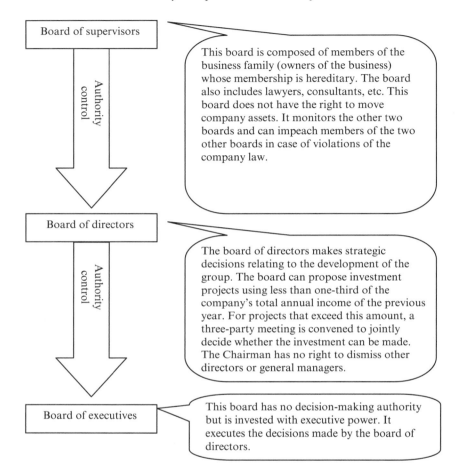

Figure 4.1   Private enterprise constitutional monarchy in the Dawu Business Group

INSTITUTIONAL INFLUENCE

Both formal and informal institutions can help shape the ways that entre-preneurs behave, set goals, and acquire and allocate company resources. Two important institutional factors have significantly influenced the Sun family business group, namely, governmental control and intervention and the business family's relationship with the community.

Governmental Control and Intervention

Government control can operate through regulations, government agencies' interpretation of laws and the enforcement of 'hidden rules'. Regulations have a formal structure. However, the interpretation of laws and regulations could be either formal or informal. Regulations and their interpretation by government agencies can be very friendly and supportive or they can be extremely hostile and restrictive. The hidden rules are even more subtle and informal, and might include giving money or other kinds of benefits to regulatory agencies. Private businesses tend to have to conform to these hidden rules if they want government support or have to go through government agencies to achieve their basic goals.[1] Private or family enterprises can encounter many kinds of government control and intervention. Most private enterprises lack the power to argue against or fight this system.

Relative to state-owned enterprises, private and family businesses face a greater level of unfriendly formal institutional constraints, which are most clearly reflected in the regulations concerning financing. Family enterprises usually need a large amount of capital, generally acquired through bank loans, to develop their businesses. Here, formal institutional constraints play a very negative role in the growth of private and family enterprises in China.

The Sun family enterprise received only two loans from banks. The first bank loan was secured after the Dawu Group was named one of the 500 biggest private companies in China by the Administrative Bureau for Industry and Commerce in 1995. At that time, the group received 2.5 million RMB in bank loans. A subsequent loan of 1.8 million RMB was given by the Agricultural Bank when Sun Dawu was awarded the title of 'Top Chicken Breeder'. But these two loans were far from enough.

Government agencies' interpretation of laws and regulations and their corresponding behaviors played a significant role in influencing the operations of the Sun family business. For example, the family enterprise had some disputes with the Inland Revenue Department, which resulted in the closure of the group's two bank accounts and the transfer of its funds. When Sun took the Inland Revenue Department to court, he was ultimately penalized with a fine. The local Trade and Industry Bureau, Health Bureau, Technical Supervision Department and other departments also created difficulties for the Dawu Group. The regulatory actions resulting from the government agencies' self-interested and erroneous interpretations of the Sun family enterprise's daily operations placed the family business in a difficult and unfortunate position. In order to cope with the adverse situation, Sun worked hard to learn government regulations and corporate law so that he could challenge interventions that he felt were unfair.

The hidden rules played an even stronger role in influencing the enterprise's daily operations. For private business owners in China, obtaining resources such as bank loans by bribing government leaders and bank officers is common. Because Sun Dawu's personal value system forbids him to bribe government agencies, the family enterprise found it exceedingly difficult to secure loans from banks.

The general manager of the group's fertilizer company tells a story about two employees of a local quality control agency who made a site visit to check the quality of Dawu's fertilizer. After they completed their investigation, they asked for 2000 RMB as a service fee. The company argued that it had not requested the quality testing service and that it was part of the agency's routine and essential duties, so the company would not pay them any fee for the service. As a result of their refusal to give money to the two agents, the quality control agency delivered an unfavorable quality report asserting that Dawu's fertilizer had a quality problem. However, when the Dawu Group requested a similar check by the provincial quality checking agency, no quality problems whatsoever were found.

On another occasion, however, Sun was forced to agree to a veiled request for money for the greater benefit of the community. In that instance, Sun Dawu had invited a local government leader to dinner several times to discuss building a road for the village, but the local leader had refused his invitation time after time. When he finally did come to dinner, he told the family that he lost a wallet containing thousands of RMB on the way, thereby dropping a broad hint for a pay-off. This is a powerful example of a government officer using the hidden rules to force a private business to satisfy his personal demands.[2] Sun struggled with the idea at first, but finally told the local government leader that 10,000 RMB would be transferred into his account immediately after the meeting.

At one stage, Sun delivered a public speech in which he spoke about the harsh institutional environment for the development of farmers and villagers and called for policy changes and institutional reforms. Those who regarded the Dawu Business Group as a 'bad boy' were more than ready to teach Sun a lesson. This radical speech inflated the government's anger and fueled their desire to punish Sun. The local government began to investigate the enterprise's informal financing structure, under which the Sun family enterprise had borrowed money from residents of surrounding villages.

Approximately 4000 people had lent money to the Dawu Group, totaling about 1.8 billion RMB. The government sued the Dawu Business Group on the grounds that Dawu's informal financing practices were against the law and charged the organization with 'illegally soliciting deposits from the public'. This lawsuit reflects the potential impact of government agencies' crooked and self-interested interpretation of the legality of family enterprises' financing behaviors. According to current Chinese Criminal Law (No. 176), 'illegally soliciting deposits from the public' refers to those behaviors that are in violation of the country's financial management regulations, specifically, illegally soliciting deposits from the public or soliciting deposits in a veiled or deceptive way, thereby disturbing the financial order. However, Sun's informal financing behavior conforms to the definition of 'lending in non-governmental circles' or 'private lending', which is protected by Chinese Civil Law. This was the case that in May 2003 resulted in Sun and his two younger brothers being sent to prison. The family business nearly collapsed during this critical period.

Community Relationships

The Sun family business has developed a mutually interdependent, long-term relationship with the community. This informal institution has been a unique resource for the enterprise through the years and has greatly helped the enterprise to grow in terms of securing labor, finance, customers and suppliers. Driven by Sun's dream of establishing a Dawu town and achieving mutual wealth for the business and the community, his enterprise has played a key role in helping the local economy and households prosper. Further, the Sun family enterprise demonstrates its commitment and sense of social responsibility to the community in many ways, such as offering free medical check-ups for farmers at the Dawu hospital and donating money to the poorest people in the community. The group has also built roads in a bid to improve local transportation.

In its dealings with suppliers and customers, the Sun family enterprise focused on building mutually beneficial, long-term relationships based on trust and loyalty. As an example, the fertilizer business gives farmers free samples of its fertilizer to enable them to test the product. This allows the business not only to prove that the quality of its product is as good as or better than that of its competitors, but is also a way to build customer loyalty. The Sun family enterprise strongly believes in protecting its customers' interests.

When Sun proposed borrowing money from his employees and villagers from the surrounding areas and offered them an interest rate that was 3 percent higher than that offered by the banks, they were more than willing to lend money to the Dawu Group. The group raised money from their employees, their employees' relatives and residents of nearby villages. The community became a very important source of financing for the group, and this greatly advanced the development of the enterprise.

When the government declared Sun's informal mode of financing illegal and imprisoned Sun and other Dawu employees, members of the community who had lent their money to the Dawu Group had only good words for Sun and the group. They believed the Dawu Group had done nothing wrong and were willing to support the family business with a strong show of goodwill and confidence. During that critical time, people from outside the community, including lawyers and the media, also came out in defense of the Dawu Group. They appreciated the Dawu Group's business philosophy and believed that the family had received unfair treatment. They were disgusted by what they regarded as an unfair trial and hoped to do their part to help the Dawu Group in this unfriendly environment.

ENTREPRENEURIAL ORIENTATION

The Spirit of the Tortoise

Entrepreneurial orientation in the Sun family business case presents some interesting patterns. The Dawu Business Group emphasizes 'stable' development rather than 'fast' growth. The business group has not developed at a very rapid pace. In Sun Dawu's words, 'We identify with the spirit of the tortoise: climb slowly, yet climb stably.' Under this principle, the enterprise does not pursue high-profit business opportunities or take great risks to get bigger, faster; rather, its first priority is to grow surely and steadily. This helps the group focus on its core businesses and establish its brand and reputation in the community and throughout the region.

The spirit of tortoise, to some extent, has constrained the group's level of entrepreneurial orientation in terms of aggressively creating and exploiting new and risky business opportunities. However, proactiveness, autonomy and innovativeness in management are largely encouraged in the enterprise. And these qualities are more frequently employed in pursuing innovations in such areas as informal financing, management and brand marketing.

Entrepreneurial Orientation (EO) as an Institutionalized Product

Gartner (1985, 697) argues that 'the actions the entrepreneurs take or do not take and the environments they operate in and respond to are equally diverse – and all these elements form complex and unique combinations in the creation (and operation) of each new venture'. The Sun family case reveals that the pattern of EO is contextualized, and that the context is primarily the different external institutional environments that help shape the ways in which resources are acquired and allocated. As institutions vary, EO varies as well. The external institutional environments that shape the possible ways that this family enterprise seeks and allocates resources include two important ones: governmental control and the relationship with the community. The Sun family enterprise had dramatically different experiences in these two contexts.

To cope with governmental control, the family enterprise's EO is reflected as implicitly or explicitly fighting against biased government regulations and the money-grabbing tendencies of local government officers. In Sun's view, many government regulations and interventions by the government are simply not right. He has tried to change the situation by presenting his ideas on how the government can support and help private enterprises grow, rather than constraining and grabbing finance from these businesses. As a consequence of Sun's reformist efforts, the family enterprise has a troublesome relationship with the government and has earned a reputation as a 'bad firm'.

The problematic relationship between the government and the Sun family enterprise, however, has steered the group's EO towards exploring alternative resource-seeking strategies. These explorations not only include seeking informal financing, but also include distinguishing the enterprise as one that is pursuing a different road to development, one that is driven by values. To the Sun family enterprise, the government is a bad role model and it refuses to become an ally or partner of a crooked government official or agency.

The group's decision to seek informal financing to build capital is a passive outcome of formal institutional constraints. The lending policies were underdeveloped and not supportive of private and family businesses. Acquiring resources through the approved channels proved difficult for family businesses. And when borrowing was not simply a pure market transaction but a money-grabbing opportunity for government agencies, the options available to Dawu Business Group were bound to be limited. The business family had to decide how to cope with 'this disturbance'. If they surrendered to it, they would be able to gain resources and legitimacy for their firms; however, in the long run, their compliance could potentially threaten the sustainability of their enterprises as it would involve illegal activities. The Sun family enterprise, however, rarely utilized government resources to develop their business.

On the other hand, the importance of the family business to the village and to local economic development and the importance of the community to the family business has led Sun and the company to realize that pursuing sustainable development and mutual wealth are far better goals than aggressively and rapidly growing the enterprise and simply pursuing profits for the family's own benefit. The Sun family business's entrepreneurial orientation of pursuing mutual wealth is largely shaped by informal environmental factors; hence, the interdependent business-community relationship they have forged. Because the Sun business family sees its destiny as linked with the community, the Sun family business relies on informal corporate financing to help the enterprise grow.

EO as an Individualized Product

Sun Dawu's personal values and spiritual beliefs have shaped the family enterprise's EO. Sun's views on the purpose of a corporation are unique. By his definition, an enterprise should not target profitability; rather, it must center on development and the pursuit of 'mutual wealth'. An entrepreneur should be willing to share his wealth with society and to transmit this entrepreneurial spirit to the next generation. Despite these views, Sun nevertheless defines his business as entrepreneurial, stating, 'Although the enterprise does not target profitability, during the past 20 years, the enterprise has never been unprofitable. Six subsidiary companies and 17 branch companies were all profitable.'

Sun's concept of entrepreneurship emphasizes the relationship between creating material wealth and creating spiritual wealth:

> Enterprises are making profits and they are also making spiritual wealth. The enterprise will ultimately be an important vehicle for the continuation of culture and spirit. And that is very important in order for employees to realize their self-worth, for an enterprise to achieve a sense of accomplishment and for the collective identity of the community. Thus, the concept of entrepreneurship in Sun enterprise finally boils down to how to behave with humanity, rather than just focus simply on making less or more money. It should echo the meaning of existence of life. (Sun Dawu, Founder)

Sun also has strong views about the right means to employ in the creation of wealth:

> Most economists would agree that creating wealth is the most important responsibility of entrepreneurs. However, in the current institutional environment, many entrepreneurs create a huge amount of wealth, yet it is through various kinds of irresponsible means. The end may be good; however, the means are illegal. (Sun Dawu, Founder)

Sun insists that creating wealth at the expense of others is by no means entrepreneurship.

What an entrepreneur needs to worry about is making sure that the enterprise is earning money in the right way, maintaining stability and being clear about how to spend money. Therefore, the role of an entrepreneur in an enterprise is to maintain responsible governance, not just earn money and manage the firm. The concept of governance is very important for an entrepreneur – it is the essence of creating an enterprise, the main purpose of doing business. In essence, an enterprise should be values-driven, having a far-reaching mission. (Sun Dawu, Founder)

Sun's ideas about entrepreneurship were further intensified after the crisis in 2003. During that time, the public began to pay attention to how entrepreneurs coped with restrictive institutional environments, and to think about what are the right attitudes and behaviors for entrepreneurs operating in underdeveloped institutional contexts. Sun offers his views on the phenomenon of 'conforming to the hidden rule' and explains how this prevalent practice has dampened entrepreneurial spirit and organizational dignity.

Entrepreneurs need to face three groups of people: workers, customers and government officials. An enterprise cannot exploit the worker and needs to pursue product quality as well achieve legitimate profits. Who would be willing to pay a bribe using their legitimate profits? The costs of these bribes will be ultimately carried by the customers. Hence, it is the customer who finally pays the bill. Seen in this way, entrepreneurial activity that involves any kind of bribing or 'conforming to hidden rules' is not entrepreneurship at all. (Sun Dawu, Founder)

Sun believes that the road he is taking is the right one, neither the 'gangster' route nor the 'red' route. However, he realizes that his chosen path is difficult for many other entrepreneurs to follow. Speaking about the influence of hidden rules, Sun observes, 'Hidden rules are influencing our society very deeply. This has even created a "reversed out" mechanism in our society where excellent and right-minded people are crowded out by less good and unethical people.'

Entrepreneurial Learning

Sun's 2003 prison sentence for allegedly 'illegally soliciting bank deposits from the public' is a sign of his unique and independent behavior within the current institutional environment. Indeed, it is very possible that Sun's attitude towards the hidden rules could put his enterprise's survival at risk. However, as the saying goes, 'he who laughs last, laughs longest'. Sun has never had stronger confirmation about how right his way of doing business is, as he had after the crisis. Sun and his family observed that even after the group came under fire, the enterprise was still able to sustain itself despite having no strong leaders and no funds. To Sun, this seemed marvelous and went far beyond his expectations. All the middle-level managers expressed their belief that the way that the enterprise had always been run should not change after Sun's release from prison as a result of his bad experience. Many believed that the Dawu Business Group had chosen a difficult but correct path – one that touched people's hearts – and thus would be able to get back on track. The survival of the Dawu Business Group proved that every positive and ethical thing that the organization had chosen to do was useful and valuable. During that critical period, the enterprise's unity and survival depended largely on the surrounding community. If Sun had chosen the path of merely pursuing profits, the enterprise would undoubtedly have crumbled after encountering such a huge crisis.

Yet something did happen to Sun himself after the crisis. Before his sentence, Sun saw government interventions and hidden rules in a negative light and spoke publicly against those who sought rents from the general public. After the crisis, however, Sun has become quieter and more discreet. Though he remains committed to his worthy mission of pursuing mutual development, Sun has become more reserved in his opinions. Why has there been such a big change in Sun? We believe this is largely due to his experiences during the crisis. Hence, entrepreneurs' experiential learning can help them reshape and change their ways of doing things (Kolb 1984).

In China's transitional economy, entrepreneurs' experiential learning can take place as a result of their relationship with the external environment, in particular, with the government and the community. Sun's personal experiences combined with those of the family in dealing with these institutional forces gave the family enterprise many different opportunities for learning. Sun and the Dawu Group learned that complying with formal institutional pressure is extremely important for the survival of private and family businesses when institutional environments influence an enterprise's growth in a negative way, even as far as engendering a corporate crisis.

The crisis gave Sun a chance to learn, in the most thorough and clearcut way possible, what a private entrepreneur like himself could achieve in China. It helped Sun understand the importance of developing a family enterprise's transgenerational potential and pushed him to consider what kind of governance mechanism would help sustain an enterprise well into the distant future. Sun eventually decided to withdraw from management of the group, but he established the private company constitutional monarchy system, an innovative governance mechanism to encourage capable family and non-family members to become enterprise leaders and help the family enterprise achieve sustainable development in the long run.

CONCLUSION

In this chapter, we have explored how the Sun family has addressed the issue of transgenerational entrepreneurship, in other words, how it 'passes the helm to the wise'. From the earliest days of the business, more than 30 years ago, to the present, Sun's grand vision of developing the enterprise by linking it to the community's welfare has helped his enterprise grow steadily. Several other factors, such as the formal and informal institutions that were in place and Sun's unique entrepreneurial orientation also significantly influenced the growth of this family enterprise. While it is not always easy for private entrepreneurs to determine what may be the right way of doing business in China during periods of institutional and economic transition, there are those, like Sun, who learned valuable lessons from their experiences. Thus, the case of the Sun family enterprise certainly deserves closer analysis.

NOTES

We thank Prof. Justin Craig and Prof. Kevin Au for helpful instructions for developing the book chapter. Bing Ren thanks the National Natural Science Foundation China (Fund code: 70732004) for its financial support. We also thank the following graduate students at Nankai University for their research assistance: Jingting Zhang, Yafang He, Yunzhou Du, Juelin Yin and Kezhi Wang.

1. This was largely the result of the self-interested and unethical behavior of regulatory agencies who took advantage of their power and position to seek collective or personal rents from private and family businesses.
2. In fact, the same local government leader used similar tactics on other occasions and other businesses when his support was sought for a particular activity.

REFERENCES

Boisot, M and J. Child. 'From fiefs to clans and network capitalism: explaining China's emerging economic order'. *Administrative Science Quarterly*, 41:4 (1996), 600–628.

Gartner, W.B. 'A conceptual framework for describing the phenomenon of new venture creation', *Academy of Management Review*, 10:4 (1985), 696–706.

Kolb, D.A. *Experiential Learning: Experience as the Source of Learning and Development*. Englewood Cliffs, NJ: Prentice-Hall, 1984.

5. Menshy Battery's Chen family: an overseas educated generation turns to export

Weiwen Li, Yuan Lu, Danming Lin and Kevin Au

INTRODUCTION

Menshy Battery is one of the most innovative companies operating today in the very small niche market for motorcycle lead acid batteries. Entrepreneurship and entrepreneurial orientation (EO) with regard to Menshy have gone through dramatic changes since its founder passed the baton to his eldest son.

The act of entrepreneurship is defined as new entry accomplished by entering new or established markets with new or existing goods or services (Lumpkin and Dess 1996). EO refers to the processes, practices and decision-making activities that lead to new entry (Lumpkin and Dess 1996). The key dimensions of EO include autonomy, innovativeness, risk-taking, proactiveness and competitive aggressiveness.

Before the leadership transition, Menshy was entrepreneurial in the sense that it was sensitive to market changes and quick enough to *explore* new industries that arose from those changes. After the leadership transition, Menshy continued to be entrepreneurial; however, its focus has changed to *exploiting* a niche market through innovation and export.

As Menshy's new entries were driven by different configurations of the dimensions of EO, the company's entrepreneurial orientation changed accordingly. When the founder was the engine of entrepreneurship, Menshy's entrepreneurial activities were mainly driven by the firm's proclivity for risk-taking and proactiveness. After the CEO succession, Menshy was able to accomplish new entries because of its autonomy, innovativeness and competitive aggressiveness.

In this chapter we will demonstrate how entrepreneurship and EO changes within Menshy are linked to the different backgrounds of its two

CEOs. This finding has two implications for family businesses doing business in dynamic environments:

(1) The knowledge and skills of the CEO will become obsolete over time in dynamic environments (Ocasio 1994).
(2) To remain aligned with environmental changes without changing its CEO, a company should build a top management team with diverse knowledge and skills (Hambrick and Mason 1984).

BACKGROUND

Culture

The Chen family is located in Chenghai, in the Chaoshan region of China, which is highly influenced by traditional Chinese culture. Even today, the Chaoshan region retains its dialect, which originated in the Han dynasty.

The family has traditionally been the basic unit of Chinese society. The relationships between family members are dictated by Confucian doctrine, according to which the father has more power than his children, the husband more power than his wife, and an elder sibling more power than a younger sibling. Traditionally, sons are more cherished than daughters and elder sons are more cherished than younger sons, even if the younger son is more talented. When the father reaches old age, his eldest son takes over the reins of the family and his sons share the family property. Filial piety is the most important social norm of traditional Chinese culture. Filial piety means not only being loyal to one's parents, but also engaging in good conduct in order to bring a good name to one's family. It is considered the first virtue among Chinese people.

Chaoshan region has a long history of entrepreneurship. During difficult times in the history of the region, Chaoshan people migrated to different parts of Southeast Asia and many started their own businesses in their adopted countries. Representative entrepreneurs include Li Ka Shing in Hong Kong and Chia Ek Chor in Thailand. This spirit of entrepreneurship was one of the factors that drove the central government to declare Shantou, the largest city in this region, as one of the special economic zones in 1981.

The Chen Family

Chen Zaixi (born in 1945) is the founder of the Menshy Group and has established four subsidiaries of the group, three in Liuzhou and one in

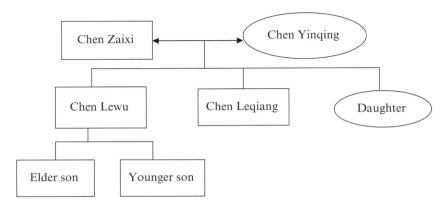

Figure 5.1   Overview of the Chen family

Chenghai. Before setting up his own businesses, he had been a village cadre in charge of industrial development.

Chen Yinqing created Menshy Electric Bicycles in 1999. She keenly promotes and is actively engaged in philanthropic activities and has been recognized for her giving by the Guangdong Federation of Industry and Commerce.

Chen Lewu (born in 1971) obtained a Bachelor's degree in economics from Sun Yat-sen University in 1993. After graduation, he joined Menshy Battery for two years, during which time he prepared his applications to US business schools. He was admitted to the Georgia College and State University as an MBA student in 1995. He became the CEO of Menshy Battery shortly after he returned to China in 1998.

Chen Leqiang is also a graduate of Sun Yat-sen University, where he majored in library management in the early 1990s. After graduating, he formed his own toy manufacturing company in Chenghai, where more than 70 percent of the world's toys are produced. In 2008, when Menshy started to prepare for an initial public offering (IPO), he was appointed by Chen Lewu as the deputy general manager of Menshy to take care of the company's financial affairs. Figure 5.1 presents an overview of the Chen family.

The Lead Acid Battery Industry

Lead acid batteries, which were invented in 1859 by French physicist Gaston Planté, are the oldest form of rechargeable batteries. The lead acid battery has a low energy-to-weight ratio, and correspondingly, a low energy-to-volume ratio compared to other forms of batteries. Despite this,

Table 5.1   Competition in the lead acid battery market in China

Rank	Company	Sales (RMB in millions)	Market share (%)
1	Chaowei	2731.96	4.55
2	Fengfan	2627.33	4.38
3	Shuangdeng	2088.63	3.48
4	Tongyi	1086.17	1.81
5	Nandu	902.44	1.50
6	Meimei	600.00	1.00
7	Shengyang	553.86	0.92
8	Longkou	513.54	0.86
9	Tangqian	393.16	0.66
10	Wangma	380.00	0.63
20	Menshy	119.42	0.20

Source: The raw data for this table are from the China Industrial Association of Power Sources.

its low manufacturing cost and its high surge currents make it attractive for use in cars and motorcycles where a large capacity is required.

Japan, South Korea and China are the three major producers of lead acid batteries. While Japanese suppliers still hold more than half of the market, companies from China are gaining ground as a result of the low price and improved quality of their batteries. There are now around 1500 lead acid battery companies in China, and their output is increasing rapidly, at a rate of about 20 percent annually. Currently, China's output of lead acid batteries accounts for one-third of world production.

While lead acid batteries can be used in various ways, the motorcycle battery market is a relatively small sector. The most common types of lead acid batteries are car batteries and industrial batteries.

The competition in this area has been intense, with over 1500 manufacturers in China. Table 5.1 lists the major domestic players in the lead acid battery market. As can be seen from the table, in 2007, the largest lead acid battery manufacturer in China was Chaowei, with annual sales over 2.7 billion RMB. While the market for lead acid batteries in China is valued at 60 billion RMB, Chaowei accounts for less than 5 percent of the market share.

The Company

With over 700 employees, Menshy Battery is now offering six series of batteries to customers from over 60 countries. In the niche market for motorcycle lead acid batteries, Menshy is the largest exporter in China and the third largest domestic player. Its products are popular among both foreign and domestic customers because of their high quality and advanced technology.

Menshy Battery started to promote its products in domestic markets only in 2006 and focuses on motorcycle batteries alone, nonetheless it has already grown to be the third largest player in the domestic market.

In addition, unlike most of its domestic competitors, who manufacture mass-produced batteries, Menshy focuses on high-quality products. Dynavolt motorcycle batteries produced by Menshy Battery are comparable to those produced by Japanese companies and are especially popular in Europe and America. Menshy Battery is now the largest exporter of lead acid motorcycle batteries in China.

FAMILY ENTREPRENEURSHIP

Entrepreneurship and EO before CEO Succession

a. Development of Menshy before CEO succession

Before Chen Lewu took over the reins of the company in 1996, the development of Menshy Battery was mainly a reflection of Chen Zaixi's entrepreneurial spirit. A brief introduction to Chen Zaixi's experience might help in understanding Menshy's development and entrepreneurial orientation.

Chen Zaixi was born in 1945 in Chenghai, Guangdong Province. He was a village cadre in charge of industrial development back in the early 1970s, when Deng Xiaoping was brought back into politics as Executive Vice-Premier to reconstruct the country's economy. Chen Zaixi did a commendable job of revitalizing local industries. However, beginning in late 1975, Deng's moves in industrial development were criticized by the Gang of Four, a radical leftist political group that saw Deng as the greatest challenge to its power. Chen Zaixi was seen as 'carrying out Deng Xiaoping's line' and was criticized and tortured by domestic leftists in 1975. Unable to bear the persecution, Chen Zaixi quit his job and became an ordinary peasant.

Deng regained power in 1977, and at the Third Plenary Session of the 11th Central Committee of the Communist Party of China (CPC) in 1978, he announced his decision to shift the focus of the Party's work to socialist modernization. Excited by this shift, Chen Zaixi decided to set up his own business together with several young people and veteran soldiers in Chenghai in 1979.

In the early days of running his own business, Chen Zaixi explored several industries in search of a business with great potential, including building materials, plastic injection molding and car batteries, before ultimately settling on motorcycle batteries.

b. Entrepreneurship before CEO succession

As can be seen from the above description, before the CEO succession, Menshy was entrepreneurial in that it continuously entered new markets: building materials, plastic injection molding, car batteries, motorcycle batteries and rubber hoses. Whenever Menshy entered a new market, it completely gave up the existing products, with the exception of its entry into the rubber hose market. Menshy entered the rubber hose market in 1995 and three years later went through a CEO transition.

Menshy's exploration of new product markets was mainly a result of the founder's business insights. Chen Zaixi was shrewd in anticipating future market trends and was quick to grab the opportunities he saw.

Continual new entries by Menshy before the mid-1990s were viable in China because of environmental munificence, which refers to the profitability or growth rate of the industry in which a firm competes (Dess and Beard 1984). During the early stages of China's economic reform, there were relatively few players in various markets. For example, when Volkswagen formed an alliance in China, it had difficulty finding producers of auto parts and accessories in the country. As a result, those who entered the auto parts and accessories market were able to make a profit easily.

c. EO before CEO succession

Menshy's entrepreneurial behavior in terms of its continuous exploration of new product markets was driven by its proactiveness and willingness to take risks.

i. Proactiveness and risk-taking   *Proactiveness* refers to how firms take the initiative by anticipating and pursuing new opportunities. This refers to a forward-looking perspective and a search for opportunities. Menshy was extremely proactive in its early stages.

Immediately after the CPC's declaration of economic reform and the open-door policy in 1978, Chen Zaixi, along with several young people, set up factories to explore different products such as building materials and plastic injection molding. These activities were truly proactive in the sense that Chen Zaixi and those who joined him were the earliest players in the relevant markets in China.

Menshy was proactive because it was extremely sensitive to market trends. Shortly after the creation of the first car alliance, Shanghai Volkswagen, Menshy saw the potential of the car industry and became the earliest producer of car batteries. Menshy also sensed the market potential of motorcycle batteries when Japanese motorcycle companies began to form alliances with domestic companies.

Risk-taking refers to the extent to which owners or managers are willing to make large commitments based on uncertain outcomes.

The development of Menshy before the CEO succession was marked by risk-taking behavior, as it frequently ventured into unknown industries. Chen Zaixi was a peasant before he started his own businesses. Though he had been a village cadre in charge of industrial development, initially Chen Zaixi did not know very much about the products he decided to produce. What he did know was that there was great market potential for these products and that he could find ways to produce them. When he decided to produce car batteries, he formed an alliance with a Shanghai company to learn the technology; and when he ventured into motorcycle battery manufacturing, he was willing to invest heavily to develop Menshy's own products from scratch.

ii. Autonomy, innovativeness and competitive aggressiveness   During this stage, Menshy showed little autonomy, innovativeness and competitive aggressiveness, mainly because of the founder's lack of trust in outsiders and his own limited knowledge and skills.

Autonomy refers to the 'independent action of an individual or a team in bringing forth an idea or a vision and carrying it through to completion' (Lumpkin and Dess 1996, 140).

In Menshy, authority was concentrated in the hands of Chen Zaixi and only those he trusted were given autonomy. As a traditional Chinese family, relationships in the Chen family were characterized by *chaxu geju* (differential mode of association) based on *shehui guanxi* (ranked categories of social connections) (Fei 1939). In this model, starting with the self at the center, there is decreasing closeness as one moves outwards from the immediate family to the extended family, to *shuren* (acquaintances), and finally, to *shenren* (strangers). When his sons were still too young to manage his company, Chen Zaixi relied on his extended family members, in particular his nephew and his son-in-law, to help him with technology management and sales, even though there might have been more capable employees in the company. Chen Zaixi appointed these two relatives as deputy general managers, with his nephew in charge of technology and his son-in-law in charge of sales.

In contrast, ordinary employees were discouraged from bringing forward any new ideas for the company.

My father once employed several engineers who were really capable but whose potential was not realized by the company. For example, one of our engineers, Wu, graduated from Northwestern University in China with a major in electrochemistry and had worked for the first battery manufacturer in China. He is an expert on lead acid batteries. But he was completely ignored in Menshy. Nobody even cared about his opinion. (Chen Lewu, 2008)

Lumpkin and Dess (1996, 142) define *innovativeness* as 'a firm's tendency to engage in and support new ideas, novelty, experimentation, and creative processes that may result in new products, services, or technological processes'.

Although Menshy was active in entering new markets, it had never been innovative when Chen Zaixi was the CEO. Chen Zaixi himself did not know very much about technology, and, at the same time, was not able to trust others who were experts to take charge of product development. He trusted his nephew to oversee research and development. However, his nephew was actually unqualified for this role:

My cousin was a junior middle school student before joining Menshy. He was first assigned by my father to be an assistant to technology consultants and engineers and to learn from them. After that, he became the technology deputy general manager responsible for research & development and quality control. How can you expect Menshy to achieve technology breakthroughs under his supervision? (Chen Lewu, 2008)

Competitive aggressiveness is defined as 'a firm's propensity to directly and intensively challenge its competitors to achieve entry or improve position, that is, to outperform industrial rivals in the market place' (Lumpkin and Dess 1996, 148).

Under Chen Zaixi's leadership, Menshy seemed to be afraid of challenging its competitors. Whenever there was intense competition in a given product market, Menshy chose to leave and enter another product market rather than engage in head-on competition. Back in 1986, Menshy and Fengfan were the only two car battery manufacturers for Shanghai Volkswagen in China. While Fengfan is now the second largest lead acid car battery maker in China, Menshy quit the car battery market in the early 1990s.

CEO Succession

Starting from the early 1990s, competition in the secondary battery market began to intensify. On the one hand, more and more private enterprises entered this product market. On the other hand, battery companies from Japan, Hong Kong and Europe, such as Panasonic and National, started setting up factories in China to serve both the domestic and international markets. In 1997, there were about 1000 companies producing lead acid batteries in China.

Menshy encountered a quality crisis in 1996. It had neglected to add antioxidants, which are critical for a battery's performance, to its motorcycle batteries, as the result of an engineer's negligence. At that time, Menshy had not established a formal management system so it did not double check the formula provided by the engineer before the batteries were produced and sold in the market. The problematic products were in the market for about half a year and they inflicted a huge blow to Menshy's brand image. Menshy thought that customers would forget about the problematic batteries and did not recall the batteries until 2000. However, customers were not as forgetful as Menshy imagined.

For all those reasons, Menshy's sales from motorcycle batteries dropped sharply from 60 million RMB in 1996 to 20 million RMB in 1998. Chen Zaixi tried his best to save his business but could not find a way to turn it around. When he spoke with his eldest son on the phone, Chen Zaixi asked him whether he would come back to help him out.

Chen Lewu returned to China from the US in 1998 and became the new CEO of Menshy three months later. Prior to his return, Chen Lewu had earned an MBA from Georgia College and State University and had worked at an information technology company in the US.

Entrepreneurship and EO after CEO Succession

a. Development of Menshy after CEO succession

Determined to pull Menshy Battery out of its quality crisis, Chen Lewu, with consent from Chen Zaixi, persuaded his cousin and brother-in-law to leave Menshy Battery and take a management position in another subsidiary of the Menshy Group.

Under Chen Lewu's influence, Menshy Battery invested a huge amount of money in developing high quality batteries and changed the brand name to Dynavolt to cater to foreign customers. Dynavolt batteries were so popular in foreign markets that Menshy rapidly rebounded from its early losses, with sales increasing from 20 million RMB in 1998 to 50 million RMB in 2001.

b. Entrepreneurship after CEO succession

As indicated in the introduction to this chapter, Menshy Battery, under Chen Lewu's leadership, had focused on a very small niche market – the motorcycle lead acid battery market. While Menshy has continued to be entrepreneurial after the CEO succession, the means of new entry have changed.

In this phase, Menshy has accomplished new entries mainly through entering foreign markets with high quality products. In order to sell its products in the US market, Menshy invested more than 10 million RMB to develop a Society of Automotive Engineers (SAE) standard motorcycle battery. Menshy also developed the Nanotechnology GEL motorcycle battery with high cranking power, which is especially popular in Northern Europe because GEL electrolytes can still be active at 18 degrees below zero whereas the electrolytes in regular batteries tend to freeze. As a result of its high quality and advanced technology, Menshy is now selling its products in more than 60 countries.

c. EO after CEO succession

Menshy has been able to accomplish its new entry into foreign markets with innovative products mainly because of its high EO in terms of autonomy, innovativeness and competitive aggressiveness.

i. Autonomy, innovativeness and competitive aggressiveness   When Chen Zaixi was the CEO, only his nephew and son-in-law could act autonomously. After Chen Lewu took charge, he persuaded them to leave Menshy Battery and trusted ordinary employees to generate new ideas for the company.

Chen Lewu once asked one of the engineers, Wu, whether he could develop a Society of Automotive Engineers (SAE) standard motorcycle battery, which had never been produced in the domestic market. Being an experienced researcher, Wu replied that it was theoretically possible. On getting that answer, Chen Lewu let Wu develop that product independently and promised funds whenever they were required. By the time this product was successfully developed, Menshy had invested more than 10 million RMB in it, even though the sales of Menshy Battery were only around 50 million RMB at that time.

Today, Menshy is extremely innovative, and aims to achieve a higher profit margin than average and to seize market share from Japanese and Korean competitors.

> To stay competitive, we have to keep our technology ahead of domestic players by at least two years. Otherwise, we might have them catching up with us and only get an average profit margin. (Chen Lewu, 2009)

One proof of Menshy's innovativeness is the development of the aforementioned Nanotechnology GEL motorcycle battery in 2004. Nanotechnology GEL batteries have great advantages over regular lead acid batteries in three respects. First, they eliminate the problem of leakage even when the battery container is broken; thus, they are much safer for motorcycles. Second, this new technology extends the battery life by 1.5 times. The usual lifespan of a regular battery is about 200 cycles, but the lifespan of a Nanotechnology GEL battery is about 500 cycles. Third, it has much higher cranking power than regular batteries. This quality is especially welcomed by motorcycle racers, who require high cranking performance, and by customers from cold countries such as northern European countries. Currently, Menshy is the only company in the world that can produce this type of battery. When this new product was exhibited in Frankfurt, nobody could believe that it was developed by a Chinese company. In 2009, Menshy leveraged this advanced technology and introduced into the market Nanotechnology GEL car batteries, which are now starting to gain popularity in both the domestic and international markets.

Menshy is now highly aggressive both in the domestic market and in the global market. Though it had not focused on the domestic market from 2002 to 2006, since 2006, Menshy has actively promoted its products to domestic customers by claiming that its products are popular in Western countries where customers demand much higher quality. Today, Menshy is the third largest lead acid motorcycle battery company in China. To out-perform its top two competitors in China, Menshy is now setting up new factories in Guangxi, Fujian, Sichuan and Jiangsu in order to compete directly with the local companies.

In the global market, Menshy continues to challenge the market position of companies from Japan and Korea. Before Menshy began selling its products in foreign markets, companies from Japan and Korea were virtually the only sources for motorcycle batteries. However, with intensive research and development, Menshy is rapidly increasing its market share and now out-innovates most of its competitors.

ii. Risk-taking and proactiveness   As shown above, Menshy had been extremely open to risk-taking before the CEO succession. After Chen Lewu became the CEO, Menshy continued to take risks, but to a lesser extent.

The decision of Menshy Battery to concentrate exclusively on foreign markets was risky. At that time, there were many competitors from Japan and Korea who possessed more advanced technology. Before Chen Lewu took the position of CEO, none of Menshy's motorcycle batteries had been sold to foreign customers. However, before making the decision to export its products, Chen Lewu had spent considerable time studying foreign markets, communicating with foreign customers and testing Menshy's products overseas. In this sense, Menshy exhibits less risk-taking behavior

Table 5.2 Menshy Battery: changes of entrepreneurship and EO after CEO succession

Entrepreneurship		Before CEO succession	After CEO succession
		Explore different product markets	Exploit the existing product market through innovation and export
EO	Autonomy	Low	High
	Innovativeness	Low	High
	Risk-taking	High	Medium
	Proactiveness	High	Medium
	Aggressiveness	Low	High

than in the past, when Chen Zaixi decided to enter into a new market shortly after he found the opportunity.

Menshy also shows much less proactiveness after the CEO succession in the sense that the company has focused mainly on the motorcycle lead acid battery market. While Chen Lewu was studying for his MBA in the US, he learned that a company should build its core competence. At the same time, he found that a considerable amount of the products sold in US supermarkets were made in China.

> Americans use products made in China. I was thinking that the products made in China should be the best. For this reason, even though our company had gone through hard times, we insisted on staying in the manufacturing industry. I persuaded my parents and top managers that in order to achieve superior performance, we should produce only one product. (Chen Lewu, 2008)

DISCUSSION

CEO Backgrounds and Changes in Entrepreneurship and EO

As shown in Table 5.2, which summarizes the key changes in entrepreneurship and EO experienced by Menshy after the CEO transition, both entrepreneurship and EO within Menshy changed significantly after Chen Lewu took over. When the founder was in charge, Menshy had explored different industries. Following the CEO succession, Menshy has been focusing on research and development in order to exploit opportunities in the lead acid battery market. Accordingly, the autonomy, innovativeness and competitive aggressiveness of Menshy have increased significantly, while there is a decrease in both risk-taking and proactiveness.

These changes are shaped by the differences in the CEOs' backgrounds. First, since CEOs are a vital resource for their companies, their knowledge and skills, especially their management skills, determine how the companies are managed and whether the companies can achieve sustainable growth (Penrose 1959). Second, according to the upper-echelon perspective, the CEO's experiences shape the management team's perceptions about the business environment and internal resources, which in turn determine how the resources are deployed, exploited or enhanced (Hambrick and Mason 1984; Meyer 2006).

Before starting his own business, Chen Zaixi was a village cadre in charge of industrial development. This specific experience provided him with basic knowledge about the economic situation in China and how the market can be an efficient mechanism for allocating resources. This knowledge helped Chen Zaixi identify opportunities in different product markets and enabled Menshy to take risks in proactively entering these markets. In this sense, Chen Zaixi's previous experience facilitated Menshy's new entries and drove Menshy's risk-taking and proactiveness.

However, as Menshy became larger, with annual revenues approaching 60 million RMB, it proved increasingly difficult for Chen Zaixi to manage the company successfully, especially when the competition in the market became more and more intense in the mid-1990s. Chen Zaixi's past experience in coordinating village industrial development and managing the small factories of the earlier days was no longer valuable. He lacked the confidence to empower ordinary employees and instead relied on his nephew and son-in-law to help him out. As neither his nephew nor his son-in-law were highly educated or knew much about research and development and marketing, they actually made the situation worse. Capable engineers remained unregarded, products were of low quality and the company's market share was shrinking. It became apparent that Chen Zaixi's knowledge and skills were obsolete in the face of a dynamic environment and his lack of trust in non-family members hindered Menshy from being autonomous, innovative and competitively aggressive.

In a similar vein, entrepreneurial activity and EO after the CEO succession are also the result of the backgrounds of the new CEO and his top management team. Chen Lewu's background is totally different from his father's. Chen Lewu earned his Bachelor's degree in economics from a prestigious university, Sun Yat-sen University, in China. He also had an MBA from Georgia College and State University and work experience with a company in the US.

His education and work experience in the US raised his understanding of international business opportunities and lowered his cognitive and practical barriers toward internationalization (Meyer 2006). In addition, the concept of 'core competence' propagated by US business schools and practiced by US companies had a big impact on Chen Lewu's cognition, so much so that he decided to build Menshy's own core competence.

> Usually, US companies concentrated on single product markets. They do not produce everything. The concept of 'core competence' has been invented and is practiced by them. When I got back to Menshy, the top managers were talking about diversification. I felt this was ridiculous. Have you ever heard of General Electric venturing into the real estate business? No. GE only made home appliances and it made the best home appliances. (Chen Lewu, 2008)

The new CEO applied the knowledge he had gained from his US business school days to Menshy and tried to build its core competence through extensive innovation and export to foreign markets. This inevitably changed Menshy's risk-taking and proactive behavior with regard to entry into different product markets.

In order to outperform competitors in the global market, Chen Lewu convinced his cousin and brother-in-law to leave Menshy and promoted two capable engineers to top management positions. These two engineers were experts on lead acid batteries but had no way of contributing to the company while Chen Lewu's cousin was responsible for research and development. After Chen Lewu took over, he asked the engineers to develop products independently. When they succeeded in developing the new products, Chen Lewu rewarded them with promotions and company shares.

In the meantime, Menshy established offices in both Europe and the US in order to compete directly with Japanese and Korean players. These are examples of management practices that Chen Zaixi was reluctant to adopt and, in some cases, of which he had never heard. Hence, the change of CEO generated new management models for Menshy and promoted greater autonomy, innovativeness and competitive aggressiveness.

One might argue that the changes in Menshy in terms of entrepreneurship and EO are simply the result of the changes in business practices in China. Indeed, the entry of multinational companies and the burgeoning executive education market have introduced advanced management practices to China. However, as there are still many companies who change their main products repeatedly in China, one might suspect that the change in Menshy is more likely to be a consequence of leadership change.

An alternative explanation for Menshy's change is that companies adopt different business practices at different stages of their life cycle. However, a careful look at the business practices of companies in China reveals that companies at different stages of their life cycle do in fact tend to retain similar business practices.

The Future

The Menshy Group has been growing rapidly and achieved above average profitability between 1998 and 2009. Menshy Battery sales increased from 20 million RMB to 120 million RMB in this period. To expand its share of the domestic market, Menshy Battery has set up two battery factories, one in Liuzhou, in the Guangxi region, and the other in Zhaoan, in Fujian province; and has plans to build another two factories, in Sichuan and Jiangsu. In the meantime, Menshy is extending its advanced technology in motorcycle battery development and manufacturing to car batteries.

As the demand for lead acid batteries is growing rapidly, there is still great potential for Menshy in this particular product market. The question is, however, whether Menshy can build a cohesive and diversified top management team to support its expansion.

In order to manage its rapid expansion in different locations, Menshy should be able to attract more capable top managers either from within the company or from outside. Subsequently, by working together, the new top management team should build a cooperative atmosphere.

We still have no firm answer on whether a cohesive top management team could be built in Menshy. Chen Lewu's training at a US business school seems to be conducive to building an effective top management team. However, his selection of his younger, less experienced brother as the deputy general manager of Menshy responsible for the company's IPO also indicates his lack of confidence in non-family members on sensitive issues.

CONCLUSION

This chapter has explored the development of Menshy, one of the earliest private enterprises in modern China. The company's entrepreneurial activities and EO changed considerably after the CEO succession.

The founder passed the baton to his son because he was not able to turn around the company in the face of a dynamic environment. The founder's strategy of continuous new entries had been successful in the company's early stages when it operated in a munificent environment. However, as more and more competitors entered these markets and the environment became more dynamic, the founder's business skills ceased to be effective.

The changes in terms of entrepreneurship and EO are the result of the new CEO's educational and work experience being different from his father's. Trained in a US business school, the new CEO is more receptive to internationalization and more familiar with the concept of 'core competence'. As a consequence, under the new CEO's leadership, Menshy focuses on the niche market of motorcycle lead acid batteries and exploits opportunities in the international market.

Another difference between the two CEOs is their willingness to trust non-family members. While the founder lacked sufficient trust in non-family members and depended on family members to manage the company, the new CEO allows the employees to act independently so long as they can bring forth new ideas for the development of the company.

The changes implemented by the new CEO successfully turned Menshy around. While qualitative case research always raises the issue of generalizability to a broader setting, the longitudinal nature of this study provides two important lessons for family businesses.

First, the knowledge and skills of CEOs will become obsolete over time, especially in dynamic environments. Therefore, in order to keep the company under the family's control, it should maximize the education and work experience of the heir-apparent such that he or she can respond to environmental changes.

Second, to stay aligned with environmental changes without changing the CEO, a company should build a top management team with diverse knowledge and skills. Even if the CEO is extraordinarily capable, he or she still needs to build a team to manage the company. In dynamic environments, a diversified top management team has an advantage over a homogeneous one, because in most cases, it provides more diversified viewpoints, generates more innovative ideas, and most importantly, is more flexible in the face of changing environments.

NOTE

This work was supported by the Chinese University of Hong Kong, Faculty of Business Administration (Direct Grant 2070415).

REFERENCES

Dess, G. and D. Beard. 'Dimensions of organizational task environments'. *Administrative Science Quarterly*, 29 (1984), 52–73.
Fei, X. *Peasant Life in China: A Field Study of Country Life in the Yangtze Valley*. London: George Routledge & Sons, 1939.

Hambrick, D.C. and P.A. Mason. 'Upper echelons: the organization as a reflection of its top managers'. *Academy of Management Review*, 9 (1984). 193–206.

Lumpkin, G.T. and Gregory G. Dess. 'Clarifying the entrepreneurial orientation construct and linking it to performance'. *Academy of Management Review*, 21 (1996), 135–72.

Meyer, K.E. 'Global focusing: from domestic conglomerates to global specialists'. *Journal of Management Studies*, 43 (2006), 1109–44.

Ocasio, W. 'Political dynamics and the circulation of power: CEO succession in US industrial corporations, 1960–1990'. *Administrative Science Quarterly*, 39 (1994), 285–312.

Penrose, E.T. *The Theory of the Growth of the Firm*. New York: John Wiley, 1959.

6. The Han family: the next generation forges a new path for the Jong-Shyn Shipbuilding Company

Hsi-Mei Chung, Kuang S. Yeh and Shyh-Jer Chen

INTRODUCTION

The Jong-Shyn Shipbuilding Company was founded by Pi-Hsiang Han in 1985 and is owned and run by the Han family. The company's decision to enter the highly value-added yacht market in 2003 can be seen both as a transfer of the founder's entrepreneurial spirit to the next generation and as a business upgrade. Utilizing the interview method, this research attempts to investigate the possible entrepreneurship development mechanism in this distinctive Taiwanese family business. From the resource-based view and the family-embedded perspective, family involvement, that is, a family's ability to adapt to change and its ability to recognize technology innovation, can have a huge influence on the transfer of entrepreneurship in a family business. Accordingly, family involvement can also influence the survival and growth of a family business. The possible implications on family entrepreneurship raised by our examination of this case will be discussed in this chapter. This case study is a good basis for a discussion of rent generation and rent appropriation issues. Furthermore, the findings of this study are meaningful and insightful in the context of entrepreneurship issues in Asian family businesses.

THEORETICAL BACKGROUND

Entrepreneurship can be defined as the recognition of new opportunities and the creation of new ventures (Aldrich 2005; Alvarez and Barney 2004; Alvarez and Busenitz 2001). Opportunities to generate or appropriate economic rents exist because of market imperfection (Barney 1986). From the resource-based viewpoint, firms with more accurate expectations concerning the future value of a strategy can avoid economic losses, and these firms will also be able to anticipate and exploit any opportunities for above-normal returns in strategic factor markets when they exist (Barney 1986; 1991). Furthermore, the ability to anticipate the future value of a strategy and to use these insights in acquiring the resources to implement the strategy is not equally distributed across the firms in an industry (Barney 1986; 1991). Therefore, entrepreneurship is likely to occur when the generation and appropriation of economic rents requires economic organization (Aldrich 2005; Alvarez and Barney 2004; Alvarez and Busenitz 2001).

The founder is often compelled by the need for achievement to explore innovative ideas and take risks in the early stages of a family business (Zahra 2005). This business becomes a family business when the founder encourages family involvement in decision-making, and when the business is eventually managed by succeeding generations (Ward 1987). Therefore, research on family entrepreneurship not only seeks to examine the role of the founder in a family business, but also aims to discover the role of family involvement and family capital in the business's entrepreneurial behaviors or in its entrepreneurship development mechanism (Aldrich and Cliff 2003; Astrachan 2003; Kellermanns and Eddleston 2006; Zahra, 2005; Zahra et al. 2004). In the case of family entrepreneurship, there is a strong link between family involvement and entrepreneurial performance, such as new venture creation, innovation and renewal, along with the ensuing financial growth and socio-economic contributions (Aldrich and Cliff 2003; Kellermanns and Eddleston 2006; Zahra 2005). A discussion of family entrepreneurship might also include the rent generation or rent appropriation dimension. Additionally, from the family-embeddedness perspective, family capital embedded in a family business is a distinctive resource that contributes to family entrepreneurship (Aldrich and Cliff 2003; Arregle et al. 2007). Although entrepreneurship has been recognized as a key factor contributing to a firm's success and sustainability, entrepreneurial transition in a family business is still an emerging topic of study in this field (Astrachan 2003; Kellermanns and Eddleston 2006; Zahra 2005; Zahra et al. 2004). Recognizing the importance of the entrepreneurial spirit in the success of a family business, the STEP project aims to explore the possible factors influencing 'transgenerational entrepreneurship' in a family business, from generation to generation. Utilizing a robust research framework, this project will provide referable value in establishing the link between family involvement, entrepreneurial performance and continuity in the context of family business.

From a resource-based viewpoint and family-embeddedness perspective, this chapter attempts to discover a possible entrepreneurship development mechanism by analyzing the case of the Jong-Shyn Shipbuilding Company in Taiwan. Specifically, we examine how family involvement in this business impacts the search for a rent-generating opportunity in the shipbuilding industry. Analysis of this case will provide valuable insights into the family's role in entrepreneurial rent generation and rent appropriation.

CASE OVERVIEW

The Company

The Jong-Shyn Shipbuilding Company, led by the Han family, was founded in 1985 in Taiwan. Before introducing this company, we will provide a brief overview of the shipbuilding industry in Taiwan and of the importance of the Jong-Shyn Shipbuilding Company in this industry.

Over the past decade, Taiwan has become a major shipbuilding country with a production value, on average, of NTD 25 billion and 200,000 tons of products built each year. In 2007, it ranked among the top eight shipbuilding countries in the world. There are approximately 90 shipbuilding companies in Taiwan. The largest shipbuilder is China Shipbuilding Corporation, accounting for NTD 20 billion of the industry's production value. China Shipbuilding Corporation is a government-owned company that has the capacity to build large merchant and military ships. It was founded in 1962 in Keelung and moved its production base to Kaohsiung in 1978.

Taiwan's shipbuilders are primarily located in Kaohsiung and Keelung. Kaohsiung has the largest port and its geographic location makes it highly suitable for the fishing industry. As a consequence, a large number of shipbuilders are located in Kaohsiung. Keelung is the center of shipbuilding in northern Taiwan. Further, several builders of offshore wooden fishing boats are located in Tainan and about 20 such builders are located in Dong Gang (Hsu 2001).

Following several mergers, only two medium-sized shipbuilders survive in Taiwan today: the Jong-Shyn Shipbuilding Company and the Ching-Fu Company. Both have implemented CAD and CAM systems and installed automated manufacturing equipment. They also have established close relationships with well-known builders and designers both in and outside Taiwan.[1]

The founding of the Jong-Shyn Shipbuilding Company, one of the leading shipbuilding companies in Taiwan today, is a prime example of seizing a good opportunity. In the 1970s, the demand for oil tankers and fishing boats surged as a result of the development of the oil and fishing industries. Meanwhile, the Ten Major Construction Projects – massive national infrastructure projects introduced by the government – were underway, and shipbuilding was one of the most crucial of these. By 1985, Taiwan's total production of ships ranked third in the world, and the shipbuilding industry was expected to continue to prosper. That year, Pi-Hsiang Han, with only a junior high school education and work experience as a technician in the China Shipbuilding Corporation, established the Jong-Shyn Shipbuilding factory with just 10 employees. He then merged with and acquired several smaller shipbuilders, including, among others, Shingao, Linshen, Shin-Tien-Er and Shin-Chuan, ultimately forming the Jong-Shyn Shipbuilding Company. This company grew rapidly under the leadership of Pi-Hsiang Han, its founder and president.

However, in 1989, the government placed curbs on the total catch allowed for fishing boats in response to diminishing fishing resources and disputes with trespassing fishermen and foreign countries. The number of ships built shrunk by 73 percent in three years, triggering large-scale shut-downs in the shipbuilding industry. President Han's response to this harsh business environment was to introduce automated equipment and focus on enhancing product quality and performance. Moreover, he also successfully won government contracts for building military ships and entered the domestic medium-sized commercial ship market, thus becoming one of the few shipbuilders to survive this critical period.

The company is involved in two kinds of businesses: Jong-Shyn Shipbuilding, which focuses on shipbuilding for the government and private companies, and Jade Yacht Shipbuilding, which was founded in 2003 and specializes in building luxury yachts. During the past two decades, the company has built more than 400 ships and earned the admiration of both the shipbuilding fraternity and its clients. The business model adopted by Jong-Shyn Shipbuilding follows the 'Original Design Manufacturers' (ODM) model. However, with regard to yacht building, the manufacturing process combines complex manufacturing techniques and custom design. Yacht manufacturing cannot be accomplished solely through automated techniques as is the case with the typical shipbuilding process. Rather, the process incorporates fine craftsmanship and design as each yacht is totally customized. Therefore, the company's entry into the yacht market and the establishing of its own brand can be viewed as an example of successful entrepreneurial activity. The involvement and dominance of the second generation of the family in this family business have been critical in the transformation of Jong-Shyn Shipbuilding Company from an ODM to a brand manufacturer.

Figure 6.1 shows that the net sales of Jong-Shyn Shipbuilding have increased steadily in the past 10 years. The same cannot be said of the net

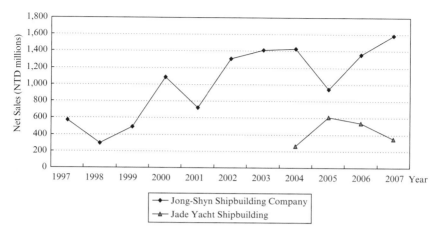

Figure 6.1   Net Sales of Jong-Shyn Shipbuilding business group, 1997–2007

sales of Jade Yacht Shipbuilding. However, the second generation leaders are not unduly worried about this situation because they realize that the incubation period for a new brand can be relatively long. Net sales growth is not the top priority currently; rather their focus is on developing and establishing the 'Jade' brand in the yacht market.

The Family

As noted in the previous section, the founder of this shipbuilding company was merely a humble technician who worked at the government-owned China Shipbuilding Corporation, and his success in this industry came from seizing an opportunity to build a shipbuilding business that arose from the government's initiative in 1985. After his successful expansion of the company in the 1980s and 1990s, he sought to transfer his knowledge and management of the company to his two sons, Eric and Memphis, and hoped that they would expand the scale and scope of the business. As is clear from the family members' roles in the company (Figure 6.2), the founder still serves as the president of the board and leads the actual decision-making of the company. The vice president positions are held by his sons Eric Han and Memphis Han. Eric is in charge of ship engineering and oversight and execution of related tasks. Memphis is responsible for finance and international affairs and also focuses on the yacht building business. President Han's nephew, Shiou-Liang Han, is the head of manufacturing operations at the Gaoding, Shingao and Jong-Shyn shipyards.

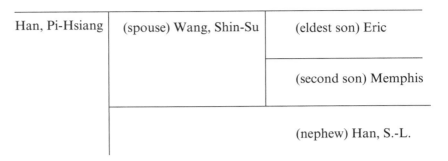

Han, Pi-Hsiang	(spouse) Wang, Shin-Su	(eldest son) Eric
		(second son) Memphis
		(nephew) Han, S.-L.

Figure 6.2   The family members in Jong-Shyn Shipbuilding

He was also previously responsible for administrative and labor safety affairs at the shipbuilding sites.

Eric, Han's eldest son, has an engineering background and keeps a low profile. He has accumulated considerable experience over the years, dating back to his frequent site visits as a child, and he also has a good grip on industry practices. He has been supervising related shipbuilding operations for several years. In order to sharpen his management skills, he acquired an MBA degree from National Sun Yat-sen University, a famous local university at Kaohsiung.

Eric also manages key relationships with companies to which Jong-Shyn Shipbuilding outsources work. Many shipbuilding industry workers in Taiwan are self-employed and they work for several shipbuilding companies at the same time. Most are qualified workers who have worked with shipbuilders in the past and many continue to serve their former employers, though in a self-employed capacity. It is important for shipbuilding companies to maintain good relationships with these self-employed workers, and this is one of Eric's key responsibilities. Jong-Shyn Shipbuilding maintains good relationships with these small businesses and often outsources work to them. Thus, rather than singlehandedly undertaking all the complex processes involved in ship manufacturing, Jong-Shyn Shipbuilding Company, by outsourcing various functions and processes to its former employees, has created a more flexible shipbuilding network and system. In several instances, Jong-Shyn Shipbuilding Company has been able to transfer some of its orders to these firms, thus fostering a mutually beneficial relationship. As a result of his profound understanding of the shipbuilding process and the industry culture, Eric is able to communicate effectively with these business partners. As a consequence, he has become a key individual in this process and successfully utilizes the network in order to expand Jong-Shyn Shipbuilding Company's operations.

The other vice president, Memphis, is Han's second son. He was encouraged by the family to pursue higher studies in the US in order to gain an international business perspective and global business insights. Memphis acquired an MBA degree from the University of California, and in his current role as vice president is in charge of finance and international negotiations and affairs. His American educational background means that his leadership style is more like that of an American manager. His international perspective and understanding of global business are his strengths and have considerably influenced decision-making in Jade Yacht Company. While procurement in Jade Yacht Company is generally handled by other professional managers, decisions on the items and quantities purchased as well as strategic decisions are made by Memphis.

Critical decisions, such as the firm's overall strategy, are generally taken by family members. Since the family members share a home, they are able to discuss the business and make key decisions whenever they choose. General operational issues and affairs are decided by almost all of the managers. The company's meetings are relatively free of formal restrictions, which reflects the fact that the top management team places great value on the 'management by walking around' approach.

When it comes to shipbuilding, each order must be viewed as a customized project because of differentiated customer needs and industry characteristics. Eric is involved in each project, deciding on aspects of design with project managers and monitoring progress. If a problem is spotted, it is addressed immediately in order to enhance quality and efficiency.

Communication between members of the Han family is frequent and harmonious. Decisions on planning and execution are generally made by the Hans, the organization structure is rather flat and vertical communication is unhindered. The Hans are viewed as being receptive to the opinions of professional engineers. In recent years, the founder and Jong-Shyn Shipbuilding management have assisted shipbuilding-related departments of universities in a number of ways. They have arranged site visits and instituted several internships, and have also provided scholarships to students in order to cultivate new generations of professionals for the shipbuilding industry. Beyond that, the firm has paid a lot of attention to corporate governance, hoping to create a transparent and fair structure for its board of directors.

The Company Structure

The organizational structure of Jong-Shyn Shipbuilding (see Figure 6.3), is functional, with the aim of ensuring flexibility and efficiency in the shipbuilding process. The sales department primarily deals with arranging,

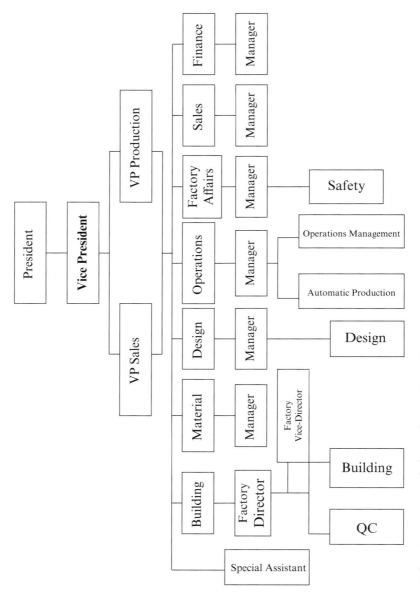

Figure 6.3   Organizational chart of Jong-Shyn Shipbuilding Company

correcting and evaluating contracts. It also establishes and maintains all procedures related to contract review and negotiation, such as bidding, negotiating with ship owners, signing contracts and so on.

The design department's core function is to design ships and review or amend contracts in accordance with customers' specifications and requirements. During the design phase, the department must ensure that its calculations and planning efforts are in compliance with governmental regulations and customers' requirements.

The main functions of the materials department are procurement of materials, supplier selection, examination of inbound materials and storage management. This department checks and confirms the quality of the procured materials and ensures that they are being used properly.

The main job of the building department is to build ships and maintain quality standards. It plans and verifies processes such as building, installing and servicing in order to meet quality requirements and is also responsible for evaluating outsourcing firms for their building capacity and quality.

The operations department is responsible for the smooth planning and progress of manufacturing operations to ensure that products are delivered to customers as per their precise requirements. This department also develops and manages statistical techniques needed for examining, testing and verifying processes and products.

CASE ANALYSIS: FAMILY INVOLVEMENT AND ENTREPRENEURIAL RENT

The following analysis of the Jong-Shyn Shipbuilding Company is based on the resource-based view and the family-embeddedness perspective, as well as the STEP model. The key question is, 'How does the family in this family business identify the entrepreneurial rent generation and rent appropriation opportunities in the shipbuilding industry?' Furthermore, the assessment of family involvement and its implications on family entrepreneurship will be conducted by asking three follow-up questions. The first question concerns the relationship between entrepreneurial orientation and entrepreneurial rent generation in the family context; the second question focuses on the relationship of the family influenced resource pools (familiness) to different entrepreneurial outcomes; and the third question considers the possible interactional influences between familiness (the resource pool) and entrepreneurial orientation.

1 What is the Relationship of Entrepreneurial Orientation to Entrepreneurial Rent Generation in the Family Context?

In the case of the Jong-Shyn Shipbuilding Company, the prominent link between entrepreneurial orientation and entrepreneurial performance outcomes is the role of risk-taking and innovativeness in identifying new opportunities. According to the product profiles provided by the company, the ships built by this company are not confined to a single size or a single use. Rather, the ships range in size from small to large. Additionally, as they encompass a wide variety, for example, tuna boats, squid boats, carriers, drift boats, ferry boats, skip boats, freight boats, shuttle boats and so on, they are used for a number of different purposes. Therefore, a potential rent-appropriating opportunity in the shipbuilding market exists in that the company has the technical skills and ability to match the requirements of different customers. In this respect, the elder son of the second generation, Eric, has valuable experience and knowledge that has been transferred to him by his father and from 'learning by doing'. Therefore, he has been able to take advantage of the potential rent-appropriating opportunities existing in the shipbuilding market.

However, a potential rent-generating opportunity cannot be exploited just through the transfer of experience and knowledge from the founder to the next generation. According to the resource-based view, the insights of a leader of a company into the rent-generating opportunity associated with a market imperfection must be combined with the ability to explore this opportunity (Alvarez and Barney 2004; Barney 1991). A risk-taking attitude and the competence to explore opportunities are the necessary conditions to generate new rents in the market. Following this argument, we can see that in the case of the Jong-Shyn Shipbuilding Company, the rent-generation opportunity hinged on the company's decision to enter the yacht market. For any shipbuilding company, entry into the yacht market is a highly risky decision because of the nature of the customers and unique customer needs of this market. The accumulated techniques, customers and knowledge of traditional shipbuilding are not transferable to yacht building. Success in the yacht-building market requires that a creative and artistic mindset is integrated with manufacturing capacity and that there is a good network of potential customers. The potential customers in the yacht market are generally not the same as those in the traditional shipbuilding market. Thus, a shipbuilding company that aims to enter the yacht market must have differentiated competencies to realize the potential value-added in the yacht market. Moreover, this value-added opportunity in the yacht building market incorporates a high risk of failure.

From interviews with the second generation of the Jong-Shyn Shipbuilding Company, it is clear that they realize that their entry into the yacht-building market is a good rent-generating opportunity which should help to overcome the problems of diminishing revenues and excessive competition in the traditional shipbuilding market. They are also aware of the challenges and difficulties of knowledge transfer inherent in this decision. Therefore, after discussions with experts in the yacht market, members of the Han family decided to acquire the new competencies required for this market by taking on different tasks. While Eric focused on manufacturing process integration, Memphis took the lead in sales and marketing and brand development.

Around this time, Louis Vuitton delegated an agent to find a qualified yacht manufacturer to repair a damaged yacht. Memphis heard about this and contacted the agent directly. The agent had no prior knowledge of the Jong-Shyn Shipbuilding Company or the Jade brand. Therefore, Memphis invited him to visit the company and remain in Taiwan while the yacht was under repair. Although the company did not profit from this order, the Han family members anticipated that their association with a famous brand like Louis Vuitton would enable them to establish their new brand, Jade, in the yacht market. The appreciation and positive feedback they subsequently received from Louis Vuitton's president can be viewed as the starting point of Jong-Shyn Shipbuilding Company's entry into the yacht market.

The proactive involvement, risk-taking attitude and spirit of innovation of the members of the second generation achieved the first step in the company's entry into the yacht market. From this case analysis, we can see that there is a close relationship between entrepreneurial orientation and entrepreneurial performance in the context of this family business.

2 What is the Relationship of the Family Influenced Resource Pools (Familiness) to Different Entrepreneurial Outcomes?

The Jong-Shyn case is typical of family businesses in that it emphasizes the importance of family involvement in decision-making and management. However, family involvement in family businesses also usually incorporates the risk of over-embeddedness and inner circle decision-making (Arregle et al. 2007; Gòmez-Mejía et al. 2007). One possible solution to the problem of over-embeddedness in a family business is that the family decision-maker can consult an outside expert before making a decision. In the Chinese family business context, emphasis on the personal authority of the founder contributes to a centralized decision-making style (Fukuyama 1995; Hamilton 1997; Weidenbaum 1996). Thus, the governance structure in Chinese family businesses is more centralized, and the focus is on establishing a cohesive family culture. Additionally, consensus between all the family members is required in decision-making. On the one hand, the high involvement of family members and emphasis on a cohesive family culture in Chinese family businesses makes it easier to achieve consensus and make key decisions. On the other hand, the cohesive culture may create barriers to the inflow of new information into the family business, thereby lowering the quality of decision-making. Therefore, achieving a balance between family cohesiveness and promoting entrepreneurship is quite a challenge for a family business, especially in the Chinese family business context.

In the Jong-Shyn Shipbuilding case, the educational background of Eric and Memphis has given them the necessary competencies to manage the traditional shipbuilding and new yacht building businesses respectively. With regard to their decision-making process, they have adopted a different approach from that of the traditional Chinese family business. For instance, they give subordinates sufficient decision-making power in day-to-day operations to enhance efficiency and employee satisfaction. In making key strategic decisions in these two businesses, they engage in discussions with all the family decision-makers and senior professional managers and seek consensus. The participation of well-educated family members and professional managers in this process ensures that there is an inflow of critical information before the final decision is made. Both Eric and Memphis believe that consensus decision-making by family members and senior managers, along with the delegation of operations management is a good formula for achieving revenue growth. The atypical nature of this family's involvement in decision-making may be one way to achieve a balance between familiness and entrepreneurial performance outcomes.

Moreover, in discussing the relationship between family influenced resource pools (familiness) and entrepreneurial orientation profiles, the Jong-Shyn Shipbuilding case shows that the family can extend its entrepreneurial orientation by assigning different roles to the next generation to enlarge the potential for both rent generation and rent appropriation. In this case, the two sons in the second generation play different roles in the business, and accordingly have different entrepreneurial orientation profiles. The elder son manages the traditional shipbuilding business established by the founder. His is more of a rent-appropriation role. The younger son, who has an MBA degree from the US, manages the new Jade yacht business. His global perspective and familiarity with the international market are advantages for rent generation in the yacht market. The different roles assigned to the second generation enlarge the possibilities for the growth of this family business. Moreover, this gives the family members of the second generation different domains to pursue and lead, and reduces the possibility of competition or conflict between them.

3   What Interactional Influences do Industry, Environment, Culture, Family Life Stage and Family Involvement have on the Family Influenced Resource Pool (Familiness) and Entrepreneurial Orientation?

To achieve successful strategic change a company needs to consider the possible interaction or alignment with the external environment in relation to control and resource integration (Van de Ven and Poole 1995). The higher the uncertainty in the environment, the higher the unpredictability of the strategy (Dess and Beard 1984); thus, the key decision-makers must change their routine problem-solving habits to manage environmental uncertainty. From the resource-dependence viewpoint, handling environmental uncertainty is an important source of power for key decision-makers (Pfeffer and Salancik 1978). In the family business context, although the family members' ability to cope with environmental uncertainty will not directly threaten business succession, the next generation can gain legitimacy by strengthening its ability to cope with the uncertainties that exist in the industry (Pfeffer and Salancik 1978). Thus, industry uncertainty and instability must factor in a discussion of the relationship between familiness and entrepreneurship orientation in the family business context.

In the Jong-Shyn Shipbuilding case, the shrinking of the traditional shipbuilding industry and the strong competition in this industry played a critical role in the company's decision to enter the yacht market. As noted earlier, compared with the high growth opportunities in the shipbuilding industry in the 1980s, the value added by fully automated manufacturing began to diminish by the end of the century. Moreover, strong competition from domestic and foreign manufacturers further reduced revenues. The decrease in revenues and in the value added solely from enhancing efficiency in ship manufacturing can be seen as possible sources of industry instability that all businesses in this industry had to overcome. In order to survive in this highly competitive environment, the search for a more promising market, for example, the yacht market, was a possible solution. The decision of the Han family to enter the high risk yacht market, which was made after a careful consideration of the industry environment, provided them with a way to grow the family business. By entering the yacht market, the Han family hoped to achieve potential rent generation and business growth through the establishment of a new venture.

THE FUTURE

Jong-Shyn Shipbuilding Company's tactic of realizing opportunities for rent appropriation and rent generation by assigning different roles to family members of the second generation is a good starting point for a discussion on family entrepreneurship. According to customers, the competitive advantage of yachts made in Taiwan are customization and workmanship. Customization means that each yacht is built to the customer's distinctive needs, whereas workmanship refers to the crafts-manship and attention to detail sought by customers at the top of the pyramid. However, the advantages that Taiwanese yacht builders have are countered by several disadvantages that need to be addressed.

The Service Model

This is the first of the disadvantages faced by yacht-builders in Taiwan. The traditional service model of Taiwanese shipbuilders was that a senior manager took the order and understood the customers' needs, and then tasked the relevant employees and departments with filling the order, with little communication and no follow up whatsoever during the process (for example, Hsu 2001). Interdepartmental coordination was ignored, creat-ing difficulties in managing the process. For example, changes made by department A might be unknown to department B, which would affect the progress of the project and its related costs. These problems would lead to higher costs in human resources and materials, which in turn, resulted in lower capacity; alternatively, they would result in decreased customer satisfaction as a result of errors. These issues posed great barriers for firms wishing to enter the high-end European yacht market.

In contrast, however, the differentiating characteristic in Jong-Shyn Shipbuilding is the family's total dedication to and involvement in the busi-ness. Family members participate in decision-making, familiarize them-selves with manufacturing techniques, are willing to confront employees and to take full responsibility. They also take responsibility for conducting coordination efforts across the organization. They respect the opinions of professionals and encourage the personal growth of employees, to the extent that they support the business ventures of former employees, thus creating a flexible organization and an extensive external network. In fact, President Han has been the chairman of the Taiwan Yacht Guild for several years, demonstrating that the Hans are respected for their profes-sionalism and organizational abilities. Based on these factors, Jong-Shyn Shipbuilding has a golden opportunity to solve problems related to cost management and customization and sail into the high-end yacht market.

Customer Development in the Yacht Market

As noted earlier, customers in the yacht market are entirely different from those in the traditional shipbuilding market. Customer relationships that have been established in the latter are of no use in generating potential customers in the yacht market. If Jong-Shyn Shipbuilding wishes to succeed in the yacht market, the second generation must understand the lifestyle and needs of high-end customers in this market. This is the second disadvantage that they must overcome in order to realize their potential within this industry.

Looking to the future, the company's management is striving to maintain a balance between retaining its flexibility and customization ability and retaining its family governance and flat organizational structure. To achieve this, it must address resource integration and building processes, enhance management, introduce information systems and create knowledge bases to foster innovation. In addition, for its top-tier customers, Jong-Shyn Shipbuilding could utilize information technologies focused on enhancing communication and coordination to effectively deliver information and link to the systems in related firms when communicating customers' needs as well as to upgrade manufacturing efficiency, thus creating a win-win situation. However, like most of the players in the traditional shipbuilding industry, it is expected that Jong-Shyn shipbuilding may be somewhat resistant to change, an issue which the Hans must expect to address.

CONCLUSION

All over the world, a family business is a business enterprise with a distinctive governance structure (Arregle et al. 2007; Gersick et al. 1997; Gòmez-Mejía et al. 200 7; James 2006; Miller and Le Breton-Miller 2005). Additionally, family businesses are characterized by distinctive family capital and family control structures (Arregle et al. 2007; Gersick et al. 1997; Miller and Le Breton-Miller 2005). The maintenance and transfer of entrepreneurship is critical for the survival and success of the family business (Aldrich and Cliff 2003; Kellermanns and Eddleston 2006; Zahra 2005; Zahra et al. 2004). Further, family involvement may play a critical role in family entrepreneurship. In addressing family entrepreneurship issues, previous research demonstrates that entrepreneurial performance outcomes along with the rent generation or rent appropriation dimension play a critical role in the growth and continuity of a family business across generations (Astrachan 2003; Kellermanns and Eddleston 2006; Zahra

2005; Zahra et al. 2004). The transfer of entrepreneurship from generation to generation is a big challenge in family businesses.

Taking a resource-based view and family-embedded perspective, this study has attempted to explore the question of family influence in family entrepreneurship by examining the case of the Jong-Shyn Shipbuilding Company in Taiwan. The entrepreneurship development mechanism (Aldrich and Cliff 2003; Astrachan 2003; Kellermanns and Eddleston 2006; Zahra 2005; Zahra, et al. 2004) of this family business is the development of a different pattern of growth in the shipbuilding industry. With regard to rent appropriation, this family business improved its efficiency and manufacturing capabilities in the traditional shipbuilding domain. Additionally, the decision to enter a highly value-added market through multiple resource integration is another possible entrepreneurship development mechanism and a good example of rent generation. The different entrepreneurship transfer mechanisms in this case provide a starting point for a wider analysis of possible entrepreneurship transfer mechanisms in family businesses. Furthermore, the findings provide insights into entrepreneurship issues in Asian family businesses.

Entrepreneurship has been recognized as a key factor contributing to a firm's success. In the family business context, family involvement in the entrepreneurship development mechanism provides the foundation essential for the growth of the family business (Aldrich and Cliff 2003; Astrachan 2003). The STEP project aims to explore the debatable and underexamined links between family influence and entrepreneurship. The qualitative case method can provide insights into family entrepreneurship. Moreover, the evidence and findings from each case can provide a better understanding of the pervasive effect of family influence on entrepreneurship. Future studies can complement such research by utilizing the survey method to provide quantitative data on the family entrepreneurship issue.

NOTE

1. For details see the Jong-Shyn Shipbuilding company website: available at http://www. jongshyn.com/english/ (accessed on 30 October 2009).

REFERENCES

Aldrich, H.E. 'Entrepreneurship', in Neil J. Smelser and Richard Swedberg (eds), *The Handbook of Economic Sociology*. Princeton, NJ: Princeton University Press, 2005, 451–77.

Aldrich, H.E. and J.E. Cliff. 'The pervasive effects of family on entrepreneurship: toward a family embeddedness perspective'. *Journal of Business Venturing*, 18:5 (2003), 573–96.

Alvarez, S.A. and J.B. Barney. 'Organizing rent generation and appropriation: toward a theory of the entrepreneurial firm'. *Journal of Business Venturing*, 19 (2004), 621–35.

Alvarez, S.A. and L.W. Busenitz. 'The entrepreneurship of resource-based theory'. *Journal of Management*, 27:6 (2001), 755–75.

Arregle, J.L., M.A. Hitt, D.G. Sirmon and P. Very. 'The development of organizational social capital: attributes of family firms'. *Journal of Management Studies*, 44:1 (2007), 73–94.

Astrachan, J.H. 'Commentary on the special issue: the emergence of a field'. *Journal of Business Venturing*, 18:5 (2003), 567–72.

Barney, J. 'Strategic factor markets: expectations, luck, and business strategy'. *Management Science*, 42:10 (1986), 1231–41.

Barney, J. 'Firm resources and sustained competitive advantage'. *Journal of Management*, 17:1 (1991), 99–120.

Dess, G.G. and D.W. Beard. 'Dimensions of organizational task environments'. *Administrative Science Quarterly*, 29:1 (1984), 52–73.

Fukuyama, F. *Trust: The Social Virtues and the Creation of Prosperity*. New York: Free Press, 1995.

Gersick, K.E., J.A. Davis, M.M. Hampton and I. Lansberg. *Generation to Generation: Life Cycles of the Family Business*. Boston: Harvard Business School Press, 1997.

Gòmez-Mejía, L.R., K.T. Haynes, M. Núñez-Nickel, K.J.L. Jacobson and J. Moyano-Fuentes. 'Socioemotional wealth and business risks in family-controlled firms: evidence from Spanish olive oil mills'. *Administrative Science Quarterly*, 52:1 (2007), 106–37.

Hamilton, G.G. 'Organization and market processes in Taiwan's capitalist economy' in M. Orrù, N.W. Biggart and G.G. Hamilton (eds), *The Economic Organization of East Asian Capitalism*. Thousand Oaks, CA: Sage, 1997, 237–93.

Hsu, T.C. 'The development of the middle-sized ship-building companies in Taiwan'. Unpublished MBA thesis, National Sun Yat-sen University, Kaohsiung, Taiwan, 2001 (in Chinese).

James, H. *Family Capitalism: Wendels, Haniels, Falcks, and the Continental European Model*. Cambridge, MA: The Belknap Press of Harvard University Press, 2006.

Kellermanns, F.W. and K.A. Eddleston. 'Corporate entrepreneurship in family firms: a family perspective'. *Entrepreneurship Theory and Practice*, 30:6 (2006), 809–30.

Miller, D. and I. Le Breton-Miller. *Managing for the Long Run: Lessons in Competitive Advantage from Great Family Businesses*. Boston, MA: Harvard Business School Press, 2005.

Pfeffer, J. and G.R. Salancik. *The External Control of Organizations: A Resource Dependence Perspective*. New York: Harper & Row, 1978.

Van de Van, A.H. and M.S. Poole. 'Explaining development and change in organizations'. *Academy of Management Review*, 20:3 (1995), 510–40.

Ward, J.L. *Keeping the Family Business Healthy: How to Plan for Continuing Growth, Profitability, and Family Leadership*. San Francisco: Jossey-Bass, 1987.

Weidenbaum, M. 'The Chinese family business enterprise'. *California Management Review*, 38:4 (1996), 141–56.

Zahra, S.A. 'Entrepreneurial risk taking in family firms'. *Family Business Review*, 18:1 (2005), 23–40.

Zahra, S.A., J.C. Hayton and C. Salvato. 'Entrepreneurship in family vs. non-family enterprises: a resource-based analysis of the effect of organizational culture'. *Entrepreneurship Theory and Practice*, 28:4 (2004), 363–81.

7. The Deague family: learning entrepreneurship through osmosis

Justin Craig, Wayne Irava and Ken Moores

INTRODUCTION

In this chapter, we introduce the idea of learning entrepreneurship by osmosis. Drawing from the experiential learning literature, we feature Australia's Deague family. Experiential learning suggests that knowledge is continuously gained through both personal and environmental experiences (Kolb 1984). However, in order to gain genuine knowledge from an experience, certain abilities are required. Specifically, the learner must: (i) be willing to be actively involved in the experience; (ii) be able to reflect on the experience; (iii) possess and use analytical skills to conceptualize the experience; and (iv) possess decision-making and problem-solving skills in order to use the new ideas gained from the experience.

As will be shown, the Deague family, in particular the incumbent leader, David Deague, have intentionally designed their family business structure to address these criteria. Specifically, consistent with Kolb's experiential learning frame, David Deague has developed a culture within the family that cultivates a willingness to provide opportunities for family members to be actively involved in the business should they wish. He has mentored his offspring in such a way that they are constantly called upon to reflect on their own decisions and on the decisions that they observe being made at all levels of the organization. In this way, family members involved either in operational roles or on the periphery are able to develop analytical skills that can be honed and applied to new situations as they arise.

The Deague family has diversified up and down the value chain and is entrepreneurially alert to business opportunities. Having survived a serious downturn in the economy in the early 1990s, David Deague understands intimately the vagaries of industry and economic life cycles. He stewards his company and family with a can-do attitude that is endemic in the organization. His eldest son and successor as managing director has worked at his side for the past 10 years, learning to understand and analyze the ways in which to ensure that the family business can build a significant diversified asset base to survive any external environmental disruption. Like many long-lived family businesses, their competitive advantage lies in quick decision-making, the lack of a management hierarchy and the relentless pursuit of wealth creation.

David Deague is committed to giving his children the best chance to succeed in business. He has in place a unique hands-on mentoring process. He has long insisted that his three sons, and when appropriate, his daughter, accompany him whenever possible to any stakeholder meeting of the organization. His eldest son, William (Will), through this process has been groomed to step smoothly into David's shoes as the leader of the business. As part of this mentoring process and as a good example of experiential learning, the physical layout of the family's office space was designed in such a way that the four male members of the family were each assigned a desk in each corner. This arrangement facilitates communication and monitoring throughout the working day. It also allows the sons the opportunity to reflect on and discuss decisions immediately with each other and their father.

The case outlines how the unyielding pursuit of innovation and creative solutions are at the heart of their business success. Using the concepts of entrepreneurial orientation (EO) (Lumpkin and Dess 1996; Miller 1983) and the resource-based view (RBV) (Mahoney and Pandian 1992; Peteraf 1993; Wernerfelt 1984), the case shows how the Deague family has been able to attain and maintain a sustained competitive advantage by being innovative and leveraging its distinct familiness.

BACKGROUND

Case Overview

Asia Pacific Building Corporation (APBC) is a proud Australian construction-industry family business that is owned and operated by members of the Deague family. Although APBC was officially established in 1992, the company's roots can be traced to the late 1800s when the Deague family's ancestors started building dwellings in the burgeoning metropolis of Melbourne. Since then, the Deague family has weathered the vagaries of a cyclical industry in a developing country plagued by a plethora of challenges to become a prominent player well positioned for strong growth across multiple industries. APBC employs approximately 150 permanent staff, of whom 100 are involved in the company's core business. Today the fifth generation of the Deague family continues the tradition of 'master builders' through a stated commitment to creativity and innovation, and the business remains 100 percent family owned.

Table 7.1   APBC business entrepreneurial initiatives

Initiative	Function
Business centers	Provides fully furnished serviced offices on lease; virtual office packages with prestigious addresses; secretarial services, including telephone answering; and executive boardrooms, meeting rooms and conference facilities
Sales and leasing	Offers short- and long-term office space, sells boutique office space and provides property management services
Hotels and resorts	Offers boutique style short- and long-term accommodation options throughout the city
Storage facilities	Offers both residential and commercial storage
Student accommodation	Offers accommodation services primarily for students
Financial group	Services include: assessment of financial position, goal analysis, calculation of comfortable investment capacity, debt reduction strategies, computer simulations, loan and finance restructuring, leveraging and gearing, and mortgage comparison and sourcing
Car parking	Offers both permanent and temporary car parking services
Facilities management	Services include management of essential services, planned maintenance, corrective maintenance, minor works, mechanical and electrical, test and inspection services, concierge and general building maintenance
Telecommunications	Provides telephone and IT services
Corporate furniture	'One stop shop' for all office furnishing requirements
Body corporate services	Services include facilities management, telecommunications and architectural design, including provision of furniture and commercial and residential fit outs

Expanding through Diversification

Though the firm's core business remains commercial property development, the company has leveraged its foothold in the commercial property development industry to launch related ventures. This diversification has resulted in a constellation of companies tied to the property industry by a common thread and in APBC's pursuit of significant entrepreneurial initiatives over the last two decades (see Table 7.1).

The primary investment of the family business is in commercial building construction, but its recent entry into boutique hotel accommodation is an astute related strategy. Importantly, each of the boutique hotels is designed such that if for some reason they are not successful as hotels, they can be sold off as individual unit dwellings. Incorporating measures to mitigate ongoing operational risks is typical of APBC's approach to engaging in entrepreneurial pursuits. Their related companies (for example, car parking, serviced offices and so on) are all cash-generating businesses.

Their current foray into the building of suburban residential dwellings has also been well thought through, in that if, because of a severe downturn in the residential property market, these houses do not sell at market predictions, they will be held by the company and rented out using the existing infrastructure for the renting of company-owned office space. The leadership is also aware that at this point of its life cycle, the organization is most likely to be successful by concentrating its energies within a confined geographical area. This strategy sees the firm's interests located in the inner suburbs of Melbourne. The family has in place an experienced non-family financial officer and an in-house legal counsel, both of whom work closely with the family leadership.

THEORETICAL BACKGROUND

Family Entrepreneurship

The first William Deague established his reputation as a leading builder soon after his arrival in Australia in 1867. Little is known about him except that he built houses and worked together with his son Claude, who continued building after his father passed away in the early 1900s. It is in the third generation, under the leadership of Claude's son William Deague (II), that the story of the family business becomes clearer. Figure 7.1 outlines the family by generation.

William (II) maintained the building tradition and established the first official family business. The business back then was known by a different name and its primary focus was on building houses and residential units. William was a hands-on type operator with a strong work ethic. His philosophy in business was, 'be tough but fair'. William was also known for his dedication. It was normal to find him at building sites at 5.30 in the morning. Even in his seventies, despite having retired, William could still be found at the construction sites.

In the late 1950s, William's son David, who was then in his early teens, left school to help his father in the family business. David recalls how at the age of 15, he was in school one Friday, and the very next day, on Saturday, he was digging trenches for a new construction. Thus began

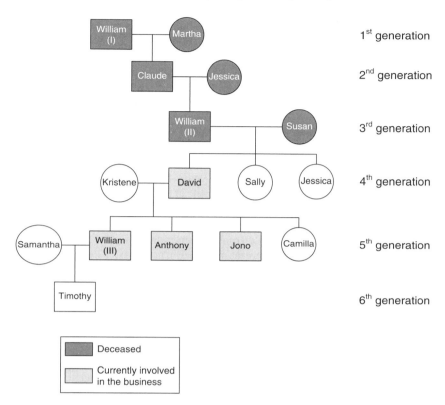

Figure 7 1   Deague family by generation

David's experiential learning journey in the family business. When not on site, the father and son team would occupy adjoining offices – learning and working together, a practice that is still evident today in the office space occupied by the fourth and fifth generations. The father and son team continued in this way for the next 15 to 20 years. The business enjoyed quick growth during this period, largely as a result of operating within a niche market and having first mover advantage due to the family's unique approach to the construction business. One aspect of this approach was their use of insights and capabilities to maximize available 'physical resources' through innovation and creativity, thereby strengthening their competitive advantage and generating wealth for the business. Thus, as early as the 1950s, innovation and creativity were resources that lay at the heart of the Deague family and formed the foundation on which the family business established a competitive advantage.

> It was about maximizing opportunities. If there was a large two bedroom and a laundry, they would convert it into a three bedroom and they would get that extra 20–30 grand, and that's how they would make their profit. So they'd look for ways that they could get an extra room . . . that sort of thing . . . so they would always look for projects where there was a bit of slack room where they could try and squeeze in, and that was their philosophy from the start . . . from there it developed. (Anthony, fifth generation)

In the late 1970s to early 1980s, the business made strategic changes by taking on its first major commercial development project – a high-rise building located in a major business precinct. The bold move was driven mainly by market trends, as for a number of years the organization's focus on building residential flats had not been viable. The change in strategy proved to be a major success for the company. Father and son applied the same unique space-saving approach that had been adopted in the construction of residential units to strata[1] title small commercial offices. The project not only made the family's name synonymous with 'strata type offices', it made them pioneers within the industry. It also marked the beginning of the shift of focus from residential flats to commercial property development. The proactive stance and risk taken by the company proved successful and commercial property development today remains a specialty of the business.

> The model we developed then we are still using today. For example, the building in which we have 600 small strata lots is probably the biggest undertaking of commercial strata in the country. It had never been done before . . . we took the risk but we were confident we could do it, and it's been very successful. (David, third generation)

David, like his father, was hard working and an expert builder. This resulted from having followed his father closely and being introduced to the practical skills required in the construction industry at a young age. However, perhaps more so than his father, David possessed an innate talent for marketing and he developed this to differentiate their operations in a crowded marketplace.

The father and son business of William (II) and David blossomed in the 1980s and the increased demand saw the business taking on one project after another. In 1989, government legislation allowed companies in the industry to increase borrowings and this led to the purchase of several buildings. However, a downturn in the market and the sudden exit of several tenants left the company with empty buildings and a burgeoning interest debt. This was the most difficult and challenging period in the history of the family business.

Events in 1989 led the company to cease all commercial development projects and the business returned to its roots – building houses and blocks of flats. However, David's determination to succeed, combined with relentless hard work, were pivotal in overcoming these obstacles, resulting in a quick turnaround by the mid-1990s. David's creative and marketing flair enabled the company to diversify and differentiate its products, thereby providing it once again with an edge over its competitors.

The late 1990s saw the regrowth of APBC and the emergence of a number of entrepreneurial initiatives, some of which exist today as subsidiaries of the parent company. These included a real estate venture, a communications venture, a facilities management company, a body corporate company, a car park company and a partnership in a cosmetics venture. These initiatives were mainly driven by David. Apart from the cosmetics company, all the other subsidiaries emerged from opportunities identified through APBC's core construction business, to which they are related.

By the early 2000s, the company had grown to a considerable size. David began to find it impossible to handle everything on his own, something that he was previously accustomed to doing. The family business had reached a stage where David realized that recruiting external managers and skilled professionals was necessary. He admits that bringing key people on board has made his life much easier.

David's three sons, William (III), Anthony and Jono, were all introduced to the family business at a young age. All three of them recall working at the construction sites during school holidays as a means of earning extra pocket money. Fortunately for David, his three sons showed an interest in joining their father in the family business. Furthermore, each possessed different skills and attributes, making David's task of managing his sons' entry into the family business and identifying the paths they would take within APBC significantly easier.

Of his three sons, David saw a bit of himself in his eldest son William (Will) who was turning out to be a natural leader among the fifth generation of the family. For the next 10 years, Will would undergo an experiential learning process within the business by literally following his father to every meeting and construction site. It was during this period that Will stepped into the role of managing director of the group.

Jono, the youngest of David's sons, officially joined the business at the age of 19. A flair for sales and marketing saw him gravitate to this area of the business.

> Jono is a born salesman and he did not get that from me. I am not a good salesman. I can sell but I cannot get people to sign. Jono can sell and sign. It is an art . . . a gift you are born with. William and I could not do what Jono does. (David, fourth generation)

Anthony earned a Bachelor of Commerce degree, and after several years of working in the business, earned an MBA degree. He is pursuing outside experience prior to joining APBC sometime in the future. The dilemma that Anthony is facing is when to enter the family business and in what capacity, given the roles his siblings occupy.

David's daughter Camilla has shown little interest in joining the family business, although it is her father's hope that she will become more involved. David believes that Camilla's qualifications in communications and public relations would serve APBC well, especially with regard to interactions with the media. David's wife Kristene served as interior decorator and bookkeeper in the early stages of the business. While she is no longer operationally involved in the business, she continues to play the role of chief emotional officer to the family.

Family Autonomy

The incumbent leader, David Deague, has, over time, given increased autonomy to his eldest son. David remains very much involved in major decisions but reports that he is increasingly willing for his son and the executive management team that has been assembled in recent years to take over from him. David is the company's creative influence and is a charismatic leader. It is clear that he is aware of the individuality he brings to the company and is careful not to overshadow his appointed successor. He has been conscious of pushing his son Will to be the company spokesperson. Senior managers of the company say they have considerable scope to voice their opinions and supply input. These observations, however, need to be made in the context of the current 'global crisis', which may require David to be more closely connected to the major decision-making process.

> I've got a very large degree of autonomy within my role. I am certainly led, I guess, but I am certainly not managed, which is a real positive for me. (Mathew, non-family OM)

Family Innovation

Innovation is APBC's competitive advantage and is driven from the top. David Deague is universally admired for his creativity. Family members and executives admire this in their leader and it is evident in all of their projects. A 'can-do', innovation-driven culture permeates the halls of the office space that houses the senior management team. Buildings constructed by APBC are known for their creative edge and use of up-to-the-minute technology. Innovation also drives the company's ability to exploit entrepreneurial opportunities along the value chain.

> It is a culture. It's not just dad, you know, who is protecting the family unit. It is the culture of these unit managers that they take on the same entrepreneurial philosophy. I think the staff are attracted by that and they start to act because they are encouraged to do it. They are rewarded when they come up with new, innovative ideas. (Anthony, Director)

Family Risk-Taking

Risk-taking is a relative concept, and APBC reports taking calculated risks. The leadership is conscious of the 'ghosts of the past', specifically, the turmoil of 1989 and the need to rebuild the company in the early 1990s. Having said that, they are still seemingly aggressive pursuers of opportunity, although it would be hard to describe these as risky commitments. Experienced non-family professional managers with capabilities beyond the skill set of the family have been employed to monitor risk and to complement the leadership's entrepreneurial pursuits. The recent economic downturn has provided the impetus for increased vigilance and monitoring of costs.

> So everything you do is a risk and you have to minimize that risk. I've come unstuck once and I don't want it to happen again. I do not want my sons to get into the mess I got into in 1989, and we do not over gear. We have a lot of our own capital in our projects now. If you don't over gear you can ride the storm. (David, CEO)

The nature of the construction industry requires organizations to be somewhat aggressive in the face of significant competition in order to be successful. APBC intimately understands what gives it a competitive edge (that is, innovation and creativity) but it also understands that this alone is not sufficient to compete successfully, particularly against publicly traded competitors. The company can only perform if it is building, and this requires it to identify and secure opportunities ahead of its rivals, and then develop unique-to-the-market, cutting-edge offerings. This capability has been developed not intentionally to outwit competitors, but rather to build a distinctive reputation in the market in which the company operates. It is the creativity and innovation displayed in the company's core business that have led to important complementary product offerings such as car parking and serviced office ventures.

Family Leadership

Leadership at APBC is transitioning from David to Will Deague and the process has been strategically managed to ensure minimal disruption. As a result of the growth of the business in recent times, both in terms of size and complexity, leadership challenges have also become exponentially more complex. The nature of the core business is relationship based, and careful management of these relationships has been of paramount importance during the transition of leadership. Non-family professional managers are in place to complement the skills of Will, the anointed next generation leader. Importantly, this process has been transparent and there is no apparent confusion in the company or the family with regard to whom leadership is being transferred.

> Will has more of the construction and head office sort of leadership. Every opportunity dad can, he ensures that Will is acknowledged as leading the company. Jono is running the sales and marketing component, which is on a separate site with different staff. So Jono is the leader of that team and that company and Will is more the leader of the core construction business. So there is a nice split, a shared sort of leadership role there. (Anthony, Director)

Family Decision-Making

Increasingly, decision-making is effectively in the hands of Will Deague, with crucial input from David and the non-family professional management. Other family inputs at a strategic level are limited at this point, although this is being addressed and will be broached in future discussions. Jono is currently involved in an operational rather than a strategic capacity, but there are ample opportunities for him to provide input because of the open nature of the office plan and the relationships between family and non-family members. Senior managers have direct access to the family.

> Decision making is quick; there are no boards. But we've created an executive committee. We discuss strategy . . . but I guess the ultimate decision comes down to dad and me. (Will, GM)

THE FUTURE

Family Continuity

David Deague has always assumed that the next generation would have the desire to continue the family business. Understanding the value of (re) building a family business post the 1990 downturn was not as important as actually building the company and the family legacy. That said, David's vision has always been to introduce his offspring to the family business, and to that end he has worked tirelessly to build an interesting and dynamic constellation of companies to enable family members to participate in a vibrant workplace. Other employees have been the beneficiaries of this passion to create an innovative workplace. The culture is one that promotes performance and rewards process innovation.

Family Relationships

Ties within the Deague family are strong. Family members enjoy each other's company and are familiar with their roles and responsibilities within the family and the business. David has spent a considerable amount of time mentoring and supporting his offspring. There is an opportunity for each member of the family to take on a role in the current or future businesses. The fact that ownership is held by the incumbent generation possibly contributes to the tightness of the relationships, which could potentially be challenged if ownership holdings were divided.

Family Governance

Family governance is not presently formalized. This has not been a problem since the strong social capital and internal bonds within the family have mitigated its lack. However, as the family moves to professionalize the business, Anthony has been approved to champion family governance initiatives and introduce them into the family over the coming years. He has had informal meetings with David and Will where he has explained the importance of professionalizing family governance, and in principle, there is support for it. To secure the support of his family members, Anthony arranged to interview the son of a prominent Australian family whose opinion he knew his family would respect. This strategy to benchmark against an aspirational business family was successful and secured him the green light to proceed.

CONCLUSION

David Deague gained much of his industry knowledge by working closely with his father in building their construction business and exploiting a niche in the strata title office market. He honed his creative and innovation skills out of necessity in order to maximize returns from refurbishments. He has employed a similar strategy in mentoring his offspring. Specifically, he has immersed them in the company from an early age and exposed them to every facet of management and leadership. Nothing that David has done in the world of business is off limits to his offspring, and he always ensured that at least one (if not more) of his children were at his side at meetings. This 'knowledge accrual through osmosis' has ensured that the next generation of Deagues has been socialized into all aspects of business.

The following entrepreneurial orientation (EO) and resource-based view (RBV) transgenerational entrepreneurship learning observations enrich the experiential learning discussion presented above:

EO Learning 1:   Subsequent generations benefit from business stress *when the lead entrepreneur is committed to building a legacy.*

EO Learning 2:   External non-family managers complement the entrepreneurial capabilities of the owning family.

RBV Learning 1:   Centralized family ownership contributes to familiness *in a positive way.*

RBV Learning 2:   Benchmarking against aspirational families will help sell issues to the family, for example, the need *for the introduction of family governance.*

RBV Learning 3:   The family is a resource for nurturing informal learning in family firms.

NOTE

1. Strata title is a form of ownership designed for multi-level apartments. 'Strata' refers to different levels. It was first introduced in Australia in 1961 as a means of addressing legal issues in ownership of apartment blocks. APBC was a pioneer in transferring this concept across to the strata of commercial offices.

REFERENCES

Kolb, D.A. *Experiential Learning: Experience as the Source of Learning and Development.* Englewood Cliffs, NJ: Prentice-Hall, 1984.

Lumpkin, G.T. and Gregory G. Dess. 'Clarifying the entrepreneurial orientation construct and linking it to performance'. *Academy of Management Review*, 21:1 (1996), 135–72.

Mahoney, Joseph T. and J. Rajendran Pandian. 'The resource-based view within the conversation of strategic management'. *Strategic Management Journal*, 13:5 (1992), 363–80.

Miller, Danny. 'The correlates of entrepreneurship in three types of firms'. *Management Science*, 29:7 (1983), 770–91.

Peteraf, Margaret A. 'The cornerstones of competitive advantage: a resource-based view'. *Strategic Management Journal*, 14:3 (1993), 179–91.

Wernerfelt, B. 'A resource-based view of the firm'. *Strategic Management Journal*, 5 (1984), 171–80.

8. The Belcher family gain legitimacy in a new industry: sailing into the unknown

Justin Craig, Wayne Irava and Ken Moores

INTRODUCTION

This chapter documents the challenges that entrepreneurial family businesses face in gaining legitimacy in a new industry. Here, we feature the founding generation of Australia's Belcher family business and trace its evolution from start-up to industry leader. The integral role the entrepreneurial founders John and Jane Belcher played in positioning a new industry, the management rights industry, is also explored.

More than half of all new ventures fail. This number is significantly higher in less established industries where a dominant logic has not been established. Though there are many contributing reasons for venture failure, the inability of new start-ups to access critical resources necessary for survival has been discussed as being pivotal in this regard. This phenomenon has been referred to as 'the liability of newness' (Suchman 1995). However, many start-ups are able to succeed by overcoming the liability of newness, and as a consequence, gain legitimacy. With legitimacy attained, the start-up is able to access additional resources, such as distribution networks to more munificent markets and more easily accessible financial capital (Zimmerman and Zeitz 2002). This situation holds true for new industries.

Various theoretical arguments have been tabled to better understand this phenomenon. For example, institutional theorists have described how successful start-ups quickly move beyond the perception of being an industry 'fledgling' (for example, Mitchell et al. 1997; Suchman 1995). These ventures attain credibility through their perceived acceptance and appropriateness, consistent with the regulative, normative and cognitive industry practices and guidelines. Thus, they assure input suppliers, output buyers and service providers of their potential for stability and a degree of permanence. This 'social judgment of acceptance, appropriateness, and desirability, allows them to access other resources (including customers) needed to survive and grow' (Zimmerman and Zeitz 2002, 415). This type of social judgment, labelled 'legitimacy', is the acceptance by buyers, suppliers and fellow competitors that they are firms of some substance. For instance, a new venture (or industry) can be considered legitimate if buyers believe that the start-up (or industry) can produce a product that can sell, can consistently maintain quality and can repeatedly deliver the product in a timely manner.

In this chapter, we will use this life cycle framework, along with concepts from the entrepreneurial orientation (EO) literature (Covin and Slevin 1991; Lumpkin and Dess 1996; Miller 1983) and the resource-based view of the firm (RBV) (Barney and Arikan 2001; Habbershon and Williams 1999; Wernerfelt 1984) to highlight how the first (and second) generation of Belchers have overcome, and continue to overcome, issues related to the liability of newness in their family business.

BACKGROUND

Case Overview

Sands Management Group (SMG) is a proud Australian family business that is owned and operated by members of the Belcher family. SMG was officially established in 1981 when the Belchers moved to Australia from New Zealand and purchased the management rights to a property on the Gold Coast in Queensland.

SMG employs approximately 80–100 staff. The daily operations of the firm and management control at the board level remain within the remit of the family despite the current absence of the second generation, namely Daniel (who is pursuing further education and gaining experience in the US) and Mathew (who will be representing Australia in sailing at the London Olympics and is preparing for that event). SMG is fully owned by the Belcher family (see Figure 8.1). Though the firm's core business remains management rights in Queensland, the company has leveraged its foothold in the industry to launch related ventures. Table 8.1 shows the three subsidiaries of SMG.

The industry within which SMG's core operations are positioned is the management rights industry. The concept of management rights originated in America and was made popular in Australia in the early 1970s. In Australia, it was first introduced in Queensland, which today has over 260,000 residential apartments operating under this system. Under such a system, a residential or holiday complex operates as part of a community

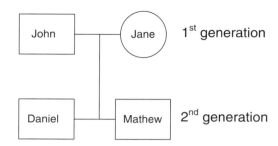

Figure 8.1   Structure of the Belcher family

Table 8.1   Overview of SMG entrepreneurial initiatives

Initiatives	Function	Ownership by SMG
Resorts and leisure	Specialized area of management rights where accommodation can be both short-term and long-term stay. In such facilities, units can be bought outright, rented or offered as tourist accommodation. This increases the complexity of their management as compared to hotels, which are owned by companies and intended solely for tourist accommodation	100%
Property	The real estate arm of SMG, which handles the development, marketing, sales and management of properties and units	100%
Diamond	A travel wholesaler that tailors accommodation to needs. The second generation was central to the development of this entity by identifying a need to address the accommodation difficulties faced by students studying at a nearby university	100%

management scheme. Owners of apartments in these complexes are often investors who wish to maintain an active involvement in the operation of their investments.

These investors, via a body corporate, then contract the management rights to a resident manager who manages the complex. The responsibilities of the resident manager mainly involve caretaking activities but he or she also has the authorization to operate a letting and leasing business of the units. Success in the industry is therefore heavily dependent on the resident manager developing good relations with the investors. Such a relationship is often difficult to administer, which is one reason why the average turn-over within the industry is under two years. In the early days of the indus-try, a management rights business was often a 'mum and dad' operation; however, today it is not uncommon to have a company as a single investor owning the management rights to properties and employing professionally trained staff to manage them. One such single investor is SMG.

The popularity of management rights continued into the 1990s, and the evolution of the concept and the industry prompted the refinement of state legislation to formalize and govern the industry. The industry also formed an industry body to protect management rights owners from legal chal-lenges to the status and operation of management rights.

In the early years, the newly established industry offered ample oppor-tunities for growth with little competition. This scenario was pivotal in assisting SMG's early development. What followed over the next 20 years was a series of successful trades where SMG bought and then sold the management rights to eight additional high-rise buildings. The decision to sell or buy was generally made between John and Jane. John would closely follow the activity in the market and the industry, and when his instincts told him the moment was right, he would make the deal and the trade would take place.

In that short period, SMG's high activity in the industry was bring-ing greater recognition to both the business and the Belcher family. In the 1980s, John was invited to chair the industry body. His involve-ment with this association allowed John to develop extensive knowledge about industry policies and body corporate laws. During his period as Chairman, John was pivotal in developing innovative marketing concepts for the industry and for tourism, which were later adopted by the state government. SMG, but more so John, was now being seen as a pioneer in an industry that had gained legitimacy.

As the industry grew, so did the competition within it; consequently, the competitive advantages that were once taken for granted were slowly eroded. SMG took a new direction by maximizing the relationships it had built over the years with developers within the industry. Working in conjunction with developers, SMG began setting up leisure/resort type accommodation. This specialized area within management rights allowed SMG to differentiate its services but also put its operations in direct com-petition with the surrounding hotels. Previously, in the management rights industry, the tourism industry was viewed as a source of opportunities for management rights rather than as direct competition.[1] SMG has been very successful in this specialized field and has overseen the successful estab-lishment of 10 large resort properties to date. Currently SMG holds the management rights to two leisure/resort type properties.

Table 8.2   SMG entrepreneurial initiatives

Year	Event
1976	John and Jane purchased their first coffee shop in NZ
1978	Purchased a second coffee shop
1982	Sold the coffee shops and moved to Australia.
1982	SMG was born. Specialized area of management rights where accommodation can be both short-term and long-term stay. In such facilities, units can be bought outright, rented, or offered as tourist accommodation. This increases the complexity of their management as compared to hotels, which are owned by companies and focus solely on tourist accommodation
	Bought first management rights to 45 units
1984	Bought second management rights (60 units)
1985	Bought management rights to 100 units and sold the previous two
1991	Bought management rights to 85 units
1993	Purchased management rights to 100 units and sold the previous 85
1997	Purchased management rights to 112 units
2001	Purchased management rights to 300 units (largest purchase to date)
2003	Subsidiary (The Travellers) formed by the second generation. This is the real estate arm of SMG which handles the development, marketing, sales and management of properties and units
2005	Purchased three more buildings (sold in 2007)
2005	Subsidiary (The House People) formed by the second generation. This is a travel wholesaler that tailors accommodation to needs. Daniel was central to the development of this entity which targeted students studying at a nearby university
2007	Purchased management rights to 113 units

Furthermore, SMG has diversified its operations by forming two new entities: a travel wholesaler and a boutique real estate agency. Both entities were established to provide complementary services and operations to SMG. Table 8.2 gives an overview of SMG entrepreneurial initiatives.

These industry-related extensions complemented and enhanced SMG's management efficiencies, resulting in economic savings and benefits for the group.

Exposure to business began early for the second generation, as is evident from Daniel's observation:

> People like me who have grown up in a family business tend to have a greater understanding of business because the issues are discussed every single evening at the dinner table and are discussed on a regular and systematic basis. People who haven't been exposed to that are often going through the same learning

curve that people like me went through when I was 13 or 14 except that they are 26 or 27. So, I would say we have a greater understanding of business. (Daniel, second generation)

After working for a while in SMG, both Daniel and Mathew decided to further their education. Their temporary absence left a void in the company that resulted in SMG bringing in external managers to fill the positions the sons had previously occupied. On completion of his Masters degree, Daniel wanted to return to SMG; however, on John's advice he decided to work abroad for two years. Mathew has just recently completed his degree and his father hopes that he will follow his brother's example. John would like both of his sons to work in SMG after gaining external work experience, a desire that Daniel and Mathew have also expressed.

THEORETICAL BACKGROUND

Family Entrepreneurship

At the time the Belchers were considering migrating from New Zealand to Australia, they were operating three small businesses that had been established in the early 1970s. These included two coffee shops and an ice-cream parlour. Being the serial entrepreneur that John was, it was certain that the family would continue to be self-employed and run their own business once they relocated to Australia. In fact, the type of business and the industry into which they would venture was already decided prior to migration. Jane recalls:

We had been here for a holiday previously and loved it. When we were here, we had found out about management rights accidentally because we stayed at one such property and we had discussed the prospect of buying them. (Jane, Director)

Soon after their arrival in Australia, the couple established SMG, a small operation employing only two people. At about the same time, they also purchased their first management rights – for a holiday high-rise apartment that signalled their first foray into the fledgling management rights industry.

When we first came over here it was more of a 'mum and dad' operation and not terribly professional. And really you just had to sit there. You registered your high-rise or whatever with all the different airlines and things and they just gave you the bookings and people walked in off the streets and it was fine. The units were individually furnished. It wasn't very standard. The management rights industry was very down-market. (Jane, Director)

Family Autonomy

The Belcher family enjoys a great deal of autonomy when it comes to managing both the operational and strategic direction of the firm. This is the result of the family's 100 percent ownership stake in the firm and its active involvement in everyday business operations. This autonomy gives the founders, John and Jane, the opportunity to continue to express their considerable entrepreneurial flair. The recent inclusion of external professional managers is having some effect on the family's (particularly the founders') autonomy. These managers, hired to temporarily occupy the void left by the second generation, have sought greater autonomy in their roles within the firm, especially with regard to control over decisions on matters pertaining to the firm's operations. These changes have been quite a challenge for John and Jane, who have singlehandedly managed the operations of the firm for the last 28 years.

> When we first handed over, we lost a little bit of control. The chain of command was very strict and we really didn't have as much contact with our workers as we had in the past, which we missed. You've got to talk to the person in command if you want something rather than talk to the person that you really want the information from, which to me was really sort of getting a little bit ridiculous. But we have learned that there has to be a chain of command. (Jane, Director)

Family Innovation

It is worth recalling that the management rights industry was still in its infancy when the Belchers founded SMG. This allowed SMG to benefit from first-mover advantages for being amongst the first firms that helped develop and legitimize the industry. Early entry into the industry allowed SMG to successfully buy and sell ownership rights for almost a decade and make good returns. Now, after more than 20 years, the industry is beginning to become saturated with an influx of competitors into the market. With this increased competition, old strategies no longer work as well as they once did. More than ever, the Belchers realize that innovation is essential if SMG is to remain competitive within the industry. Rather than trading management rights (as they successfully did in the past), SMG is using its established relationships in the industry, for example, with body corporate and construction companies, to add value to the buildings and services they manage. John realized that the units they managed could also be marketed as holiday accommodation and thus turned what was previously a purely management rights style accommodation into more of a resort style one. SMG's innovative strategy allowed the company to realize that body corporate property could be used to create services, thus increasing the value of the buildings and giving greater returns to both the body corporate and SMG. This strategy, which was based on the strength of their relationships, was new in the industry and is turning out to be very successful.

> We've introduced a lot of things here. It would be the first time that any man-agement rights owner has got the body corporate to pay for something that we are charging the guests and where we are giving all the money back to the body corporate. Since the body corporate can't run a business, they funded the putt-putt. We're running it and giving them all the money, which is a new thing in this kind of business, that is, to be able to help the body corporate with an income source that they could use to fund further projects. We are probably one of the only management rights owners that have put a lot of money into refurbishing, like putting the new pizzeria and bar by the pool. We got the body corporate to give us exclusive use of the area and we paid for that. Sure, we are making money but we are also upgrading the building so that the units are more valuable and the business is more sustainable. So in that way, we're prob-ably one of the forerunners of the management rights industry. (Daniel, second generation, Director)

Family Risk-Taking

The current stance adopted by SMG is comparatively conservative. In the past SMG was more aggressive in the market with the trading (buying and selling) of management rights ownership (10 properties over a period of 20 years). Over time this aggressive stance has evolved into a more cautious approach to business activities. Today, with the founders nearing retire-ment and with increased competition within the market, SMG has opted to focus resources on strengthening the firm's current business activities. Potential business investments and projects that SMG decides to consider are now subject to feasibility studies, whereas previously this process was far less formal. SMG's reduced risk-taking stance may also be influenced by the increased inclusion of non-family professional managers, who have been employed to monitor risk and to complement the incumbent leader-ship's entrepreneurial proclivity. The increase in non-family professional managers has given rise to more formal structures and procedures that have led to changes in the way SMG has functioned. These have contributed to SMG's current (comparatively) conservative entrepreneurial stance.

> We only invest in projects if we have done an awful lot of background work on them. We would not, especially now, go into a risky situation without doing

the background work. We have made one mistake and that was through an unusual set of circumstances, I must admit. Our normal business practice is to go into something very thoroughly before we enter it.

                     (Jane, Director)

Family Proactiveness

SMG has always been proactive in the way it has conducted its business. John and Jane were particularly proactive (even naive) in their early forays into a new industry. Their proactive stance ultimately gave the firm first-mover advantages as the industry evolved. John was very proactive in looking for opportunities in the market. With larger, better resourced companies entering the market, SMG has used its reputation and the relationships it has developed over the years to gain access to development projects in the early planning stages. This gives SMG an edge over competitors in acquiring the management rights to these buildings. Furthermore, SMG was one of the first companies to turn its management rights properties into resort style accommodation. Such a move revolutionized the management rights industry because it positioned body corporate entities directly in competition with hoteliers and resort owners.

  SMG does not openly engage in aggressive competition, preferring to focus its efforts on strengthening and improving its business activities. This is not to say that the firm does not monitor what other players in the market are doing; rather, the focus is primarily on refining internal operations and working continuously on process improvement to raise the quality of the company's services.

Family Leadership

The founders, John and Jane, have developed complementary leadership roles. Jane gets on well with the staff and is often consulted by them as a mediator on work-related issues. John's leadership is respected because of his knowledge and experience within the management rights industry. Their combined leadership strength resides in their ability to create a work environment where employees are valued for their contributions.

> They treat the business like it is a family. It is one of the biggest things in terms of staff involvement. They know everyone in the firm even though they have 100 employees. They know the kids, they know who is pregnant and they know who is dating whom. There is a real sense of a family. Within the company everyone feels like they are part of the family. I think that would have to be the biggest leadership strength – making the staff feel that they are an important part of making the business work. (Mathew, second generation, Director)

Family Decision-Making

The Belchers control 100 percent of the capital decision-making and distribution in SMG. Non-family managers are occasionally consulted on important decisions that influence operations or the strategic direction of the firm, but ultimately these decisions remain the prerogative of the Belchers, John and Jane in particular. The family has also set limits on the capital senior managers can spend without the family's approval.

Decision-making involves input from the second generation and non-family members of the recently established company board, which comprises three family directors and two non-family directors. The presence of non-family professionals within SMG has led to increased formality and governance in the firm's daily operations, resulting in a more active company board.

Family Values

Today the family understands that it is not in business primarily for the money. Rather, hard work, passion for the business and family bonds are elements that override the objective of wealth creation. The firm's culture is also one that regards employees within the organization as part of one big family. Continuous communication and interaction between the founders and owners and the front-line staff have helped to nurture this familial culture. The Belchers also agree that should an incoming generation have a passion for pursuing interests outside of SMG, they will be encouraged to do so. Passion for the business is a necessary condition for entry into SMG.

There is a common understanding among the family members that the family is more important than the business and this is critical in maintaining strong family relationships. Nevertheless, differences have occurred between the first and second generations, primarily with regard to levels of authority and role clarity. The reorganization of SMG's internal processes and structures is helping to iron out these differences. Jane has always played the role of chief emotional officer and has helped mediate between her husband and sons whenever required.

> I think with anything it's your relationship that's important – you have to get on, you have to trust each other and know that you're looking after the future direction of the business. I guess one of the values is that it's all family. It's an extended family. (Mathew, second generation)

THE FUTURE

The founders gained much of their industry knowledge and experience as a result of being intimately involved in the formative years of the industry's development. SMG and other early entrants into the industry helped the industry develop into what it is today. As president of the first industry body, John played a pivotal role in the creation of laws and regulations that governed the industry. John's knowledge has thus been of immense value to SMG.

SMG has been recently transitioning from being founder managed to being professionally managed. The shift to external management was necessary given the age gap between the first and second generations. Governance is certainly required to clarify the roles and responsibilities and the communication channels within the family and between the family and management. An external board consisting of three family members and two independent advisory members has been championed by the second generation to facilitate the transition of the business and make it easier for the founders to deal with the separation of management from family and ownership. Family governance is informal at present. The small size of the family has mitigated the need for family governance but this will likely come into play as the family grows, for example, when in-laws are introduced into the family.

CONCLUSION

The key to the Belcher family's success lies in the way in which they have been able tolerate ambiguity and help legitimize a new industry. This resilience is a characteristic of long-lived family businesses, many of which have pioneered what are today mature industries. The preceding discussion has focused the lens on the life cycle challenges of a new industry, and when integrated with entrepreneurial orientation (EO) and resource-based view (RBV) concepts, this allows for rich, transgenerational entrepreneurship learning observations, which we now present:

EO Learning 1: The greater the control of the family over the firm, the more likely it is that the firm's EO is a reflection of the owning family's EO stance.

EO Learning 2: Professional executives from outside the family complement the 'can-do' attitude of entrepreneurial leaders by assisting in professionalizing and legitimizing the family business.

EO Learning 3: Multiple generational inputs into the business provide additional resources that can benefit the ease of transition from one generation to the next and strengthen the entrepreneurial contributions of the family to the business.

RBV Learning 1: Intuition, while often criticized for its lack of formality and rigor, is a valuable resource on which most family businesses are birthed and thrive during the formative years of the business. This is a tacit resource which contributes to survivability and sustainability.

RBV Learning 2: External professional managers can provide an interim administration when there is a large age gap between the generations of the family owners, that is, between the incumbent and the incoming.

RBV Learning 3: Relationship building is an important element in strengthening and building familiness resources by creating differentiation and competitive advantage.

NOTE

1. A thriving tourism industry resulted in more tourists coming to the area. If they enjoyed the visit, they would often consider either moving to the area permanently or purchasing a place where they could stay whenever they visited. Often it was to the management rights operators that these tourists would speak when considering the option of purchasing getaway homes, which they would occupy when they next visited, or, at other times, rented under management rights.

REFERENCES

Barney, Jay B. and A.M. Arikan. 'The resource-based view: origins and implications', in Michael A. Hitt, R.E. Freeman and J.R. Harrison (eds), *Handbook of Strategic Management*. Oxford: Blackwell Publishers, 2001, 124–88.

Covin, Jeffrey G. and Dennis P. Slevin. 'A conceptual model of entrepreneurship as firm behavior'. *Entrepreneurship Theory and Practice*, 16:1 (1991), 7–25.

Habbershon, Timothy G. and Mary L. Williams. 'A resource-based framework for assessing the strategic advantages of family firms'. *Family Business Review*, 12:1 (1999), 1–25.

Lumpkin, G.T. and Gregory G. Dess. 'Clarifying the entrepreneurial orientation construct and linking it to performance'. *Academy of Management Review*, 21:1 (1996), 135–72.

Miller, Danny. 'The correlates of entrepreneurship in three types of firms'. *Management Science*, 29:7 (1983), 770–91.

Mitchell, Ronald K., Bradley R. Agle and Donna J. Wood. 'Toward a theory of

stakeholder identification and salience: defining the principle of who and what really counts'. *Academy of Management Review*, 22:4 (1997), 853–86.
Suchman, Mark C. 'Managing legitimacy: strategic and institutional approaches'. *Academy of Management Review*, 20:3 (1995), 571–610.
Wernerfelt, B. 'A resource-based view of the firm'. *Strategic Management Journal,* 5 (1984), 171–80.
Zimmerman, Monica A. and Gerald Z. Zeitz. 'Beyond survival: achieving new venture growth by building legitimacy'. *Academy of Management Review*, 27:3 (2002), 414–32.

9. Incremental entrepreneurship: best practice professionalization across generations

Mervyn Morris

INTRODUCTION

This chapter will introduce Australia's Dennis family – a case of 'incremental entrepreneurship' in the business transition from the first to the second generation. Following the second generation's formal involvement and ownership in the business, Dennis Family Corporation (DFC) undertook a major professionalization process to formalize the family business and ensure its continued success. The members of the second generation have successfully sustained the entrepreneurial spirit of their family business (albeit in a different style), adding value to the firm in an 'incremental' manner.

Throughout the chapter there will be a strong emphasis on the family element of DFC and the roles that each family member has played. Bert Dennis, as the founder and incumbent leader of the firm, has witnessed major changes to the business he built from the ground up. His children, in particular his son Grant Dennis as the primary next generation issue champion, have seen the changes from another perspective – ensuring the business remains within the family into the second generation and beyond.

The professionalization process was sparked by a commitment from the second generation to continue to 'make a real go' of the family business rather than simply liquidating and distributing the assets. The dedication of all the family members to this objective has ensured the success of this process, and ultimately, the longevity of the firm.

Although DFC has become more 'professional', it has not lost its entrepreneurial character; rather, it has improved the ways in which entrepreneurialism is fostered and pursued in the company.

In essence, this case outlines how the implementation of appropriate governance and management practices has allowed the Dennis family to overcome the challenges and maximize the opportunities associated with owning and operating a multigenerational family firm. From a theoretical perspective, this case uses the concepts of entrepreneurial orientation (EO) (Lumpkin and Dess 1996) and the resource-based view (RBV) (Habbershon and Williams 1999; Barney 1991; Wernerfelt 1984) to demonstrate how the firm has leveraged its familiness to foster an enduring spirit of entrepreneurship and to maintain a sustained competitive advantage.

BACKGROUND

Dennis Family Corporation came from humble beginnings as a small civil engineering consulting partnership in Melbourne, Australia, in the 1960s. This partnership was dissolved in 1965 and Bert Dennis became the sole owner of the company which would ultimately become DFC.

To better understand the beginnings of this company and its entrepreneurial successes, it is necessary to delve into the personal history of its founder, Bert Dennis.

After the untimely and tragic death of his father when he was very young, Bert's early years were spent in poverty. If it wasn't for the fact that Bert's mother was an extremely strong-willed and resilient person, he and his siblings would have surely ended up as wards of the state. She was determined that no one would break up her family. She lived in fear that the social security department would take her five children from her and place them in a home or put them up for adoption. As a result, the family shifted frequently. There was also another reason for their nomadic existence. Since they were staying mostly with Bert's mother's brothers and sisters, and as there were five children in the picture, their welcome would wear out quickly. At one point, they lived in a tent on the banks of the Murray River for nearly 12 months. Life was exceedingly tough in those years. The Second World War was in progress, a lot of commodities were being rationed and the country was in the middle of a devastating drought.

Bert's mother would not allow herself to be defeated, but she had moments of despair. Bert recalls:

> I remember on a couple of occasions coming into the house unexpectedly, to find her sitting at the table with her head in her hands, quietly sobbing. By the time I was 13, I had lived in 15 different houses; and by the time I finished school at 21, I had gone to 19 different schools. People often remark that things would have been tough in those years. They certainly were for mum, but for myself, I wouldn't change a moment of it. With mum working constantly, no grandparents to speak of and no father, I had little supervision and made my own way. Because I had to fend for myself, it taught me to be very self-reliant

from an early age – very determined and capable. Having no money meant that if I wanted something, I had to either make it myself or repair someone else's cast-offs. I also saw changing schools often as an advantage because if I had a poor teacher, or more likely one I could not get on with, I only had him or her for a short time until we moved on. (Bert Dennis, company founder)

In hindsight, Bert found his early self-reliance and determination were tremendous assets. When he was 14, he set his sights on becoming a member of the state under-17 schoolboy baseball team. The only condition was that he had to be a schoolboy, which meant that he had to go on to senior school and do a diploma course. He started the diploma course and not only made the baseball team, but was elected captain. When the baseball championships were over, he was part way through the course and thought to himself, 'I am this far through, so I might as well finish', which is exactly what he did.

Even when he completed the diploma course in civil engineering, he was still not quite sure that he really wanted to become an engineer. It wasn't until he was working at the Heidelberg council and discovered that becoming a consulting civil engineer could be profitable, that he decided that he wanted to join the engineering profession. At the age of 22, he applied for an assistant engineer's position at the City of Chelsea. It was only during his interview before the mayor, town clerk and city engineer that he realized that they had incorrectly described the position in the advertisement and what they were actually seeking was a deputy city engineer. Legally, they could not appoint him until he was 24 years old, had passed the requisite exams and had four years' experience. Bert recalled, 'I got the job and I was then, at 22, in the position I wanted to be in by around 35 years of age.'

Eighteen months later he applied for a job with partnership prospects with a retired city engineer, Oscar Flight, who was 65 and who wanted to start a consulting practice. Flight had the contacts that Bert was seeking and needed someone to do the hands-on work. Bert got the job. Oscar Flight retired from the practice at 70, and at the age of 29, Bert became the sole proprietor of O.T. Flight and Associates Pty Ltd. In 1965, Dennis Pty Ltd was born.

Engineering continued to be the main focus of the business until the late 1960s when it began to invest in residential land, utilizing the technological base gained from engineering and motivated by the long-term growth patterns in that industry. Through the 1970s, the corporation's focus centered on the residential and development industry and on investment properties.

Following the property downturn in the early 1980s, home building became an important adjunct to the corporation as market fundamentals moved towards completed homes on the fringe of Melbourne, Australia's second largest city. As a further strategy to overcome the volatile cycles of the construction industry, attention was given to spreading the risks by actively seeking opportunities in other Australian states.

With regard to the family, at this stage Bert and his wife Dawn had four adult offspring whom they had groomed into competent business professionals. They were confident that their children would be successful following their own separate paths if that is what they decided to do. But they also felt that it would be good if they could all combine their strengths and build a sustainable family business for the current and future generations. They did not want to pressure their children into joining forces and were keen to make sure that whatever happened was fair to all parties. They were well aware of the challenges that confront family businesses when control, management and ownership issues overlap.

Bert and Dawn decided to ask their children whether they would prefer them to work towards a structure that would ultimately result in the liquidation of the assets that had been built over the past 25 years and then divide the funds equally between them or whether the children would prefer to amalgamate the associated businesses with the parent company and take on the challenge of professionalizing this new entity. Their children, Adele, Grant, Natalie and Marshall, expressed a unanimous desire to amalgamate and 'make a real go of it'.

This triggered the beginning of a major, 10-year professionalization process which would see DFC transform into a highly successful, multigenerational family firm with best practice governance and management structures and processes effectively implemented.

Today the company is reaping the benefits of this process, and although it still has a major interest in the consultancy practice, it is the biggest private land developer in Victoria and constructs around 1700 houses every year. DFC operates in four Australian states, exports houses to New Zealand and is involved in joint venture projects in China.

FAMILY ENTREPRENEURSHIP

The true family-oriented nature of this business is evidenced in the first instance of husband and wife cooperation in the 1960s, when Bert and his wife Dawn together began renovating old houses, while, at the same time, growing the consultancy business. From houses they went on to invest in bigger and better properties; meanwhile the consultancy flourished.

Bert's early years had instilled in him a very strong commitment to

Building Communities

Figure 9. 1   Values and essence of DFC

family, which has added value to the business in two key respects: first, family members are closely involved in the business; and second, employees are well looked after as part of the wider 'Dennis family'. These values are reinforced in the words that form the core essence of the company: 'Welcome to our family' (see Figure 9.1).

Third generation members of the family are now beginning to enter the business: one holds a full-time position while three others have part-time roles in addition to their university studies (see Figure 9.2).

All three generations of the Dennis family consider the company to be entrepreneurial as the following quotes reveal:

> Up until the early nineties, the business, if I could say the business, was on a very entrepreneurial, you know, deal by deal basis without any real direction. (Interview with Bert Dennis, company founder, 12 February 2008)

> Yeah, I think so, I think entrepreneurial absolutely. (Interview with Adele Levinge, Company Director, second generation, 13 February 2008)

> Yeah. Because I think there's an element of risk in every decision. (Emily Levinge, third generation, 11 February 2008, responding to the question: Would you consider the business to be entrepreneurial?)

There is, however, a recognition that the nature of the entrepreneurship has changed across generations, as is evident from the following excerpt:

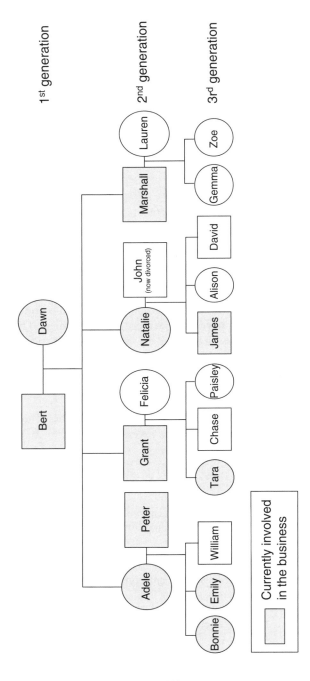

Figure 9. 2   Dennis family by generation

I think focused entrepreneurialism. I wouldn't say less, I'd just say more focused. (Interview with Grant Dennis, second generation, Company Chairman, 21 February 2008)

The founder of the firm, Bert Dennis, is quite clear that he 'fell' into residential development almost by accident. His original career plan, formulated in 1957, envisioned a career in local government, where he would be able to retire by the time he was 40 and undertake consultancy work. However, after taking control of the consultancy practice in the 1960s, he also began renovating houses in his 'spare' time.

> So we renovated that house and then we bought another one and renovated that and we finished up buying a dozen houses and we began renting them out. We'd buy derelict houses, renovate them and rent them out, and the rent would pay off the mortgage, so that worked very well. Then we got into about '72 and we sold all those houses and then made bigger and better investments. (Interview with Bert Dennis, company founder, 12 February 2008)

Bert and his wife and partner in the business, Dawn, did the renovations themselves, thus acquiring many of the skills required for building houses as well as developing a knowledge of how the building industry worked. Bert's local government experience, coupled with his consultancy experience, also gave him insights into the workings of councils with regard to land rezoning and subdivisions. None of this was the result of conscious planning – it was simply Bert doing what he felt was necessary to maintain both a certain standard of living for his family and a sense of security. But this did not mean that he had a blinkered approach to the industry in which he worked. He was well able to see and to take advantage of an opportunity:

> I could see the potential down in Werribee, half an hour from the center of town. It's flat, it's good building land and it was where the future of growth was going to be, so I went hoofing down there and tried to convince them to buy. (Interview with Bert Dennis, company founder, 12 February 2008)

He had previously dealt with the two people he was trying to convince to buy the land as part of his consulting activities. His risk-averse nature is demonstrated by his unwillingness initially to buy the land himself and accept the full risks associated with developing and marketing the land. He ultimately demonstrated his faith in what he perceived as a good opportunity:

> I must have pushed Charles and Hal fairly hard to convince them that it was a good buy and Charles finished up saying, 'Well, if you think it's such a good buy, why don't you put your money where your mouth is and join with us?' I

did, and we formed a company. (Interview with Bert Dennis, company founder, 12 February 2008)

This was the mid-1960s and these events brought together the disparate elements of the broad experience Bert Dennis had been gaining since leaving school. His experience in renovating houses, his understanding of local council rules and regulations and his need to understand how to finance building projects all found expression in this new partnership. This initial purchase provided the foundation (and model) for the future Dennis Family Corporation. Subsequently, financial circumstances in the early 1980s forced the two partners, Hal and Charles, to reassess their commitment to the partnership, with the result that they decided to bow out and Bert Dennis became the sole owner of the firm.

Bert Dennis possessed specific skills that had been developed as the result of his different endeavors (council engineer, engineering consultant and house renovator) and these skills could have been used in a variety of different ways. He could have, for example, concentrated on any one of the three specific skill sets that he had developed and been able to attain a measure of economic security. Instead, Bert Dennis combined the skills he had developed and applied them to creating a land development business. He was convinced that a market existed for his 'products' even though such a market was as yet non-existent and there were those who doubted if it ever would exist. Subsequent events proved Bert Dennis right and indirectly provided the foundation for Dennis Family Holdings, although that was not the intention at the time. Bert Dennis was simply doing what he thought was the best he could do for his family – and this involved him in entrepreneurial actions. When he was asked if he had a preference for land or houses, Bert's reply was succinct: 'Whatever was going' (Interview, 12 February 2008). He thus established a model which was adopted by the company he formed and by the second generation of the Dennis family.

The Second Generation

The next entrepreneurial phase in the life cycle of the company was led by Bert's son, Grant Dennis. On his return from the US in 1984, Grant, along with his brother Marshall, proceeded to learn the business from Bert at a time when DFC was still engaged in residential and commercial development. In 1992, the founders of the company gave the second generation the opportunity to wind up the business or to consolidate the myriad of holdings into entities distinct from family activities. There was unanimous agreement from the four members of the second generation to continue the business, and as a result, all four were made equal shareholders with

Table 9.1   DFC major development projects, 1995–2004

1995	Burnside, Victoria: 1300 households and a community shopping center
2001	Rose Grange, Victoria: 1600+ lots, plus parks, waterways and easy access to school and shops. Projected population: 4700+. Awarded the Housing Institute of Australia Green Smart Development medal in 2004
2001	The Hunt Club, Victoria: 2400 lots, plus parks, wetland, commercial precinct and retirement village. Projected population: 6600+. Awarded Best Residential Land Estate by the Urban Development Institute of Australia
2002	Manor Lakes, Victoria: new suburb of 7000+ lots, including parklands, waterways and a commercial center. Project population: 21,000+ at completion
2004	Northquarter, Queensland: 700+ lots planned, including regeneration of a wetlands area. Projected population: 2,000+

the founders. Each member of the first and second generation now owned one-sixth of the company.

When Grant Dennis returned from overseas, one of his first major decisions was to open a branch of the company in Brisbane, Queensland, in order to expand their market. Plans for another member of the second generation to move to Perth to undertake a similar venture did not eventuate. DFC was still using the model that had been developed by the founder, but now they were applying it to a new market in Brisbane.

The application of this model can be seen in the examples of the developments undertaken by DFC during this time in Table 9.1.

With each successive Victorian project, the scale increased. When DFC commenced its projects in Queensland, however, it reduced the risks associated with entering a new marketplace in a couple of ways. First, there was a significant incubation period (nearly 10 years) between the establishment of the Queensland branch of the company and its first significant project there; and second, the size of the project was relatively modest, more closely resembling an earlier project in Burnside, Victoria, in 1995.

One of the key issues that changed DFC's entrepreneurial perspective was the conscious decision, taken in 1992, to run the business as a family business and to be able to pass the business on to succeeding generations. Each of the four members of the second generation embraced this objective and it was one of the key reasons for the adoption by the company of an inherently conservative approach to risk assessment. Adopting such a position as a business also meant that decisions could be taken from a long-term perspective as there was no imperative to produce profits within much shorter time cycles.

DFC looks at new projects over a period of decades, rather than months or years. This is evident in the Queensland venture. Although the Brisbane office was set up in 1994, the first major project did not commence until 2004. The company has also developed an internationalization strategy that focuses on the US, China and Europe with plans to divide 45 percent of the company's activities equally between the three regions. This strategy has been stalled in recent years as the result of a number of disparate factors, but each member of the company is aware that this is a future strategy.

Integrating the Third Generation

There are currently four members of the third generation of the family involved in the company. Only one is working full time, as an apprentice carpenter; the other three are pursuing higher studies and work part time in the company's head office during their vacations. The first and second generations of the family have a number of different strategies for incorporating the third generation into the 'culture' of the company.

Members of the third generation are actively introduced to the family's ways of doing business, and each has direct access to the key decision-making activities of the company, either informally as a family member, or formally as an observer at company board meetings.

> Yeah, we actually get to see what goes on and listen to what goes on behind those double doors. I guarantee that no one else in the business who is not in there knows what goes on. I don't even know what goes on sometimes, but it definitely helps, because you physically get to experience it. It's not, 'well this is what we talked about today, I know you weren't there' – it's 'sit down and listen and try to see if you can understand'. I've probably been here a year, and my level of understanding has increased so much. (Interview with Emily Levinge, third generation, 11 February 2008)

While members of the third generation are being actively encouraged to take an interest and participate in the family business, there are no explicit pressures on them to do so. There is a general recognition that they are still in the early stages of their lives.

One of the few potential areas of difficulty for the third generation might be that of providing the necessary opportunities for them when they feel ready to accept specific responsibilities within the business. If there are no opportunities available or if there is implicit conflict with existing senior managerial staff, the family member might simply elect not to take on a role in the business.

This conflict did not arise with the second generation of family members because of the way the company had been structured. All the second generation family members sit above the management structure and to one side, so that while there is the occasional foray into operational matters, the bulk of their time is taken up with strategic issues.

At this stage it is simply too early to predict how the third generation will be integrated into the family business. As noted above, only one of the four third generation members interviewed, James Postma, works full time, and that is as an apprentice carpenter with a building contractor. The other three third generation members (Emily Levinge, Bonnie Levinge and Tara Dennis) are all full-time university students, with only part-time involvement in the family business.

THE FUTURE

The Dennis family continues to improve its professionalized business model as a means to achieve its overarching mission: 'To build a long-term, sustainable and profitable family business for present and future generations.' Family members remain committed to working on a number of long-term transgenerational issues to ensure that the integration of the next generation into the business is as successful as possible. Many such issues are dealt with by the family council – a family governance structure which allows purely family-based issues to be discussed outside the boardroom.

> One of the tasks still to be finalized is to put in place a commercial exit strategy, because at the moment the structure does not have an exit strategy. But in reality, if a family member decides to leave the business, then we should have a commercial exit strategy in place that again delivers the rightful amount to that family member who wants to leave but also does not prejudice the financial performance or financial ability of the company. (Grant Dennis, second generation, Company Chairman)

Other issues that are still to be worked through include: (1) preparing criteria for the third generation to join the business, (2) Bert's formal exit from the business, and (3) a succession strategy for board members.

> Currently at the family council level, we are discussing what the entry-level criteria are for subsequent generations – so many years of tertiary education, so many years of experience outside the family business before involvement in the family business, etc. One thing that is for sure is that family members working in the family business will be measured on their performance just like any other employee. (Grant Dennis, second generation, Company Chairman)

Another challenge that the family faces is one that they did not anticipate. That is, now that the family is so enmeshed in the business, they must be careful not to lose their focus on the family as it exists outside the business.

> One thing that I have noticed recently is that family members need to appreciate their role as family members and not be always focused on being family business members. For example, when we get together socially, it is important that we are conscious not to fall back to discussing work related topics continually. There is a forum now for that. For example, dad has a role to play as a grandfather and he needs to appreciate the importance of that role just like I have a role as a dad, a husband and a brother. It is great that we have worked this hard on the business and we are starting to see the results, but we cannot forget that our role as family members is ultimately more important. What I am saying, I guess, is that we have to continue to work on the family as well as on the business. (Grant Dennis, second generation, Company Chairman)

Grant offered one final piece of advice: 'I think that in the early days, all of us would have underestimated the time and effort involved in going through the professionalization process and doing it properly. If I were to give advice, that's exactly what it would be, "Don't underestimate how challenging it will be, and at times how difficult it will be", but the benefit that we are getting now is immeasurable.'

CONCLUSION

The long-term approach to, and effective implementation of, the Dennis Family Corporation's professionalization process has added value to the business in a number of ways. Perhaps most importantly, the entrepreneurial nature of the firm has been maintained across generations. This incremental entrepreneurialism is now embedded in the culture and business model pursued by the firm, albeit in a sharpened and more institutionalized form.

The following entrepreneurial orientation (EO) and resource-based view (RBV) related transgenerational entrepreneurship learning observations have been drawn from the Dennis family case study:

EO Learning 1:   The *institutionalization of entrepreneurship* helps ensure its preservation across generations.

EO Learning 2:   The *entrepreneurial spirit of next generation members* is vital to champion issues to the incumbent generation.

RBV Learning 1:   A *collective commitment to continuity* of the firm contributes to familiness in a positive way.

RBV Learning 2:   The *investment horizon* for family firms can, and should, span generations.

RBV Learning 3:   Professionalizing the family business can ensure that *familiness is translated into sustainable competitive advantage.*

REFERENCES

Barney, Jay B. 'Firm resources and sustained competitive advantage'. *Journal of Management*, 17:1 (1991), 99–120.

Craig, J.B. and K. Moores. 'How Australia's Dennis Family Corporation professionalized its family business'. *Family Business Review*, 15:1 (2002), 59–70

Habbershon, Timothy G. and Mary L. Williams. 'A resource-based framework for assessing the strategic advantages of family firms'. *Family Business Review*, 12:1 (1999), 1–25.

Lumpkin, G.T. and Gregory G. Dess. 'Clarifying the entrepreneurial orientation construct and linking it to performance'. *Academy of Management Review*, 21:1 (1996), 135–72

Wernerfelt, B. 'A resource-based view of the firm'. *Strategic Management Journal*, 5:2 (1984), 171–80.

10. Twin brothers in arms learn the family business

Justin Craig, Wayne Irava and Ken Moores

INTRODUCTION

In this case, Moores and Barrett's (2002) family business learning and life cycle framework has been used as the foundation, along with entrepreneurial orientation (EO) (Lumpkin and Dess 1996; Miller 1983) and the resource-based view of the firm (RBV) (Mahoney and Pandian 1992; Peteraf 1993; Wernerfelt 1984), for a review of an intriguing Australian second generation migrant family business.

In their book, *Learning Family Business: Paradoxes and Pathways*, Moores and Barrett present the findings of their research into how owners of successful family businesses learn to manage various transition phases in their businesses and in their lives. The two are closely entwined. Using a combination of qualitative and quantitative techniques, Moores and Barrett reveal how owners of a broad spectrum of family-owned businesses in Australia *learn* business, learn how to *run their* business, learn how to *lead* their business, and finally, how they learn to *let go* of their business. They use the organizational life cycle model to frame their discussion.

The organizational life cycle framework is appropriate for understanding the uncertainties in the business environment and how organizations cope with them, because, as theorists and practitioners alike have found, there are no universal principles that will guarantee the survival and success of a firm. Moores and Barrett (2002) use this framework to argue that changes follow a predictable set of developmental stages. These stages occur as a hierarchical progression that is not easily reversed and involve a broad range of organizational activities and structures.

In the case of the Battaglia family, this chapter will demonstrate how the twin siblings have learned business and learned to lead their family business while the incumbent generation learns to let go. Interestingly, the case will canvass some of the conflicts between the twin brothers and their conflicts with the patriarch. Insights gleaned from the study will be related to, for example, how siblings approach and handle differences of opinion between themselves and between their generation and the incumbent generation.

BACKGROUND

Case Overview

Base Group Development (BGD) is a medium-sized, second generation family business in the property development industry. The core focus of the business is residential and commercial property development. BGD originally started as a subsidiary of the parent company Base Development Corporation (BDC), which, over the years, gradually ceased operations and evolved into BGD. To date BGD has built several residential developments and luxury mansions. In 2008, the firm employed approximately 15–25 people. The Battaglia family retains 100 percent ownership and dominates the management of the firm. There is a strong desire to keep the business within the control of the family. Two of the founder's three children currently head operations and management in BGD. Ownership control remains with the founder and his wife, both of whom are also board directors for BGD. While the focus of this chapter is on the firm's Australian operations, the family also has significant investments in Argentina. In addition, one of the entrepreneurial diversified businesses has recently set up operations in mainland China. Subsidiaries of BGD are shown in Table 10.1.

Table 10.1   Overview of BGD subsidiaries

Initiatives	Function	Ownership by BGD
IT company	Founded and managed by Bruno (second generation). Supplier of computer software that manages portfolios, trades stocks, conducts stock and market research, etc.	100%
Supply Corporation International	Founded and managed by Mick (second generation). Suppliers of building materials, especially finishings and trimmings for buildings	100%
Modeling agency	Fashion model agency (since sold)	100%

The Founding Generation

Base Development Corporation (BDC) was founded by Stefan Battaglia, an Italian immigrant who arrived in Australia in 1954 at the age of 17. He had no formal education and could not speak, read or write English. Stefan had a passion for buildings and construction and naturally gravitated to this industry in his search for employment. Unsuccessful at finding work, he took to walking up and down the streets armed with his basic building tools, knocking on doors and asking people if there was anything they needed fixed. From these humble beginnings he slowly progressed to more specialized work, including cement rendering, form-work and steel work. With this experience under his belt, he was able to obtain a job with one of the largest construction firms in Australia at that time. It was there that Stefan began to perfect his trade. After working for this company for several years and observing the increasing demand and opportunities in the building industry, Stefan, the aspiring entrepreneur, started his own construction company, BDC, in 1967. This is how Stefan *learned business*.

Once the business was established, Stefan arranged for two of his brothers, who were then living in Italy, to join him in Australia. His brothers joined BDC and a partnership in the business was formed.[1] The partnership was successful until his two brothers married. Family bickering and jealousy (especially amongst the in-laws) led to the dissolution of the partnership. Stefan then entered into another partnership with a construction company and a real estate company. This partnership did not last long either. The partnership was dissolved and Stefan started his business again, this time in partnership with his wife, Tina. It was then that things changed and the business started to grow significantly.

From humble beginnings and slow growth during the 1970s, BDC experienced significant growth in the 1980s, thanks to the boom in the construction and development industry. By the early 1980s, BDC had grown into a medium to large company and had secured contracts with prominent developers. At one stage, Stefan had 200 men working for him, mostly immigrants like himself who had come to see Stefan as a leader among the burgeoning immigrant population. BDC had now grown to a size that enabled it to undertake developments stretching interstate. According to Stefan, hard work was behind the success of his family business. He embraced the philosophy that service should never be considered an afterthought and that customer care was the foundation of the company's developments.

In the mid-1980s, three events unfolded that had significant impacts on both the family and the business. First, in 1984, Stefan relocated both the

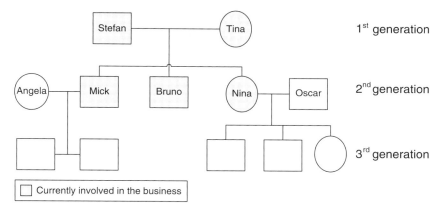

Figure 10.1   Battaglia family by generation

family (which now included three children) and the business to a neigh-boring state that was fast emerging as a popular residential and tourist destination and where the construction industry was flourishing. Second, Stefan was no longer content with building other developers' projects and was in the process of transforming what was until then a purely construction company into more of a property development company. To prepare for this shift, Stefan had begun banking land that he was positioning for future development. To maintain cash flow, he bought a medium-sized motel (importantly, on a very good future development site), which the family lived in and managed. The third event came in 1988, when Stefan was involved in a car accident that threatened both his life and the continuation of the family business. Stefan was in a coma and Tina found herself in the difficult position of singlehandedly looking after her young family while also protecting the family's significant assets from an increasingly uncompromising finance lending community. The twin boys and their sister learned valuable life and business lessons during this time.

It was a difficult period for both the business and the family. Stefan's three children, Bruno, Domenico (Mick) and Nina (see Figure 10.1), were still in school and not ready to operate the business in their father's absence. Tina, who had played an administrative role in the business, now had to focus on her husband's recovery. Although a cousin of the family was brought in to oversee operations and keep the business running,[2] without the entrepreneur and founder at the helm, the business entered a dormant period. After his recovery Stefan returned to the business, but as Mick recalls, 'after the accident, Dad pretty much retired'.

Entry of the Second Generation into the Business

In 1996, after spending most of their weekends driving around looking at properties with their father, Stefan's twin sons Bruno and Mick decided it was an opportune time to rejuvenate the family business. Both sons had recently completed their schooling. In keeping with Stefan's intentions for the business prior to his accident, a property development company, Base Group Developments (BGD), was established as a subsidiary to BDC. The boys regarded BGD as the continuation of the legacy created by their father and fashioned it accordingly. As BGD grew and developed, the family business was being reborn via the second generation under the watchful eye of the first. The boys were learning valuable business lessons.

BGD's first development project was a success for the company and was managed by the twins, with some help from their father. Bruno points out, 'We learned our craft from our father. He guided us and he always had the last say.' The boys' first project was a learning experience because it taught them a great deal about the industry and about working with each other. It was also the first step towards establishing their commercial reputation. By 2000, BDC had ceased its operations and had evolved into BGD. BGD was being led by the second generation, with Bruno taking on the leadership role of Managing Director (he was *learning to lead* the business). Mick's forté was turning out to be sales and marketing, and he was beginning to gravitate towards this side of the business. Stefan had reduced his operational involvement in BGD, but as the majority shareholder, he was consulted on all aspects of the business and had the final say on major decisions. The twins, who were still in their early twenties and had little experience, were comfortable with that arrangement, but they were acutely aware that Stefan was finding it difficult to *learn to let go*.

After five years of working together on several development projects, the twins realized that while they shared the same passion to grow the family business, each had separate interests that they wanted, and needed, to explore. The brothers decided to diversify into new areas according to their independent interests. Bruno's interests included developing a share market trading portal, setting up a fashion modeling agency and various information technology related pursuits. With these new concerns placing increasing demands on Bruno, Mick moved into the role of Managing Director of BGD (he was *learning to lead*), a role Bruno had played for the previous five years. Mick's wife Anna also stepped in to help her husband by overseeing the management rights for BGD's properties.

With a reduced operational role in BGD, Bruno had time to pursue his entrepreneurial interests. Bruno was able to secure the licensing rights to a global fashion modeling agency, a move that was seen as a coup in the modeling and fashion industry. According to Bruno, it was his sister Nina's passion for design and fashion that partly influenced his decision to diversify into modeling, an industry totally unrelated and alien to BGD. Nina had no interest in construction and development and had very little involvement in BGD though her husband Oscar had been contracted to work for BGD on several occasions. Bruno also saw opportunities in the IT industry and decided to venture into this arena as well, eventually launching a subsidiary company to BGD.

Mick, who was now leading BGD's core operations, was becoming increasingly aware of the growing competition within the property development market. Mick realized that BGD's development projects were heavily reliant on suppliers of building materials and dealing with them was turning into a costly exercise for BGD. This motivated him to launch BGD's own subsidiary supply company to reduce time lags, costs and reliance on suppliers. The subsidiary would supply building material to BGD as well as to other property developers. The related diversification provided a cash flow business for BGD, strengthened BGD's reputation and network within the industry and allowed Mick to hone his talent in sales and marketing. BGD could now control the costs and delivery times of building materials for its building projects.

From an operations perspective, Stefan and Tina now have little involvement in either BGD or its subsidiaries. However, together with their two sons, they form the four-member board of directors for the group and are currently *learning to be a family business*.

THEORETICAL BACKGROUND

Family Entrepreneurship

The Battaglia family is a good example of a migrant family whose patriarch arrived in Australia from Europe in the post-World War II years with nothing but hope. Stefan Battaglia, along with his wife Tina, were pioneers in seeking better working conditions for migrants and they are revered to this day by many for their significant contributions to migrant communities. The public stance they took on improving working conditions and pay was pivotal to their early success and exerted a profound influence on the current generation.

The Battaglia family has experienced its share of business and family hardships. These adversities have strengthened its resolve to be successful in business, stand united as a family and make a valuable contribution to the broader society. The founder and family patriarch, Stefan Battaglia, openly states that he prefers that his sons experience failure en route to success. Though he has carefully monitored their progress and encouraged their foray into business at an early age, he has also ensured that they are not sheltered from the sometimes harsh realities of the business world. Stefan takes a 'common sense' approach to business and this has meant that his sons have had considerable latitude in presenting opportunities to the family for funding support. Where potential business opportunities have been in industries unrelated to BGD's core operations, additional informal monitoring processes have been implemented. Both sons have demonstrated their entrepreneurial zeal by launching business partnerships with non-family members, all of which have failed. Though he has not explicitly stated as much in interviews, Stefan, through his own experience with partnerships both with family and non-family members, would have expected this outcome. In hindsight, the sons view this experience as a part of how they *learned business* and *learned about the value of family business*.

> That is what I love about my family because they never stopped us from doing anything. Whenever I thought they did, in hindsight they never did. They were just winding me up (testing me) to see how serious I was about it. So they were not really holding me back. (Bruno, Co-Managing Director)

Family Innovation

Survival in the mature but cyclical construction and development industry requires a significant focus on innovation. To that end, there is considerable evidence of product and process innovation within the Battaglia family group. With competitors having access to similar technologies and with market-driven price point restrictions in place, survival depends on creativity and innovation. Supply Corp International, a related diversification venture beyond the group's core business, is an example of an entrepreneurial next generation business that has effectively leveraged family reputation and product and process innovation to build a sustainable competitive advantage. Other non-related diversifications away from the core business (IT and fashion) are more aligned with the new venture creation process.

> I think we are innovative with our product and processes; development and everything else is pretty much according to the norms of the development

property industry. I think our difference now is finishes. We can provide much better finishes for our buyers at a much more efficient cost than what we used to do before. (Mick, Co-Managing Director)

Risk-taking has been openly encouraged in the Battaglia family. Though it has not been specifically quantified in dollar terms, a considerable amount of the money that the family has allowed the next generation to invest in relatively high risk ventures points to their tolerance on this issue and is a signature of this family's propensity for risk-taking. That said, there are now clear indications of the need to establish more stringent decision-making processes, a point agreed on by both generations as they proceed to professionalize their operations.

In terms of taking risks, Stefan always told his sons to never fear failure but to learn from it. (Tina, Director)

Family Proactiveness

The Battaglia family has the benefit of the incumbent generation's shrewd understanding of construction industry cycles. It has banked land during lean times and is not tempted to make forays when market indicators are not strongly in favor of the developer. It is during such times that the family has explored opportunities in industries related and unrelated to its core business. This paradoxical strategy has proven successful and is a clear demonstration of its use of patient capital.

The family uses the vagaries of industry cycles to its advantage. This is a form of *proactiveness* as the family members are intentional and deliberate opportunity scanners who move only when the conditions are most favorable. This strategy in their core business is complemented by the exploitation of related entrepreneurial opportunities, an example of which is Supply Corp, the industry supply company. This offshoot business allows them multiple opportunities to be proactive as their customers in this venture are in many instances their competitors in their core business. Whether this was intentional or just a fortuitous outcome is not established; nevertheless, the benefits are numerous and apparent.

On all our projects, we did it our way and we did it based on what we believed was good for the community. We always tried new products. All our developments are different . . . never so far out there to the point that you are a pioneer, I guess, but up there with respect to quality. Yes, I would say that the family is proactive in this sense – very proactive in the main fundamentals of property development which is location, build ability, marketing and quality finishes. (Bruno, Co-Managing Director)

Family Leadership

Leadership of the Battaglia family is unique in many ways. Stefan has a strong influence over the family and he has led his sons by stealth and seemingly remains committed to this approach. The fact that projects for which his sons have been responsible have been successful has not meant that Stefan has altered his approach very much. It is apparent that at times he has been frustrated by the failure of the unrelated diversifications to provide agreed upon returns. To a certain extent, his controlling leadership style has been necessary to this point. However, the recent unification of business entities and consolidation required to pursue future core business opportunities have somewhat softened his approach. The sons, while openly frustrated by their father's leadership approach in the early years, are now quick to defend it as necessary for their learning, for nurturing the next generation and for building the family's assets and wealth.

Tina Battaglia is the spiritual leader and chief emotional officer of the family. Her strength in these roles has been a revelation through the course of this research process and cannot be understated. She possesses a real sense of family and community, values that can be traced back to her Peruvian culture. Her deep understanding of family members and other stakeholders with whom the family interacts is abundantly evident. That said, Tina is also a keen student of the property industry and does her own independent research on the market. Her role in this capacity is pivotal to how the family as a unit operates, a point that is further explored below.

The twin sons currently share leadership of the company, a process that has evolved over more than 10 years of working together and can now be appreciated fully. Bruno took responsibility for the family's projects early in life, a situation whose roots can probably be traced to the time of his father's car accident when Bruno, at age 14, joined his mother in numerous negotiations to keep creditors and banks from bankrupting the business. His early project leadership was directive and necessary to counter the influence and expectations of his father, a demanding patriarch. He unashamedly set high performance standards for his twin brother, Mick, who upon reflection admits that he was not as focused as Bruno at that time. Though there has not been a deliberate change, the roles and responsibilities held by the brothers have reversed over time. Mick became more focused around the time of his marriage, thus allowing Bruno to take a back seat. This has been the situation until very recently. Currently the twins are acting as joint leaders with distinct responsibilities and a sense of clarity that has helped them plan with a shared vision.

The shifting situation between the brothers over the years, it appears, has been a source of considerable frustration to their parents and has required them to remain tolerant as they witnessed the divergent behavior of their offspring. The current outcome is a testament to their resolve to let their sons learn and grow in the business and is a distinguishing characteristic of this family.

> It is much harder to be a leader for the family. I think our family is going through a transitional period. Bruno was leading the way for five years when we started. The last five years, I have been leading the way. We both acknowledge the past and we respect each other's contribution and that's excellent. We need to focus now on today for tomorrow. And when you talk about today and tomorrow, it's important to take away the family emotions and start focusing on the business and where we have to be and where we need to go and respond accordingly to that. And that's been difficult. (Mick, Co-Managing Director)

Family Networks

The Battaglia family has been able to build and maintain strong industry and political networks. Stefan had a major impact on migrant families who were struggling to attain a foothold in Australia and the return on this commitment has been the family's significant standing in the community. It also has meant that the family has attracted its share of partners who have behaved opportunistically and attempted to profit from their relationship with the family. This has now been addressed and considerable due diligence is undertaken before a decision is made to enter into partnerships or joint venture arrangements. The Battaglia family has also leveraged its reputation to build strong relationships with financing institutions and remains loyal to only a few financiers.

> It wasn't about failed businesses, it was about failed partnerships. But what he built was a strong brand . . . Stefan Battaglia. He had the networks and the contacts. He also had the ability to leave those partnerships because of his name. (Tina, Director)

Ownership is concentrated in the hands of the founders. This was a deliberate strategy, in effect until the sons reach the age of 35. The founders believe that at 35 the sons would have had sufficient time to demonstrate their worth to the family business and at that time conversations around ownership can occur if necessary. Currently, given the unity within the family, there seems to be no reason for a change in the ownership structure. The agreed aim from this point on is to grow wealth for the family unit that will benefit everyone.

The long intentional apprenticeship or incubation period required of the next generation has advantages and disadvantages, as reported by both generations. Tina openly expressed her concern that one or both sons would not return to the family fold in a contributing way once they pursued their own ventures. At this point both sons understand their parents' wisdom in giving them considerable scope to pursue entrepreneurial ventures using family funds without seeming to be overly concerned with financial results. The family now considers the importance of financial and non-financial results and can see how costs can be amortized over the life of the business. The family is currently positioned to benefit from its strong foundation and from the considerable trust and mutual respect amongst all the family members. They remain prudent investors who rely heavily on their understanding of the industry life cycle in their core business.

Family Business Decision-Making

The family decision-making process has evolved over time and is complex for a combination of reasons. Though Stefan makes the final decision, he expects family members to fight for his approval. The family understands this process and it seemingly bodes well for better decision-making, or at least for assumptions to be clearly understood. The sons have learned to live with this situation, and although this was the cause of considerable conflict between the generations in the early days, there is now a mutual respect among family members that eases the angst around decision-making and authority. Tina is an important sounding board for Stefan and her sons and is a major influence on the outcomes of major strategic and operational decisions. She acts as a filter between operations and family. She has accrued intimate knowledge of the property industry and spends a considerable amount of time studying the property market and identifying potential opportunities. This makes her a valuable voice of reason when decisions are being made. Her sons understand her considerable influence and knowledge and seek her counsel, particularly on issues related to property industry trends.

> Daily decisions go through me at the moment. My father will ultimately have the final say on major decisions but everyone has an input. We prefer to get consensus. (Mick, Co-Managing Director)

THE FUTURE

Relationships between and within the generations are complex in the Battaglia family, as they are in all family businesses. The twins' relationship is probably the most intriguing, with the two having diverged and converged on several matters over the years. The first project they undertook together was Mick's idea and concept, and both he and Bruno united to prove to their father that they were capable. It was 'make or break' time for them and it was an 'us' against 'him' approach. They converged and this development was a success. Soon after, they diverged and their relationship was tested as their motivations were not aligned. Despite this divergence, their second project was again successful. This divergence continued for a time, during which they pursued their different interests but remained connected. Recently they have converged again and appear to have a similar relationship to the one they had during their first project. However, this time around, their relationship with their father is far better because in his eyes they have proven themselves. He is satisfied that they have *learned business*.

> There were times I thought I could never work with Mick again, but we stayed in there because we didn't want to show the family that Mick and I fought. Dealing with Mick was difficult because we had to deal with a lot of emotional issues; we had to really learn to respect and trust each other, to understand that there will be situations where things will get confused. But we worked it out and now we're cool. Mick's the best partner I'll ever have. (Bruno, Co-Managing Director)

Governance up until now has been informal. Family members agree that to have forced formal governance structures upon the family earlier (when the twins' thinking and behavior diverged and entrepreneurial activities were being pursued individually) would not have proven wise. Recent family unity sees the family in a far stronger position to formalize governance structures and to benefit from the introduction of such structures.

> I think trust within the group is key. I think corporate governance was something that was lacking within the group. And it has been a journey in the last few years to formalize that. We are almost there and I think that having one line of direction, one line of communication was a problem before. And I believe that today, all the directors are now realizing that they have to stick in one line and be responsible for their areas and for the group as directors and shareholders. So I think yes, that's what we are lacking but we're getting there. (Mick, Co-Managing Director)

The individual insights that the twin brothers have gained about themselves and their relationship during their times of divergence and convergence are arguably the most valuable lessons that have contributed to their understanding of being brothers in business. Both brothers now consider themselves as having a richer understanding of each other's strengths and weaknesses because of the forced apprenticeship they have undertaken en route to their thirty-fifth year. Though unintentional, their progress in *learning to lead* their business mirrors Moores and Barrett's (2002) 4-Ls model.

CONCLUSION

The evolution of the Battaglia family provides a rich example of how next generation members of a family business learn and are mentored and prepared for their roles as leaders. This individual learning and organizational life cycle approach introduced by Moores and Barrett (2002), when integrated with entrepreneurial orientation (EO) and resource-based view (RBV) concepts, allows for several transgenerational entrepreneurship learning observations, which we now introduce:

EO Learning 1:   Next generation entrepreneurial success is enhanced *when failure is openly tolerated.*

EO Learning 2:   Partnership arrangements between family business members and non-family members or entities to exploit entrepreneurial ventures often do not work *and therefore require contractual conditions favoring the business family.*

RBV Learning 1:   Informal family governance initiatives are not a requisite for strong familiness and the introduction of formal family governance initiatives *should align with the cohesion levels of the family (in other words, formalizing family governance during a period when the family is not cohesive may lead to negative familiness F–).*

RBV Learning 2:   Joint leadership by siblings is more likely to lead to positive familiness (F+) when each individual has experienced similar but not the same business experiences and has thus had *the opportunity to gain insight into his or her own, and the sibling's, strengths and weaknesses.*

RBV Learning 3:   Building family wealth rather than individual wealth promotes familiness; yet, members of the next generation need to be given *considerable scope to explore new ventures as separate entities but funded by the family.*

NOTES

1. This is typical of family firms where the family functions as a resource pool which the business can access. Here the family provided human resources via Stefan's two brothers to help him run the newly established family business.
2. Once again reinforcing the point made in the earlier note.

REFERENCES

Lumpkin, G.T. and Gregory G. Dess. 'Clarifying the entrepreneurial orientation construct and linking it to performance'. *Academy of Management Review*, 21:1 (1996), 135–72.

Mahoney, Joseph T. and J. Rajendran Pandian. 'The resource-based view within the conversation of strategic management'. *Strategic Management Journal*, 13:5 (1992), 363–80.

Miller, Danny. 'The correlates of entrepreneurship in three types of firms'. *Management Science*, 29:7 (1983), 770–91.

Moores, Ken and Mary Barrett. *Learning Family Business: Paradoxes and Pathways*. Aldershot: Ashgate Publishing Company, 2002.

Peteraf, Margaret A. 'The cornerstones of competitive advantage: a resource-based view'. *Strategic Management Journal*, 14:3 (1993), 179–91.

Wernerfelt, B. 'A resource-based view of the firm'. *Strategic Management Journal*, 5 (1984), 171–80.

11. GMR Group: a case of serial entrepreneurship

Kavil Ramachandran, John Ward, Sachin Waiker and Rachna Jha

11.1 INTRODUCTION

With the opening up of the economy in 1991, India emerged as one of the fastest growing economies in the world. Acknowledging the need for a sound infrastructure base to support this rapid pace of socio-economic growth, the government of India initiated several policy measures to promote investments in the infrastructure industry, among which encouraging public-private partnerships for infrastructure development was one.

Grabbing this opportunity to deliver sustainable development through public-private partnerships, the GMR Group made a foray into the infrastructure business in 2000. Within a span of nine years, the Group successfully positioned itself as one of the leading infrastructure companies in the country, with interests in airports, energy, highways and urban infrastructure.

Named after its founder and the current Chairman, G.M. Rao, the GMR Group was built upon the entrepreneurial energy of two generations. Starting from a very small trading base, the Group went global through the infrastructure route and started institutionalizing entrepreneurship in the family and business. The family and business also adopted and practiced good governance principles.

11.2 BACKGROUND

The Company

The GMR case underlines the need to have proactive approaches to sustain entrepreneurship in the family. Entrepreneurship flourishes when a favorable environment is created both in the family and the business. Among the multiple models of family entrepreneurship possible, the GMR Group followed a model whereby family members led the process of identifying new opportunities and were involved in managing the new ventures through the start-up stage and then left it to non-family professional managers to build upon the strong foundation they had laid.

Grandhi Mallikarjuna Rao, along with his brothers, inherited a commodity trading business at Rajam, Andhra Pradesh, in 1978. He quickly realized that his brothers were not interested in investing in new opportunities and that their risk profiles were quite different from his own. A decade later, in 1988, he parted ways with his brothers and set off to chart his own course in the national arena. Progress was rapid and Rao diversified into ferro alloy manufacturing, sugar production and breweries before finally emerging as a major player in the infrastructure sector.

By 2010, the GMR Group had become one of the major diversified infrastructure organizations in India with large-scale interests in infrastructure (energy, roads and airports) and manufacturing (agri-business, mainly sugar). The company had an annual turnover of 45.67 billion INR (1 US$ = approximately 46 INR) as compared to 10.62 billion INR in 2005–06, representing an annual growth rate of 44 percent. During the same period, consolidated net profit grew from 940 million INR in 2005–06 to 1.58 billion INR in 2009–10, at an annual growth rate of 14 percent, and total assets grew at an annual rate of 64 percent from 43.76 billion INR in 2005–06 to 319.74 billion INR in 2009–10. As per the 2009–10 annual report, the company's sectoral assets were valued at 149.34 billion INR.

The Group's Businesses

In 1989, the Group commissioned an ISO 9001 certified ferro alloy plant with an installed capacity of 25,000 metric tons per annum. The unit manufactured carbon ferro chrome for the stainless steel industry and exported 75 percent of its output to Europe, Korea, Japan and China. The Group forayed into agri-business in 1997 by establishing a sugar plant at Srikakulam in Andhra Pradesh, and followed this by commissioning two integrated sugar complexes at Haliyal and Belgaum in Karnataka in 2008. The Group also entered the breweries business in 1996, but exited it shortly afterwards, having made considerable profits.

Identifying entrepreneurial opportunities in the infrastructure space offered by economic liberalization, the Group entered the power sector in 1998, the airports business in 2001 (though airport work started only in 2005) and the highway sector in 2002.

In the power sector, the Group successfully commissioned three power plant projects with a combined capacity of 808.5 MW in 1998, 2001 and 2006 respectively. Five other India-based projects, with a total capacity of 2480 MW, were scheduled to be completed by 2012. The Group acquired a 50 percent stake in Intergen NV (a US-based power generation firm with a global presence) and a 10 percent stake in South Africa's Homeland Mining and Energy Ltd. It also embarked on two major Nepal-based projects. Several new initiatives taken up subsequently, including participation in coal mine projects in Indonesia and South Africa, reflected the Group's hunger for further growth.

The Group completed two road projects under the government's Golden Quadrilateral Plan in 2005. Three additional projects (two toll-operated and one annuity-based) had been completed on a Build, Own, Transfer (BOT) basis by 2008 and another was completed in 2009. As of 2010, the Group had six operating assets – with 421 km – and four assets under development – with 409 km

In 2008, in collaboration with its Malaysian partner for highway projects, the Group completed the construction of a new airport at Hyderabad under a 30-year BOT arrangement, renewable for another 30 years with the government. In May 2008, the Group also signed an agreement with the Turkish government to rebuild and operate Istanbul's international airport; the project was completed in October 2009, a full year ahead of schedule. 'We are the first Indian company to build an international airport at a non-Indian location', Rao said. The Group took up a project to modernize and expand Delhi International Airport in time for the Commonwealth Games in 2010 and completed it in 37 months, well ahead of schedule. In early 2009, GMR began developing a multi-product Special Economic Zone (SEZ) that is expected to be completed by 2014. Later, the Group ventured into developing an exclusive SEZ for the aeronautical industry and two 'aerotropolis' developments, at Hyderabad and Delhi airports. In June 2010 a consortium led by GMR Group, won the bid to develop Male International Airport in the Maldives.

The infrastructure projects were created as special purpose vehicles (SPVs), except for the airport projects which had consortium shareholders; however, all were subsidiaries of GMR Industries Ltd (GIL). These projects were professionally run as public-private partnerships (PPPs). In PPP projects, private entities take the responsibility of completing infrastructure projects for the government on a BOT basis, thereby assuming the full risk of financing, developing, operating and maintaining the infrastructure along with the responsibility for drawing traffic. In return, contracting companies are granted the commercial right to collect tolls (user development charges), as in the case of some road projects for instance, from the users for a fixed tenure, usually running for two decades or longer. GMR Group's business collaborations were with well-known global infrastructure companies that were working on PPP projects in their own countries.

The Family

All the male members of the GMR family – Rao, his sons Raju and Kiran and son-in-law Srinivas Bommidala, commonly known as S.B. – are involved in the business. Rao set a retirement age of 70 for himself with the intention of passing on the Group's leadership baton to a member of the family after he stepped down. Though the women of the first and second generations of the family are not involved in the business, they remain deeply committed to fulfilling the Group's social responsibilities through the GMR Varalakshmi Foundation (GMRVF), the Group's corporate social responsibility arm (see the Corporate Social Responsibility section below for more details).

G.M. Rao's son-in-law, Srinivas Bommidala (S.B), who hailed from a well-known business family in Andhra Pradesh, was the first member of the family to join the Group. Before joining his father-in-law's company, S.B., a B.Com graduate, had worked in his own diversified family business and in 1994 had started up his own aquaculture business. S.B. married Rao's daughter in 1992. In 1995, when Rao obtained a license to set up a 100 MW power plant in Chennai, he asked S.B. to help him out as he was busy managing Vysya Bank and other businesses. S.B. moved to Bengaluru in 1995 to work closely with Rao. 'Since my childhood, I was determined to do something big and I found Rao sharing my dream for the future', said S.B. Rao's sons, Raju and Kiran, were in college at that time. S.B. led the Group's foray into the infrastructure sector and played an instrumental role in setting up its first power project.

During 1995–96, S.B. worked hard to get clearances for the Chennai power plant from the central government in Delhi. He subsequently moved to Chennai and lived there until 2000 to oversee completion of the Group's first power plant, the GMR Power Corporation Pvt. Ltd. He shared the responsibility of managing the development of DIAL with Raju, Rao's elder son. From 2008, as Business Chairman, Urban Infrastructure and Highways, S.B. handled the responsibilities of property development, construction of a Special Economic Zone and road projects, in addition to the Delhi airport project.

G.B.S. Raju joined the family business at the age of 22 in 1996 after obtaining a B.Com degree. Initially, he played a crucial role in shaping the overall strategy and positioning of the organization and later looked after the development and implementation of various Group projects. He took the initiative to install India's first and the world's largest floating (barge mounted) power plant, GMR Energy Ltd, in Mangalore, in 2001. Through a combination of various revenue models, Raju successfully steered the Group's entry into the road business (an overall road network of 421 km). Raju also led the Group through GMR Infrastructure's maiden IPO in 2006 and has been on the board of directors of GMR Infrastructure Limited since its inception. He was a Director of DIAL and GMR Hyderabad International Airport Ltd (GHIAL) and led the property development business of both airports and of the entire Group. He also oversaw the construction of the new terminal building at Delhi airport. From 2008 onwards, apart from being the Group CFO, Raju also looked after the Group's corporate services, such as HR and finance, as well as international business. In 2009, he served as the Group Chairman, Corporate and International Business.

Kiran Kumar Grandhi, Rao's younger son, completed his B.Com degree in 1996 and formally joined the Group as a Director in 1998, after working in Group companies for two years. He was deeply involved in developing strategic tie-ups, including a joint venture with PSEG Global Inc. for the Tanir Bavi Power Project; a life insurance joint venture with ING and Vysya Bank that the company later exited; a joint venture with Malaysia Airports Holdings Berhad for the GHIAL project; and another with United Engineers of Malaysia to bid for the Golden Quadrilateral road projects of the government of India. He also played a significant role in helping the Group bag two smaller road projects. As a member of the Group Executive Council (since discontinued), he oversaw operations and served as the business development head of the Group's airport business. Kiran was also heavily involved in developing an organizational structure and professionalizing the management process by installing proper systems and processes.

Dr Marshall Goldsmith, a globally respected executive coach and family business advisor, served as a personal coach to the four male members of the GMR family involved in the business. He said:

> One of the greatest entrepreneurs I have ever known is Mr G.M. Rao. Rao's colleagues marvel at his constant curiosity. One commented that 'he travels through life', constantly observing. He makes notes on all kinds of potential opportunities, which people might not even notice. He does not just observe – he acts! He immediately follows up with messages to staff that say 'please check this out'. While many of his observations do not turn into business opportunities, some do. This is one of the reasons behind his success.

The Company Structure

From the beginning, the GMR Group sought to retain its identity as a family-owned, professionally run business organization, and in early 2001, the family took the decision to keep the holding company private, under family control. The family corpus was held in an investment company called GMR Holding Pvt. Ltd (GHPL). As per the family constitution, several changes to the organizational structure were proposed and were in the process of being implemented.

First, the entire family holding was to be distributed among four discretionary trusts (DTs) that would be created for four branches of the GMR family. Each DT would hold 25 percent of the shares of the holding company and be managed by husband and wife as trustees, with Rao as a common trustee. The family would have right of refusal on the sale of shares by any DT outside the family. Intra-family sales would be allowed only under exceptional or unavoidable circumstances, at a 20 percent discount on market valuation.

Second, a separate shareholders agreement was to govern voting and management rights. The board of the holding company, which would be the apex decision-making body for the Group, would comprise four members of the family and two independent non-family executives. It would drive the company's strategic initiatives and approve business and annual operating plans, besides developing a pool of future leaders.

Third, GHPL was being reconstituted to have an independent board of directors and active management committees which would engage in rigorous deliberations to arrive at key business decisions. The organizational culture was to be participative and involvement-oriented. Open dialogue, free interaction and two-way communication between the family CEO and other non-family professionals would be encouraged.

On the succession front, the three (next generation) successors would choose unanimously the next Chairman from amongst themselves when Rao steps down at the age of 70. In the event of a disagreement on this matter, a family appointments board consisting of two independent directors and a 'deadlock facilitator' would be entrusted with powers to resolve the issue. The family agreed to follow all corporate governance practices and to professionalize operations so that the family members could gradually move from running operations to strategy making (Figure 11.1 presents the Group's organization chart).

In essence, G.M. Rao's thrust is on combining the best of the family's entrepreneurial spirit with a dynamic team of non-family professional managers in a values-driven organizational culture, in order to

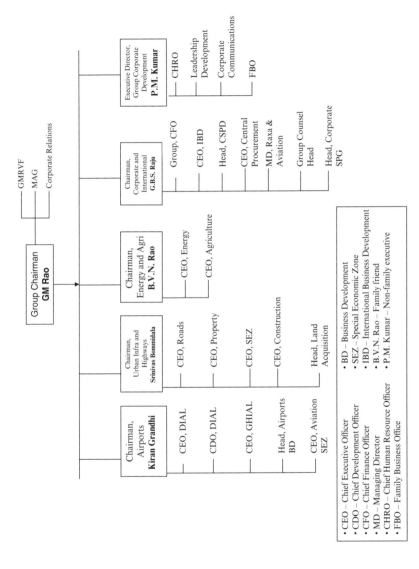

Figure 11.1   Group organization chart

consistently meet the Group's vision of 'building entrepreneurial organizations that make a difference to society through creation of value'.

11.3   FAMILY ENTREPRENEURSHIP

Hailing from a small village in Andhra Pradesh in South India, G.M. Rao, founder and Chairman of the GMR Group, has often been referred to as a serial entrepreneur. His entrepreneurial drive can be traced back to his childhood when he first dreamed of doing 'something different, something big'. Rao, who was the first among the three boys of his family to pass the final exam at the secondary school level, went on to earn a mechanical engineering degree, worked in a paper mill after graduation and later went on to work for a time with the state public works department.

In the 1970s, Rao's father, a successful dealer of jute, bean and oil products, divided his wealth equally between his four sons. Each received some property and approximately 0.3 million INR. The Rao brothers pooled their earned and inherited resources to begin a commodity trading venture (mainly jute) in 1978. However, as noted above, Rao split with his brothers in 1988 due to differences over their willingness to take risks. Finding himself solely in control of his own destiny and high on entrepreneurial energy, Rao set out to do 'something big'.

In 1985, Ramesh Gelli, then Managing Director of Vysya Bank was looking for a successful Vysya community entrepreneur with a rural background to join the bank's board. He chose Rao for this position. Between 1987 and 1989, when Gelli and the board were under pressure from the Reserve Bank of India (India's central bank) to double the bank's existing capital of 6.0 million INR, Rao bailed out several of Vysya Bank's rights issues of equity shares which were undersubscribed, gradually increasing his stake in the bank to 35 percent.

In 1993, when Gelli quit the bank with several of the bank's core staff to set up the Global Trust Bank, Rao was left with no choice but to run Vysya Bank himself. His full-time involvement with the bank compelled him to relocate his own firm's headquarters from Hyderabad to Bengaluru in 1995. Soon after, Rao brought Bank Brussels Lambert (BBL) on board, giving it a 5 percent stake, and began upgrading the bank's systems and processes with the new partner's help. In late 2002, BBL was acquired by ING, with Vysya Bank as part of the deal, and Rao received 5.6 billion INR for his stake. It set the stage for Rao's subsequent moves, giving him a significant capital base to aim for bigger things. Looking back on his rich experience with the bank, Rao said, 'Vysya Bank was my turning point as it exposed me to the modern world of finance and broadened my outlook on business.' Rao served as the Chairman of Vysya Bank from 2002 to 2006 and became Chairman Emeritus of the bank for life upon his retirement in 2006.

Following establishment of the Group and its diversification into ferro alloy manufacturing (1991–92), sugar production (1995), breweries (1998) and infrastructure development, the Group came into the limelight when it won bids for building a new airport in Hyderabad and for modernizing Delhi International Airport. Elaborating on the reason the Group chose to focus on airports, Rao said, 'we were the first among the private sector in power, but we realized that there was a lot of uncertainty and that the mega power project policy had not taken off. So we needed to get into other areas in infrastructure to hedge our bets. We chose airports.'

By 2009, the Group had successfully completed both the airport projects. It had established a strong presence outside India as well, in countries including the UK, the Netherlands, Australia, Turkey and Mali. Importantly, the Group won the bid for modernizing Istanbul's Sabiha Gokcen International Airport in Turkey. GMR Group also purchased the 'Delhi Daredevils' cricket team franchise of the Indian Premier League (IPL).

Rao initiated an organizational restructuring process in 2004. To shift the focus of family executives from operations to strategy, the family brought together the two manufacturing businesses of sugar and ferro alloys under GMR Industries, placing the entity under a non-family executive. GMR Infrastructure Ltd, comprising operations in power, roads and airports, went public in 2006.

Growth Factors

(a)   Opportunity identification
Ramachandran (2003) identified two key characteristics of an attractive entrepreneurial opportunity. These were: (1) the extent of the criticality of the need, and (2) the level of discontent customers had with the key features they wanted. The best opportunities were those that were high on criticality and discontent. The GMR family most often focused on opportunities that met these criteria. For instance, earlier efforts to meet India's infrastructure requirements had been woefully inadequate both in quantity and quality, creating a strong sense of discontent among the public and making the need for superior infrastructure critical.

In the earlier phase of his career, G.M. Rao identified and pursued local and regional opportunities for business growth in sectors such as jute, ferro alloys, banking and sugar. His company made considerable profits in each of these businesses. However, the major breakthrough for the company came with the opportunities presented at the national level, after the opening up of the infrastructure sector to private investment. Anticipating the huge growth potential of the infrastructure sector, the family entered the energy, road and airports sectors, a move that enabled the Group to scale greater heights.

(b) Role clarity

As the Group expanded into various sectors and individual responsibilities increased, Rao engaged McKinsey & Co. in 2006 to reorganize the Group's corporate structure. This was the time when S.B., Raju and Kiran felt the need for further role clarity in terms of business responsibilities. Rather than allocating responsibilities to everyone himself, Rao asked them to do an analysis of each other's capabilities, strengths and weaknesses and decide amongst themselves what each would do. Based on that analysis, they agreed the division of the portfolios, while Rao kept himself out of the whole exercise. They also decided that every three years, their roles would be rotated so that each of them gained experience in all areas of business.

(c) Family governance

In 1999, after attending an industry association conference on family business, Rao realized the importance of 'keeping the family together' for the perpetuation of the business across generations. At the conference, he learned about the possibilities of leveraging the special strengths of the family, anticipating and ring-fencing the risks, and fostering the value of stewardship among family members for the long-term success and sustainability of the family business. As S.B. recalled, 'Rao had initially planned to divide his assets equally amongst Raju, Kiran and myself, giving 30 billion INR to each of us. But after attending the family business conclave, he gave up the idea.' Over the next two to three years, he took a deep interest in understanding the dynamics of family businesses with a view to creating mechanisms for ensuring effective family governance.

In November 2000, Rao persuaded all the family members to attend a national conference on family business in Jaipur. Determined not to let go of this opportunity to embark on family governance initiatives, Rao used this shared experience to form a family council consisting of the four male members working at GMR and their wives. The council was tasked with deliberating upon the values, mission, vision and key policies that should go into a family constitution. Rao also invited Professor Joachim Schwass of IMD Business School, an internationally known family business advisor, to guide the family in developing a governance model over the course of a two-day retreat with family members.

P.M. Kumar, who had served as an advisor to the Group on corporate HR and organizational development since 1998, was entrusted with the development of family governance in 2003. He drove the process of establishing the governance structure, policies and processes within the family, to the point of getting the family ready to draft a family constitution. At that stage, they engaged Peter Leach, a family business advisor from BDO, London, who facilitated the process of drafting and adopting the family constitution. After several rounds of family meetings to understand the process, address doubts and reinforce motivation, the family was energized about creating a written family constitution that would include values, key policies and processes. The family discovered that their largest challenge was managing individual aspirations, for instance, ensuring each family member's operational freedom under the GMR umbrella while maintaining family cohesiveness. Throughout the process, the family kept its focus on maintaining harmony. As S.B. suggested, 'Relationships are the most important. Money will come and go. I have seen it all. So, "trust, express and communicate" is what I believe in.' The family worked hard to reach a consensus and understanding that would form the basis of the constitution.

The hard work paid off when the family signed the constitution on 3 March 2007 at Sarsika Palace Resort in Rajasthan, as part of the GMR Corporate Leadership Conference that was attended by all the family members. The constitution's signatories were the four male members of the family and their wives. Thus, the GMR Group became the first Indian family business to have a written constitution – a detailed document on the rights and duties of family members with respect to the business. 'The family was aiming to create a long-term, sustainable governance structure and set policies to serve the family in the current generation and beyond', Rao said. The constitution was not a formal legal document, but 'by signing it each family member confirmed his or her commitment to it', according to Rao. The aim of the effort was to strengthen and sustain bonding among family members. In the same year, Rao engaged a few family counselors to help the family members live the constitution in letter and spirit.

Along with family and business values, the constitution also articulates the Group's mission and vision as well as key processes. It provides for a family code of conduct and laid out the rules and qualifications for the entry of family members into the business along with their remuneration and perks. The constitution also provides for retirement and succession plans.

'One implication of these policies was that to join the business, the future generations would have to have prescribed qualifications, including outside experience, and they would be appointed subject to suitable vacancies and merit', Rao said. The performance appraisal system for family members and non-family professionals would be one and the same.

There was also an induction process that every newcomer was required to undergo. Family members were not directly appointed to senior positions, nor did they report to other family members. They were required to work outside the family firm for about three years before joining the business. A total of 12 months' internship is compulsory, which could be completed during their undergraduate years (for example, a series of three-month summer stints). Even in the second generation, Kiran had over two years of work experience before joining the Group. Like any newcomer, he underwent an induction process and worked on many projects (during 1996–98) before assuming greater responsibilities. For example, his exposure to treasury during his six months' training in Singapore during the 1999 Asian financial crisis helped him understand the nuances of financing and capital management.

The women of the first and second generations of the family, that is, the wives of the four male members working in the Group, had decided not to work in the business in order to take care of their children. However, they could, if they choose to, take up part-time jobs outside the family business or start their own businesses, provided such work did not interfere with their care giving responsibilities. The constitution further stipulated that only bloodline descendants (both male and female) of future generations are eligible to join the business, but not their spouses. The only exception, of course, was S.B. in the current generation.

(d) Family fund

It was proposed that a family fund (in the form of a trust) be established to maintain financial equity among family members. The fund is to be used to meet specific common expenses, such as the education of junior family members, medical expenses, the provision of monetary help for relatives in need, family investments, family venture capital, home-building loans, weddings and gifts, pensions and other expenses. In short, the fund is aimed at meeting essential security and developmental needs, with separate sub-funds for each. The family fund was to be built from contributions from the discretionary trust at the agreed percentage of distributions of the trusts and income on assets vested with the fund.

To make his mantra of 'keeping the family together' work in practice, Rao also included several formal organizational structures in the constitution. These included the family council, the family business forum, the non-business family forum and the family office. The family agreed that the constitution would undergo a formal review every five years. Constitution-related proposals from at least two members from different units would go to the family business forum for comments before the proposals were submitted for approval by the family council.

In April 2007, soon after signing the constitution, the family felt the need to have professional counselors help them in their development as individuals and in building mature, healthy relationships with each other. Professional counselors, including a US-based leadership expert and coach, an organizational psychologist, an emotional intelligence expert, and a spiritual behavioral coach were engaged to work with the family members through Individual Development Plans (IDPs). These exercises were intended to help them maintain a mature and non-toxic worldview and develop emotional intelligence, openness and constructive communication skills to foster bonding in relationships, which was crucial to living out the values specified in the constitution. However, Rao planned to reduce the family's dependence on consultants in a phased manner. In 2008, the family organized a series of training programs on managing differences or conflicts of interest with the intention of making family members skilled enough to resolve issues through dialogue, without outside help.

(e)   Corporate Social Responsibility (CSR) initiatives

Apart from taking up organizational growth and family governance initiatives, the GMR Group also committed itself to serving the needs of marginalized sections of society. To fulfill his social commitments, Rao established the GMR Varalakshmi Foundation (GMRVF) in 1991. GMRVF shares the same mission as the GMR Group: 'to build entrepreneurial organizations that make a difference to society through creation of value'. The Foundation was established as a section 25 company under the Companies Act (1956) and focused on developing various programs in the areas of education, health-care and community-building for local communities in need, typically those near Rao's hometown of Rajam or located in areas where the Group had business operations. All subsidiary companies of the Group contribute 3 to 5 percent of their profit after tax to the Foundation.

GMRVF is a professionally managed institution headed by a non-family CEO, with a board of directors consisting of family and independent non-family members. All first and second generation female members of the family serve on the board of the Foundation and take part in its initiatives.

Entrepreneurship: A Core Family and Business Value

The family developed two separate, though overlapping, sets of core values (see Figure 11.2) for the family and the business. These values were major instruments for protecting the culture and continuity of the family business. The constitution articulated and elaborated on each of them.

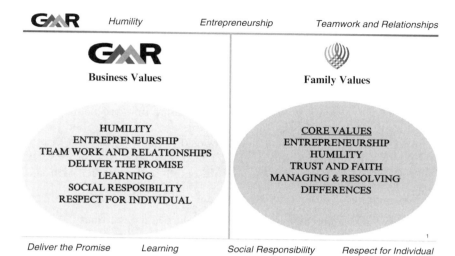

Figure 11.2   Core values

For the GMR Group, risk-taking and the ability to accept failures as learning opportunities are the key aspects of entrepreneurship, as specified in the family constitution. The constitution described entrepreneurship as 'encouraging one to take *calculated risks* and accepting that one will learn from failures along the way; to have the ability to *live with ambiguity and convert potential problems into opportunities*. This will enable the family to take the business to greater heights in *this generation and beyond*.' This definition of entrepreneurship was articulated over the course of several discussions held during family council meetings. Each (male) member of the family was asked to describe in words his personal experience and understanding of entrepreneurship. Thereafter, everyone's views were collated and the above definition arrived at through consensus.

(a)   Risk management/taking calculated risks

Risk management was one of the major business strengths of the GMR Group, and was especially useful during the diversification phase. The Group Executive Council (GEC) was set up in 1998 and later replaced by the holding board. It comprised four family members, non-family executives and independent members and advisors. The GEC approved all the new proposals and budgets, and the independent and non-family executives had equal say in approving or disapproving them. The GEC was treated like an independent board, and the non-family members' views were respected as much as those of family members. Rather than dismissing the objections raised by anyone, efforts were made to reach consensus by convincing the entire group. This arrangement had dual benefits. As the family respected the views and opinions of non-family GEC members while taking decisions, the non-family members, in turn, respected the ownership concerns, participative and consultative approach of the family towards decision-making and problem solving. The board presently works on similar lines to the GEC. The family members, before submitting a new proposal to the board, hold discussions in family business forum (FBF) meetings until any proposal is unanimously approved and can be presented to the board with one voice.

(b)   Living with ambiguity and converting failure into opportunity

Whenever the Group entered a new and previously unexplored sector or field (be it power, breweries or airports), the family members did not know clearly and definitively what they were aiming at or what the implications of the project would be. In other words, they accepted ambiguity. The idea was to do something different and big, learn on the job and execute it efficiently. Also, each failure was treated as an opportunity to learn so that it would not be repeated in the future. Quality was never compromised in terms of hiring the best resources for the business. For instance, about 320 million INR was spent on engaging 15 international consultants to prepare the bidding proposals for the Delhi and Mumbai airports.

(c)   The need for developing the entrepreneurial abilities of the next generation

The family realized that there was a possibility of the risk-taking ability of members of the next generation declining gradually if they, as managers of the existing ventures, focused exclusively on their growth and became too structure-oriented and controls-driven. It was possible that they would avoid taking risks out of fear of failing. The constitution recognized the need to educate future generations about the history of their company and the hardships that their fathers, uncles, and above all, the founder endured in building this legacy. This knowledge was necessary to foster a sense of pride in their predecessors' achievements and a desire to imbibe their entrepreneurial drive and also to create a feeling of emotional ownership towards the company. In order to support individual entrepreneurial ideas, the family would create a venture fund for future generations under the overall family fund (see above).

(d) Overcoming limited resources and making the best possible use of available resources

In the early days (between 1975 and 1998), when the business was in the start-up stage, Rao could not afford to hire experienced professionals. He persuaded his college friends and executives from Andhra Bank to join him. These people were the co-builders of his enterprise at a time when his family members were not ready to the join the business. Though they came from different backgrounds, such as mechanical engineering, banking and so on, they learned the same business principles along with Rao while on the job. Even then, G.M. Rao demonstrated the ability to attract and retain employees and to encourage them to learn on the job and take calculated risks.

11.4 CONCLUSION

The Forbes 2011 list of the richest people in the world put G.M. Rao's net worth at USD 2.6 billion. The business that Rao started some 30 years ago with 300,000 INR, had, by 2009, grown into one of the leading infrastructure companies in India. All the four family members demonstrated high entrepreneurial orientation with strong organization-building capabilities. The Group had ambitious plans to sustain the same level of growth through business opportunities in India and abroad.

Rao, who started his entrepreneurial career with a rather nondescript jute yarn business followed by a foray into banking, had by 2010 become not only a billionaire on the Forbes list but also had controlling interests in India's most desirable assets – three world-class airports. He was conferred with several awards over the years including the prestigious Indian *Economic Times*' 'Entrepreneur of the Year' award in 2006. The jury members described the GMR Group as 'an entrepreneurial company with good governance'. They were impressed with Rao's blazing speed and more importantly, the quality of his work. GMR's work on most of the Group's infrastructure projects, including Hyderabad airport, was ahead of schedule. The jury members observed that 'infrastructure building in India was one of the toughest jobs to do and Rao in that context had done an outstanding job'.

This case study focuses on how the GMR Group has successfully generated and sustained entrepreneurial performance over the last 30 years and across two generations. G.M. Rao, a first generation entrepreneur, built an entrepreneurial legacy for his successors. What is remarkable is that he boldly entered a number of new and often unrelated businesses (jute, power, sugar, ferro alloys, breweries, highways, airports, SEZ and so on) and succeeded in making profits in each of them. Mechanization of the jute processing mill, transformation of a 73-year-old traditional bank (Vysya Bank) with the introduction of modern IT systems and the construction of a world-class airport at Hyderabad are important achievements that reflected the family's entrepreneurial acumen and innovativeness. The Group's social activities, in the areas of education, health, livelihoods and community-building through GMRVF, are also commendable. The Group remained competitively aggressive through the years. On-time project execution and financial engineering have been the hallmarks of success for the Group. In addition, their proactiveness and ability to manage risk brought accolades and success to the founder and his company.

Rao believes that the second generation business leaders from the family have successfully imbibed his entrepreneurial spirit, business acumen, native intelligence and willingness to learn, and that the subsequent generations will inherit these qualities as a family legacy. Having identified entrepreneurship as the defining characteristic of the Group, the founder and his family aimed to institutionalize it in the organization in a professional manner. Rao, as a first generation entrepreneur, took care to develop and nurture the entrepreneurial abilities of his sons and son-in-law. The top executives of the Group were also facilitated in developing the spirit of entrepreneurship through an organization-wide leadership development program in which world-class national and international coaches were engaged.

Interestingly, while according to the early business model, family members planned to move out of operations gradually, while continuing to remain equally involved in identifying opportunities and chasing them, opportunity identification did not remain the family's prerogative. Even non-family employees were encouraged to spot opportunities and discuss them with the board. For instance, whenever Rao came across a press release or newspaper notification of a potential business opportunity, he would circulate it amongst the staff with post-it slips saying, 'Please examine and let me know.' Core business values, entrepreneurship being one of them, were displayed on posters, printed on calendars and diaries and animated on the Internal portal so that they were disseminated widely throughout the organization.

Rao understood that a successful business could be run with the help of a well-governed family. He hoped that the family governance structures he implemented would keep the family together and ensure that his entrepreneurial drive permeated throughout the organization for generations to come. He also hoped that, in the future, his company would be led by young and dynamic individuals, who would build upon his strong social networks and the company's growing financial base with their entrepreneurial drive and farsighted decision-making.

REFERENCE

Ramachandran, K. 'Customer dissatisfaction as a source of entrepreneurial opportunity', *Nanyang Business Review*, 2: 2 (July–December 2003), 22–38.

12. The Shakti Group: keeping the entrepreneurial spirit alive in the second generation

Kavil Ramachandran

The Shakti Group traces its origins to India's independence in 1947, when the founder of the company along with his family migrated from Lahore, Pakistan to Hyderabad in South India to start a new life. Naresh, the second of three sons, took the lead in exploring a number of different entrepreneurial opportunities before he hit on the idea of manufacturing cooking masalas (spice mixes) and pickles. This business, which he ran with his two brothers, grew at a steady pace for many years, and after the entry of the second generation into the business, its growth multiplied several fold. However, conflicts within the family eventually led to a split and resulted in the closure of the factory and a freeze on the trademark. This proved to be a temporary setback and Naresh quickly revived the company under a new avatar – Shakti Products (Pvt.) Ltd. His three sons took the lead and ventured into new areas, while continuing to grow the traditional business. The Shakti Group case demonstrates the hunger of an entrepreneurial family to grow in spite of a family division. Moreover, members of the second generation proved themselves to be entrepreneurial managers by identifying and pursuing emerging opportunities while building the traditional business.

BACKGROUND

Naresh moved to Hyderabad in 1947 with his two brothers, parents and several close relatives when he was 12 years old, a part of the great wave of migration that was sparked by India's independence and partition. The extended family had 13 members. Despite his youth, Naresh was compelled to start earning a living to help support his family as the other members were either too young or too old or were not used to working for wages. He started out by making bakery products at home and selling them on the street in a handcart. The business did not take off, and in 1950 he decided to open a restaurant. This venture was not a success either. In 1955, he began selling masalas and pickles from a kiosk he had set up under the staircase of a shop. Here too luck was not on his side. His kiosk was torn down when the building was demolished for a road widening project. He continued to experiment with masalas and develop new varieties, and also operated a canteen until 1964, when he started manufacturing the masalas. He had gotten married the previous year, in 1963 at the age of 28, and believed that his prosperity began after his marriage.

In 1967, Naresh worked in a rented room, manufacturing a variety of cooking masalas under the name Bhojan. Food King was the only other major brand of masalas in the market at that time and catered primarily to the middle and upper classes of society. It offered a range of products in the premium category and had attractive packaging. Also, Food King was more popular in North India than in the South. Bhojan offered competing products at prices at least 10 percent lower than Food King, thereby catering to the needs of less affluent customers who wanted greater value for their money. In 1970, Naresh shifted his manufacturing operations to a 125 square metre factory in an industrial estate in Hyderabad's Old City area. Though he was not formally trained in preparing mixes of spices and herbs, his olfactory sense was well developed and he was well able to smell and identify the ingredients of a good masala mix.

Around this time, the first signs of discord between Naresh and his elder brother, Mohan, became visible. Their father had expired and a disagreement arose between the two brothers over the family's property and inheritance, specifically over Mohan's refusal to divide household utensils and gold. In 1972, Naresh moved out of the family home with his family, his mother and his younger brother Madan and his family and settled in a house in another part of the city. His elder brother Mohan's family of seven continued to live in the former family home. Their mother shuttled back and forth between the two houses.

Mohan continued to run the masala and pickles retail shop while Naresh focused on manufacturing. He had brought Madan into the manufacturing business after the latter had completed his education and worked elsewhere for a while. As the business expanded, Naresh's mother insisted that Mohan should be brought into the fold as well. However, instead of bringing him into the manufacturing side of the business, Naresh formed a separate partnership firm in which 50 percent of the shares were held by Mohan and the remaining split equally between himself and Madan. This firm, Bhojan Agency, was essentially a shell company set up to provide a regular income to Mohan as his share in the profits and thus to accede to his mother's wishes.

The business grew steadily, and in 1977, Naresh moved operations to a bigger factory in the same industrial estate. The mark up from manufacturing to marketing was not more than 5 percent. By 1988, their turnover had reached about Rs 200 million which prompted Naresh to set up Bhojan Products Private Ltd (BPPL), retaining an ownership ratio of 3:2 between the two brothers (Naresh 60 percent and Madan 40 percent). According to Naresh, this structure not only ensured that he retained control over the business but also guaranteed that his three sons and Madan's two sons would have equal shares of 20 percent each when the question of succession arose in future. Bhojan Products, the partnership firm that owned the trademark, licensed it to the new company for an annual fee, which was revised upwards several times over the years.

The first opportunity to diversify the business arose out of necessity. The family had begun to realize that the poor supply of metal containers was proving to be a major constraint to their growth. Naresh, in partnership with a friend, set up 20 small factories over a period of time to manufacture and supply containers. By operating several small factories, they were able to keep each one below the excise duty threshold and avoid regulatory restrictions. They also built a new manufacturing facility in Nacharam, in the outskirts of the city, as the business continued to expand.

ENTRY OF THE SECOND GENERATION

Kishan, Naresh's eldest son, joined the business in 1985 after completing his B.Tech degree and was trained in mixing and blending the ingredients, the most critical aspect of the business. However, Kishan developed an allergy to some of the ingredients and decided to move into finance and administration, with the result that his younger brother Rajan turned his attention to learning the blending formulae. Kishan subsequently went to Boston to pursue a second degree in the biomedical field in 1987 and returned to India in 1992. Rajan quickly mastered the art of blending and decided to devote himself entirely to the business after he graduated from college. His role was multifaceted and covered several aspects of business, including production, expansion of new facilities, technology development and fabrication of new machinery to meet the needs of the business. In 1990, Manish, Madan's elder son, returned from the US after graduating in computer science and joined the business where he helped to supervise production. Rajan continued to work with his father on blending. Jayesh, Madan's younger son, returned from England in 1995 and began working in the factory, though he was not given any specific responsibility. Meanwhile, Mohan's sons Nirmal, a biomedical graduate, and Rajesh, a B.Com graduate, had joined their father on the marketing side at Bhojan Agency. Their grandmother proposed that one of Mohan's sons be inducted into the manufacturing business while the other remained in marketing. In accordance with her wishes, Nirmal was brought into the manufacturing business, where he held administrative responsibilities in the areas of operations such as excise, packaging and government related activities.

The early 1990s witnessed a major revision in the company strategy. While the younger generation pushed ahead with new ideas, the older generation supported their experimentation and entrepreneurial enthusiasm. They believed that collectively they had the will and energy required to considerably accelerate the growth of the business. During this period, they made some significant changes in their packaging, retail promotional materials, advertising and even their logo.

Another important initiative the company undertook was to automate production processes. Because of the peculiarities of the business and the widespread use of traditional methods of manufacturing, ready-made machinery was not available to upgrade the processes or technology used in this business. The family had little choice other than to buy whatever piece of equipment was available and ask machinery suppliers to design and develop new machines to meet their additional requirements. Unfortunately, most of these efforts did not bear fruit. Finally, they created a new tool room and formed an engineering team to work with machinery suppliers to design machines as per their requirements. After several rounds of design changes, they succeeded in automating their production and packaging processes and were thus able to stabilize product quality. This was a major turning point for the company. Until then, they had lagged in production for want of appropriate equipment while the market for their products had been rapidly expanding. After automating their processes, they were able to reduce order-to-dispatch cycle time from 7–10 days to just 1–2 days. From 1992–2000, the company steadily improved production as the market for Bhojan products grew. Equipped with new technology, they explored an alternative form of packaging for their products using small pouches. While they continued to sell their products in the traditional tin containers, they expanded significantly by using pouch technology, which was 75 percent cheaper than tin containers. Also, customers found the pouches much more convenient to use.

By 2000, the company's turnover had increased enormously, from Rs 200 million in 1987 to Rs 1 billion; it grew further, to Rs 2 billion by 2003. They introduced a range of new products and expanded their territory to cover new areas such as Eastern India. This was a major development for the business. Until then, Bhojan's territory had been largely restricted to South India and a few states in the West, where it had been a relatively quiet player. They also expanded their production facilities, increasing the built up area by approximately 20 percent year on year over three years. In 2003, they had 8000 square metres of built up area for their manufacturing operations. It was a major transformation for a company that had started operations in a 100 square foot room. For Naresh personally it was a very long way from his modest beginnings when 13 members of his family lived in one room and had to convert their bathroom into their kitchen after the family had finished bathing in the morning, and when as a bachelor his bed was a bench at the side of the road.

DIVERSIFICATION OF THE BUSINESS

The family took a major step in business diversification in 1992 when Manish and Kishan took the initiative to establish Shree Technology Private Ltd (STPL), a company that focused on offering software development and IT education and Internet services. In 1997, Kishan and Nirmal set up another company, Shree Biomedicals Private Ltd (SBPL), to market the health-care products of a European company with whom they had entered into a partnership. The second generation members of all three branches of the family were shareholders in both STPL and SBPL, though Naresh's branch (with three sons as against the others' two each) held the majority of shares. Both STPL and SBPL were self-sustaining businesses that did not make substantial profits.

Naresh and his brothers drew equal salaries although most of the key decisions were made by Naresh. Everyone accepted that Naresh's entrepreneurial capabilities were the reason behind the company's growth. All the members of the second generation earned the same salary, regardless of their responsibilities. This amount was directly deposited in their respective bank accounts. They were paid out-of-pocket expenses by Naresh as per their needs. As the head of the joint family, Naresh met not only the family's expenses but also the expenses towards maintenance and repair. He kept signed cheque books of all the children in his custody and informed them when any funds were withdrawn from their bank accounts. There was full transparency and trust among all the family members in this matter and nobody objected to this practice. In order to generate cash for other investments, the group declared liberal dividends.

DISCORD AND DIVISION

Though both BPPL and Bhojan Marketing had unbalanced ownership structures (Naresh held 60 percent while Madan held 40 percent of the shares in the former, and Mohan held 50 percent of the shares in the latter with the rest divided between the other brothers), the family had accepted this decision and no one raised any objections to it. However, when the second generation had settled into the business and the question of the senior members' retirement arose, the situation became complicated. Mohan's sons proposed restructuring the entire ownership structure so as to divide the business equally among the seven cousins of the second generation. By and large, the family had not anticipated any restructuring in their holdings as they expected the children of the second generation to inherit their fathers' shares. Naresh, who had built up the company and was the technology expert, felt that it was important that he and his branch of the family retained control of the business for the sake of the unified family. While Naresh had a good relationship with Madan, the same was not true of his relationship with Mohan. This was due in part to the falling out that took place between the brothers following their father's death. With the issue of succession on the table, a new conflict arose between the brothers, this time with the equation changed. While Naresh believed that he should have the controlling stake in the business and due recognition for his contributions, his two brothers thought it fair that ownership be equalized in the second generation.

In 2001, their differences grew to such an extent that interactions between Naresh's family on the one side and Madan's and Mohan's families on the other ceased. Between 2000 and 2003, the Madan-Mohan faction had been making preparations to take the matter to the court, a development of which Naresh and his family were completely unaware as they were busy with the management of Bhojan, now solely run by them. In May 2004, Naresh received an ex-party order from a local court asking for the dissolution of the partnership firm. Shortly thereafter, Manish began manufacturing products under the Bhojan brand name, claiming that it was his right to do so. Naresh applied to the Supreme Court and secured a freeze on the use of the brand name. The factory in Nacharam was closed in 2005 under orders from the Supreme Court of India. In January 2005, even before the Supreme Court ordered a freeze of the trademark in March, Naresh's branch had set up a new company, Shakti Products (Pvt.) Ltd and launched a range of products using the original ingredients and blends under the Shakti brand. In about three years, he was able to match BPPL's 2003 turnover of Rs 2 billion. Naresh had started working on this new option as far back as 2002, sensing that the two sides would not succeed in resolving their differences. Meanwhile, his brothers started manufacturing and trading stationery products. In February–March 2005, they launched a new brand of cooking masalas under the name 'Masti', competing with Bhojan, and later on with Shakti .

As for STPL and SBPL, the family division and legal battle had taken its toll and affected the performance of these companies. The promoters of the European partner called for a meeting with Kishan and Nirmal and divided their marketing territories into two. Kishan took charge of several states and made a turnover of Rs 50 million in 2009.

NEW DIRECTIONS

Naresh's branch of the family continued to diversify. They formed Shakti Health Care Private Ltd in 2004 and obtained a Radiant Clinic franchise from the Radiant Hospitals Group. Around this time, Naresh's youngest son, Tapan, returned to India and began playing an active role in the company's health-care business. They invested approximately Rs 20 million in infrastructure, building a 6500 square foot facility against the basic franchise commitment of a 3000 square foot facility. Shakti added new specialty areas such as dental, physiotherapy, ENT and orthopaedics. They focused on creating high quality facilities and built additional rooms for training and meetings as well as office space for directors and central managers. They gradually installed mammography equipment and built a full-fledged operation theatre, a 24-hour ICU, a pathology lab with NABL accreditation and a 10-bed inpatient facility. The annual turnover of this company in 2009 had reached Rs 50 million.

Though the second generation had by this point taken over management of the business, Naresh was still involved to some extent as he continued to oversee financial matters. Kishan looked after marketing and administration, including the audit and legal departments, while Rajan was in charge of operations, purchase, new product development and equipment. Tapan looked after Radiant Clinic and Kingles (discussed below) and provided general backup to the others as needed. He did not show any aggressive interest in taking on additional responsibilities.

The second generation pursued a number of entrepreneurial opportunities, further diversifying the business. They launched a herbal health drink under the brand name 'Kingles' in 2004. This business turned over about Rs 50 million in 2009 and made a small net profit. In 2006, the family decided to enter the packaged foods business when they learned that a snack manufacturing company in Delhi was closing down. They acquired Great Nuts along with its production facilities and trademarks and started producing and marketing a variety of processed nuts in 2007. The annual sales of this business increased from Rs 10 million in 2008 to Rs 40 million in 2009. They also made plans to introduce new products such as roasted peanuts and light snacks. In 2009, they bought 50,000 square feet of land on the outskirts of the city and built a facility that they could rent out for events such as weddings and other large functions.

In 2010, Kishan was entirely in charge of product marketing and was partly responsible for finance, which was still largely Naresh's domain. Rajan took care of technology, performance and production and Tapan looked after administration and the Kingles, Great Nuts and Radiant Clinic businesses. The total turnover in 2009–10 was Rs 3.50 billion, of which 95 percent came from Shakti.

DEVELOPING FAMILY GOVERNANCE

Naresh's family was a close knit one, with all three children living together with their father in a newly built home on the outskirts of the city. They were devoted to their work and spent a considerable amount of time exploiting potential market opportunities. Their close relationship with a professor of family business management first made them aware of the need for family governance and the challenges involved in perpetuating and sustaining both the family and the business over time. They attended a variety of training programs on family business and were completely convinced that they should adopt a professional approach to addressing family and business challenges. They realized that they might not be able to enjoy the fruits of their current activities unless they addressed governance challenges sooner rather than later. The split that had occurred in their own family taught them that they could not afford to allow history to repeat itself. However, they are yet to take concrete steps in developing family governance.

Index